MANIFESTING SPIRITS

MANIFESTING SPIRITS

Jack Hunter

AEON

First published in 2020 by
Aeon Books Ltd
PO Box 76401
London W5 9RG

British Library Cataloguing in Publication Data

A C.I.P. for this book is available from the British Library

ISBN-13: 978-1-91280-788-8

Typeset by Medlar Publishing Solutions Pvt Ltd, India
Printed in Great Britain

www.aeonbooks.co.uk

*For Rosie, Nils, and Alice, and everyone
who has helped and put up with me over the
long years spent writing this book.*

*This book is also dedicated to the memory
of Edie Turner, whose pioneering explorations
have been a source of continuous inspiration.*

CONTENTS

CHAPTER SIX

CHAPTER SEVEN

ABSTRACT

This book is an exploration of contemporary trance and physical mediumship with a particular emphasis on issues related to altered states of consciousness, personhood, performance, and the processes by which spirits become manifest in social reality. A major component of the book is given over to an examination of anthropology's evolving attitudes towards the "paranormal" as a component of the "life-worlds" of many people across the globe. The book works towards developing a non-reductive anthropological approach to the paranormal, and mediumship in particular, that does not attempt to explain away the existence of spirits in terms of functional, cognitive, or pathological theories, but that rather embraces a *processual* perspective that emphasises complexity and multiple interconnected processes underlying spirit possession performances. This non-reductive approach is arrived at through a combination of ethnographic observation during séances, and interviews with trance and physical mediums at the Bristol Spirit Lodge, a private non-denominational spiritualist home-circle in Bristol, literature reviews covering the anthropology, psychology, neurophysiology, and parapsychology of spirit possession, and cross-cultural comparison with other mediumistic traditions to uncover core processes.

ACKNOWLEDGEMENTS

I would like to say a very big thank you to Dr Fiona Bowie, Dr David Shankland, and Dr Camilla Morelli for helping to steer this book towards completion. My thanks also go to Lisette Coly and the Parapsychology Foundation, the Society for Psychical Research, the Read-Tuckwell Scholarship at the University of Bristol, and Anneli Thomas for their indispensable financial support of my writing and research. I am also grateful to: (in no particular order) Dr Fabian Graham, Dr Emily Pierini, Dr Mark A. Schroll, Dr David Luke, Dr Hannah Gilbert, Dr Sarah Roberts, Dr Cal Cooper, Dr Diana Espírito Santo, Dr William Rowlandson, Dr Angela Voss, Prof Charles Emmons, Prof Patric Giesler, Prof Jeffrey Kripal, Prof David Hufford (and all at Esalen), Dr Wendy Dossett, Prof Bettina Schmidt, Prof Ronald Hutton, Dr Margherita Margiotti, Prof Stanley Krippner, Prof Patric Gielser, Prof Charles Laughlin, and Dr Serena Roney-Dougal for their continued encouragement and support. Thanks also to George Hansen, Shannon Taggart, Patrick Huyghe, and Greg Taylor for their Fortean assistance and contributions over the years. Big thanks also go to my

A-Level, Access, and undergraduate students who have had to endure my frequent tangents on mediumship and the paranormal in their religious studies, psychology, and sociology lessons at college. Finally, I am immensely grateful to all my family and friends for their encouragement throughout this process.

NOTE

This book was written over a long period of time, beginning in 2009 with my first encounter with mediumship at the Bristol Spirit Lodge while still an undergraduate student; it was finished as a doctoral thesis at the end of 2017, and finally transformed into its current form in 2020. Over the years I have been active in writing academic and popular articles about my research and ideas, which have appeared in various journals, magazines, and blogs. Revised, edited, and expanded portions of these articles form the basis of many of the chapters in this book.[1] I have always considered my research to be an ongoing process—as something that I am always working at—and always intended that these articles would become, in one form or another, *this* book.

---

[1] Portions of Chapter 1 have been revised and expanded from the Introduction to Hunter (2012b). Chapter 2 features elements of Hunter (2010). Chapter 3 is a fully expanded version of Hunter (2011a), 3.9 is an expanded version of Hunter (2014b), and 3.10 features elements from Hunter (2012c). Chapter 5 contains elements of Hunter (2015b). Chapter 6 features revised sections of Hunter (2012d). Chapter 7 is a fully revised and expanded version of Hunter (2014a).

INTRODUCTION

Anomalous experiences in a garden shed

Spiritualism is the name given to a complex of beliefs and practices that emerged in America in the middle of the nineteenth century. It is often confused with the more general term "spirituality", but while we can probably say that all Spiritualists are "spiritual" (to some extent) we cannot say that all "spiritual" people are Spiritualists. Spiritualism is built around the idea that it is possible to communicate with discarnate spirits (usually of the dead). This dialogue is facilitated through special individuals known as "mediums"—people who provide a psychic link between the world of the living and the world of the dead, often through the cultivation of altered states of consciousness. There are two ways in which the term "spiritualism" is frequently used—either as referring to the *general* belief that it is possible to communicate with spirits (spiritualism, with a little "s"), or in reference to a formally organised religious movement (Spiritualism, with a capital "S"). The Spiritualist movement began as a paranormal event centred upon three teenage sisters in New York State in 1848, and rapidly blossomed into a global religious movement. Today, in the UK, where the fieldwork that underpins this book was conducted, Spiritualism is epitomised by the activities of the

Spiritualists' National Union (SNU)—the official body regulating Spiritualist churches, and the mediums that serve them, across the country.
This book, however, is primarily concerned with spiritualism (with a
little "s"), specifically the kind of spiritualism practised at the Bristol
Spirit Lodge—an independent mediumship development circle, now
based in Clevedon, near Bristol, that has no formal links to the SNU.

A séance, from the French for "sitting", is a loosely-structured ritual during which a medium initiates contact with the spirits so as to
enable a dialogue with the gathered "sitters"—lay folk who regularly
come to ask questions of the spirits. It was as an undergraduate student
in the winter of 2009—the final year of my degree in archaeology and
anthropology at the University of Bristol—that I first attended a séance
at the Bristol Spirit Lodge. Much to my surprise, the Lodge itself was
a specially constructed wooden shed at the bottom of a neat garden in
Filton, a suburb of Bristol.[2] What I experienced in that unassuming garden shed entirely exceeded my expectations and challenged my initial
preconceptions—if truth be told, I didn't really know what to expect, or
what I was getting myself into.

There had been a heavy snowfall during the night that gave the day
a brilliant glow in the bright early morning light. Everything felt crisp,
the air was cold, and I felt alert, if a little nervous—not least because
I had to trek along treacherous ice-covered pavements to get to the Spirit
Lodge, which was about a twenty-minute walk from my student accommodation. I was the first to arrive. Christine (the founder of the Lodge)
expressed her concern that I wasn't going to turn up. She was glad that I

---

[2] Although it was not on my radar at the time, recent developments in my thinking—
especially revolving around the ideas explored in *Greening the Paranormal* (Hunter,
2019)—have drawn me back to a reconsideration of the role of the garden itself as an
"ante-chamber to the netherworld" (Conan, 2007, p. 7), indeed there are long traditions
worldwide of using gardens in this way, for spiritual purposes. This is not quite the place
for a complete exploration of this intriguing rabbit hole, which will be taken up in a future
publication, but I did recently ask Christine about this, and her answer provides some
interesting food for thought:

> "… initially when the 'shed' was built and sitters left the house and walked
> to the shed I personally felt that it increased the 'fun' and 'adventure' ele-
> ments … what we were about to do felt like a 'secret' … As we adjusted to
> the shed I'd personally often sit out there with the door open and look out
> into the garden … which felt kind of 'spiritual' … like the 'shed' was natural
> … an integral part of nature. The same effect was recreated here when we
> moved house" (interview with Christine, August 2019).

had though—some of her regular sitters would not be attending because of the weather, but the morning's séance was still scheduled to go ahead. They needed someone to make up the numbers. She directed me through into the dining room, where she had laid the table out with named place mats for the expected guests. I was offered a cup of tea, and drank it as I chatted politely to Christine about what I should expect to experience during the séance. She told me it was best *not to expect anything at all!* As I sat pondering this, feeling very much out of my comfort zone, and looking around the dining room (in which Christine had a glass-fronted bookcase containing numerous books on mediumship, Spiritualism, and popular science), the doorbell rang. Christine rushed to answer. It was Sandy, the medium who would be sitting this morning, followed shortly by Margaret and Lynne, two of the Lodge's regular sitters. The atmosphere was warm, informal, and friendly—it was clear that Christine, Margaret, Lynne, and Sandy were very close and that they were enjoying themselves in familiar surroundings. In all respects they seemed to me to be "normal" twenty-first-century British women. As we sat around Christine's large dining room table I listened to them sincerely and very matter-of-factly describe their own séance experiences while drinking tea and eating biscuits—weird apparitions, anomalous movement of objects, ectoplasmic materialisations, and other paranormal events. I became increasingly apprehensive, but tried not to let it show. I didn't know what to expect, and the thought of potentially experiencing *real* paranormal phenomena was both thrilling and a little bit frightening.

Once we had all finished our tea, Christine gave us a quick runthrough of the séance protocol. We were asked to remove all jewellery, and to completely empty our pockets of any loose change before going out to the Lodge—the metal, we were told, could interfere with the spirits' attempts to materialise. Under no circumstances were we allowed to bring electronic equipment into the Lodge for recording purposes—no mobile phones, no hand-held tape recorders, no concealed video cameras—nothing. Christine explained that she would be making her own recording of the séance, which would be uploaded to the Lodge's website along with numerous others in their archive. We all agreed to these terms, left our belongings on our place mats, and followed Christine out into the garden.

Inside the Lodge, Christine, Margaret, Lynne, and I sat in a semi-circle on padded office chairs with blankets on our laps to keep us warm. It was cold in the small building. We took off our shoes and placed them neatly under our chairs. Sandy sat in a high-backed Parker Knoll armchair that was positioned in a curtained-off corner of the room known as the "cabinet"—a direct descendant of the early Spiritualist spirit cabinet séances of the Victorian era. She wore a red fleece jumper and loose jogging trousers with stripy rainbow-coloured socks to keep her body warm while she was in trance. Once we had settled in our seats, Christine read the opening prayer from a laminated sheet attached to a clipboard. The stationery caught my attention—if she had been wearing a white lab coat at this moment Christine would have been indistinguishable from a research scientist—this was not something that I had expected, particularly in the context of a prayer. Somehow I had managed to find myself in the *interstices between science and religion*. When the prayer ended she pressed play on a small CD player and switched off the lights, before gradually turning up a red light using a makeshift dimmer switch attached to a piece of wood. The big red light bulb, which was hooded over with dark card so that it could be directed into the cabinet like a spotlight, generated a warm, womb-like, and slightly eerie glow. Although the light levels were low in the Lodge, everyone could clearly be seen sitting quietly with blankets on their laps, and we could all see Sandy sitting between the curtains on either side of the cabinet. She shut her eyes and started her trance induction process.

Sandy sat motionless in the cabinet to begin with, her arms resting lightly on her lap and her head just slightly tilted forward. We watched in silence for a couple of tracks on the CD, as Sandy sat breathing deeply. Then something unusual started to happen. Her face appeared—at least from my own subjective perspective—to *change*. It became increasingly difficult for me to focus on her features, which seemed to shift and fade. While Sandy descended deeper into her trance state, breathing heavily in the gloom of the red light, I saw small flashes of white and blue that flickered in front of my eyes, and at one point thought that I saw the face of the entranced medium morph and transform to resemble someone else entirely—an oriental monk's face—before the mask-like apparition slid spookily down the medium's face and chest, dissolving as it descended. At one point her features seemed to shift weirdly—to distort—and it looked as though her head had disappeared completely, leaving a dark empty space just above her shoulders.

I will state from the outset that I could not tell whether these experiences were *objectively real* (that is, correlating with objective/physical transformations of the medium's features, for example) or whether they were some form of hallucination, perhaps induced by the red light, or some other combination of factors. Either way, the aetiology of the experience doesn't really matter at this juncture (though we will consider it in greater detail later). For the time being it is enough to say that they were, at the least, genuine *experiences* (if nothing else) that seemed to accord well with the beliefs and expectations of my informants, and so (for me at least) they represented a partial validation of the world view they had told me about over tea and biscuits before the séance. My first encounter with trance mediumship, therefore, demonstrated that, in the context of the séance room at least, anomalous experiences *do occur*—whatever their ultimate causes and ontological underpinnings may be. The uncommon experiences I had in the Lodge on that cold morning are one of the main reasons I continued to pursue research into the spirit mediumship practices of the Lodge and its members beyond my undergraduate dissertation.

In addition to my own *semi-subjective* visionary experiences (I say *semi*-subjective because my "vision" of the oriental monk's face was later corroborated by Margaret during a conversation at the end of the séance), there was another aspect of the séance performance that particularly caught my attention: the trance state of the medium. It was clear to me from the beginning of the séance that Sandy was experiencing a genuine altered state of consciousness—her eyes remained tightly shut throughout the séance, while her hands and legs twitched and moved spasmodically. When distinctive spirit personalities eventually started to speak through her body, her entire physical and behavioural demeanour was transformed, as were her vocal tones.

Inside the cabinet, behind the folds of the curtain we could see Sandy's arms and legs moving about in the red light. Her hands contorted as she pushed her body backwards into the heavy chair. Before long she was making grunting, growling, and coughing sounds—sounds that I didn't expect the quiet and polite woman I had met an hour or so ago to make. The growling and gurgling noises continued for a while, as Christine tried to coax the incoming spirit to talk to us. Christine reassured the visiting spirit that Sandy's spirit-team would help to make talking easier. She turned and explained to me that this was only the second time *the Soldier* had made himself known to the circle, so his connection with the group was still quite weak and he did not yet have a rapport with the sitters. Sandy's movements were erratic—her arms and legs pulled and pushed the chair as the spirit voice frustratingly strained to grumble through. The few words that were discernible seemed to suggest that gravity felt strange to the Soldier—that he was no longer used to physical weight that comes with being embodied in matter. He tried to express to us just how strange it was that he had never noticed what gravity *felt* like while alive—he had simply taken it for granted. Unfortunately the Soldier wasn't able to say much more than this—his connection was too weak for a sustained dialogue.

As the séance progressed, Christine turn up the music when it became clear that the spirit no longer wanted to talk, or was no longer able to. Each time a spirit left her body Sandy would go limp and fall back into the chair. After the Soldier's deep vocalisations she had some trouble with her throat. Her primary spirit control, Joseph (the spirit of a twelve-year-old Native American boy), expressed his dislike of the taste of *ectoplasm* in the medium's throat, which he explained had been necessary to allow the Soldier to speak in such a startlingly different manner to the medium's normal voice. When the spirit was talking, so we were told, an ectoplasmic voice box was formed in the medium's throat, which was controlled and manipulated by the incorporating spirit. He explained how ectoplasm is a semi-physical substance that is used by spirits to manifest in our physical world—in a sense it may be thought of as a *bridge between spirit and matter*.

After a brief musical interlude another spirit made itself known to the group. His name was Elf—a regular visitor to the Lodge with a strong and distinctive personality, not like the Soldier. Elf was very active through Sandy's body, his motions were playful, cheeky, and childlike in many ways. He wasn't afraid of telling Christine to "Shut up!", for example, and was clearly performing the archetypal role of the *trickster* during the séance (Hansen, 2001). Christine explained to Elf that there was someone new in the circle (referring to me) who hadn't met him before. He responded with what I came to realise was his own characteristic indifference—Elf simply didn't care what I thought of him and cheerfully repeated the lines:

> I am me, I am free, I just be,
> I am me, I am free, I just be,
> I am me, I am free, I just be …

In retrospect I wonder whether there was an important message about the nature of spirits contained in Elf's whimsical statement, offered up very early on in my inquiry. After a while Elf went on to explain how sometimes Joseph, Sandy's primary spirit control, would only allow him to occupy certain parts of Sandy's body, specifically her knees and legs. It was apparently possible for Elf to inhabit Sandy's legs, for example, at the same time as another spirit was using her vocal chords to talk with the sitters. This accounted for the medium's often erratic-looking behaviour while in trance. In his high-pitched voice, Elf explained his purpose in communicating was not philosophising, or teaching about the spirit world—he preferred to leave that task for other more interested spirits. Instead, Elf's primary motivation was fun. He also told us that he was *still* (evidently he had been working at it for some time) attempting to make Sandy's physical body levitate above the ground. He was adamant that one day he *would* succeed in performing this extraordinary feat.

Several other spirits came forward that morning before Joseph decided that the sitting should be drawn to a close. The connection to the spirit world was severed for the time being, and the spirits receded back from where they came. The close of the séance was signalled with more music—this time a short instrumental piece performed by Hank Marvin and The Shadows. The proceedings were capped off with Christine's reading of the closing prayer. Once Sandy had safely returned to normal consciousness, after a few moments of drowsy confusion, the lights were switched back on, and after her eyes had adjusted, we all went back into the house for tea, cake, and conversation. The snow outside made the early afternoon winter sunlight exceptionally brilliant in contrast to the mysterious red gloom of the séance room we left behind. I felt invigorated, but didn't know why, and wasn't quite sure what I had just experienced.

When we were in the house I asked Sandy what it felt like to go into trance. She said she didn't know what to say. She couldn't put it into words. When I asked about the types of mediumship she was developing she responded by saying, "I have been *told* I practise physical, trance, and transfiguration mediumship. I know spirits talk through me, some things have moved in my presence when in trance, and I aid healing." Her comment suggested that she was not conscious, or at least wholly conscious, of her mediumistic activities during séances. This inability to recall events that take place while in trance is referred to in the parapsychological literature as "mediumistic amnesia" (Rock, 2013, p. 7), and is a cross-cultural feature of many mediumship practices and traditions. In anthropology and religious studies, the amnesic quality of the medium's experience has classically been used as a point of distinction between the practices of spirit mediums on the one hand and shamans on the other. During the mediumistic state, the medium's consciousness is displaced by that of the spirit occupying their body—in essence, the medium is no longer present. For the shaman, however, their primary role and function is to *bring back* information from the spirit world—in order to perform this function the shaman must be able to recall their trance excursion (Eliade, 1989; Jokic, 2008b). In reality, however, this distinction is not always so clear-cut.

These features of Sandy's mediumship performance also accorded well with classic anthropological accounts of spirit possession and other ecstatic magical and religious practices, recorded in vastly different cultural contexts around the world (Lewis, 1971; Bourguignon, 2007; Schmidt & Huskinson, 2010; A. Dawson, 2010; Hunter & Luke, 2014). It was also evident from this first séance at the Bristol Spirit Lodge that their practices, and the experiences that arise from them, aligned with accounts of spirit mediumship from the history and literature of psychical research (Gauld, 1982; Rock, 2013). Combined with the apparent sincerity of my informants, these correspondences suggested that I was dealing with a *genuine human experience*. In other words, with Sandy I felt sure that she was not trying to fool me—she was not "pretending". Sandy seemed to me like a modern-day Oracle—sitting in the corner of the darkened séance room, providing a conduit for communication between the mundane world of suburban life and the extraordinary world of spirits and the dead.

Another element of my early encounters with the Bristol Spirit Lodge that caught my attention was the apparent complexity of the spirits themselves. Far from being abstractions with little real-world relevance, the spirits I encountered at the Bristol Spirit Lodge were both *immanent* and *tangible*. Indeed, they were manifested in three-dimensional space through the bodies of their entranced mediums. These spirits could be talked to and questioned directly, and even interacted with physically through their hosts. I would eventually come to see that each of the spirits at the Lodge presented themselves (physically and psychologically) in a surprisingly distinctive and consistent manner across weeks, months, and even years of development. Through this process the spirits were able to build up a friendly, usually jovial relationship with regular sitters at the Lodge. Furthermore, these spirit entities apparently possessed a real form of active agency the world. The spirits were clearly able to affect change in the social world that surrounded them—they were social actors quite capable of influencing the actions and behaviours of the social circle that built up to support and develop them. It became clear to me quite early on that the spirits and the group were mutually sustaining one another in a sort of symbiotic feedback relationship.

To briefly summarise, the following were my primary reasons for wanting to pursue further research into the practices of the Bristol Spirit Lodge beyond my initial undergraduate dissertation (Hunter, 2009):

1. The apparent *genuineness* of the medium's altered state of consciousness, indicative of an underlying experiential dimension to spirit mediumship.
2. The apparent *immanence* of the spirits I encountered in the field. The spirits were not lofty abstractions, but *tangible realities*—talking to us directly from the corner of the room we were sitting in.
3. The apparent *complexity* of their personalities (not in all cases, however).
4. The spirits I encountered were at the very least *socially real*, in fact they were the main social actors in an ongoing discourse between the living and the dead.
5. My own subjective experiences, which seemed to resonate with the beliefs and experiences of Lodge members.

All of this led me to the conclusion that there was something much more complex going on in this suburban garden shed than the usual explanations of fraud, trickery, delusion, and pathology could adequately account for (Hunter, 2009). Indeed, there seemed to be more going on than the dominant anthropological models of social functionalism and cognitive science could comfortably explain (at least in their simplest forms). This book, therefore, represents the fruit of my labour in trying to gain a deeper understanding of what this phenomenon actually is, what it means, how we might best go about interpreting and understanding it, and how best to approach questions of experience and ontology in ethnographic research. This is achieved through the development of a non-reductive interpretive framework that emphasises *complexity* and *multiple dimensions of process and meaning.* In other words, an approach that sees spirit mediumship as multifaceted, involving multiple simultaneous processes (psychological, physiological, sociological, psi, spirits, etc.), and that does not seek to reduce the significance of spirit mediumship to purely functional, psychological, sociological, or cognitive explanations.

CHAPTER ONE

Problems and approaches

No account of the Universe in its totality can be final which
leaves these other forms of consciousness quite disregarded.
—William James, *The Varieties of Religious Experience*
(2004, p. 335)

Ontological frustrations

This book is about mediums, spirits, and how we know what is *real*—its
concerns are, therefore, *epistemological* (how we come to *know*) and *ontological* (about what *exists*). It is also ethnographic, making use of participation and observation in real-life social situations to help answer these
sorts of questions. This situates my work, to a certain extent at least,
within anthropology's recent so-called "ontological turn" (Carrithers,
Candea, Sykes, Holbraad, & Venkatesan, 2010; Holbraad & Pedersen,
2017), though it is a position I have arrived at through a slightly different lineage of scholars. Martin Holbraad and Morten Pedersen, two key
theorists of the ontological turn, write that it:

> ... is meant as a call to keep *open* the question of what phenomena
> might comprise a given ethnographic field and how anthropological

1

> concepts have to be modulated or transformed ... to articulate them (2017, p. 11)

In other words, it is about taking seriously the world view of our fieldwork informants—not as systems of cultural *beliefs*, but rather as gateways into different *worlds*. This book is also about anomalous experiences (those experiences that do not seem to fit within the accepted boundaries of Western materialist science) and their role in the development of self concepts and models of the mind-body relationship. A useful definition of anomalous experience is offered by psychologists Cardeña, Lynn, and Krippner (2000). An anomalous experience, they write, is

> an uncommon experience (e.g. synaesthesia) or one that, although it may be experienced by a substantial amount of the population (e.g. experiences interpreted as telepathic), is believed to deviate from the usually accepted explanations of reality. (p. 4)

This book is also, therefore, *phenomenological* and *experiential* (situating it within the remit of the anthropology of *experience*, and the anthropology of *consciousness*). It is grounded in ethnographic and auto-ethnographic participation in the activities of a private non-denominational spiritualist home-circle called the Bristol Spirit Lodge, but also builds on this with an exploration of broader theoretical issues in the anthropology of spirit possession, the anthropology of personhood, performance studies, consciousness studies, and parapsychology.

One of the principal aims of this book is to offer a suggested route for social-scientific engagement with topics that have, until relatively recently, been considered "taboo" in academia—specifically considering the *ontological reality* of spirits, psi phenomena and the paranormal (and not simply dismissing them, or attempting to explain them away in terms that undermine or negate the "native" interpretation), and the *processes* by which they are brought into social reality (but not *just* social reality). This is in contrast to the examination of *belief*, which has been the traditional focus of the social sciences when engaging with the paranormal. Parapsychologist George Hansen writes:

> Academe does not totally neglect the paranormal. Sociologists, anthropologists, psychologists and folklorists are allowed to study *beliefs* about paranormal events, but there is a taboo against

attempting to verify their reality. In academe today serious consideration of the supernatural is limited to the arts and humanities. Yet even there we find ambivalence; the accounts studied are of "long ago" or "far away" and usually explicitly fictional (or metaphorical). The fact that no academic departments study the reality of the claims subtly implies to the students that the phenomena are not real. (2001, p. 185)

Hansen's observation resonates with the attitude expressed by renowned ethnographer E. E. Evans-Pritchard (1902–1973) in his book *Theories of Primitive Religion* (1965). In the opening chapter, Evans-Pritchard clearly delineates the research remit of the anthropologist of religion—*belief not ontology*. He writes:

As I understand the matter, there is no possibility of knowing whether the spiritual beings of primitive religions or of any others have any existence or not, and since that is the case [the anthropologist] cannot take the question into consideration. (p. 17)

This book seeks to push beyond this kind of bracketing out of questions of ontology—arguing that social scientific research methods and insights can contribute to these debates. It is also a response to the sense of frustration expressed by anthropologist Edith Turner (1921–2016) in her seminal paper "The Reality of Spirits: A Tabooed or Permitted Field of Study" (1993), which was written following her own anomalous experience while participating in the *Ihamba* ceremony of the Ndembu in Zambia. The paper is also a broader reaction against the kind of approach advocated by Evans-Pritchard above. She writes:

Again and again anthropologists witness spirit rituals, and again and again some indigenous exegete tries to explain that the spirits are present, and furthermore that rituals are the central events of their society. And the anthropologist proceeds to interpret them differently. There seems to be a kind of force field between the anthropologist and her or his subject matter making it impossible for her or him to come close to it, a kind of religious frigidity. We anthropologists need training to see what the Natives see. (p. 11)

The frustration expressed here is the result of Turner's desire to move *beyond* the forms of phenomenological bracketing employed in the social sciences, which in their admirable effort to describe experience *as it presents itself* without the imposition of preconceived ideas, nevertheless continues to "pull away" from the actual implications of experience at the last minute and revert to a reductive materialist explanation. This book seeks to push against this perceived limitation. As an illustration of this attitude, phenomenological anthropologist Michael Jackson (1996) writes:

> What makes the phenomenologist uneasy is the assumption that beliefs and ideas have to have some kind of ahistorical, supraempirical validity if they are to be workable. But ideas can be meaningful and have useful consequences even when they are epistemologically unwarranted. (p. 13)

I agree with this sentiment to a certain extent—beliefs do not *necessarily* equate to something that "really exists" and can be meaningful to believers without an "existing" referent—but it also raises a fundamental question—what if *some* beliefs and ideas *do* possess "some kind of ahistorical, supraempirical validity", as Edie Turner seems to suggest? What if some beliefs *do* refer to something *real*? What if the experiences of spirit mediums *can* tell us something about "reality", or about the nature of consciousness, or give insights into the processes of self formation? In an effort to provide a route to overcome Turner's frustration this book also presents an historical overview of trends in anthropology's engagement with the paranormal leading up to the present study. Furthermore, to continue the draws on parapsychological research on spirit mediumship to explore this *possibility*.

To balance these many different strands I have sought to use and develop a methodological framework that I have termed "ontological flooding" (Hunter, 2015a, 2015b, 2016a, 2016b), which itself has emerged from and through my attempts to make sense of my own encounters with spirit mediumship. Ontological flooding is essentially a position that emphasises complexity and the interaction of multiple contributing factors in any given situation or phenomenon. From this perspective, no single explanatory framework or ontological scheme is able to give a fully satisfying account of what is taking place in a given ethnographic context, though they may give indications of particular contributing *processes of becoming*. In order to *really* understand what is taking place in a mediumship séance in Bristol, for example, we would have to draw on a wide range of perspectives—from performance studies to parapsychology and shamanistic studies, to neuroscience and intercultural psychiatry, all of which interact as a *system*—rather than hope to find a "simple" functionalist, cognitive, or pathological explanation.

By approaching my subject matter through the lens of an "ontologically flooded" perspective—open to multiple possibilities and emphasising complexity over reductive simplicity—I seek to demonstrate that the usually invisible world of spirits, and the anomalous experiences that hint at their existence, not only have considerable implications for those who engage with them on a regular basis (the conclusion that is often arrived at in traditional anthropological examinations of the "supernatural" in other societies), but that through taking their experiences *seriously* in themselves we might also learn something about the nature of consciousness, the self, and indeed "reality"/"realities" more generally (Henare, Holbraad, & Wastell, 2006, p. 9). As Martin Holbraad suggests: "Rather than using our own analytical concepts to make sense of a given ethnography (explanation, interpretation), we use the ethnography to rethink our analytical concepts" (Holbraad in Carrithers, Candea, Sykes, Holbraad, & Venkatesan, 2010, p. 184).

Defining the paranormal

The term "paranormal" was first employed early in the twentieth century by psychical researchers—scientific investigators of psychic experiences—as a replacement for the more loaded term "supernatural", which had been used in its Latin form *supernaturalis* by theologians since the Middle Ages to refer to the *explicitly religious* phenomena documented in the Bible and other religious texts (Bartlett, 2008). Miracles, such as Moses's vision of the burning bush in the Old Testament, Christ's resurrection from the dead in the New Testament, the revelation of the Qur'an to the Prophet Muhammed (Pbuh), or Guru Nanak's extraordinary aquatic journey to the court of Waheguru, for example, have all been understood as manifestations of the power of an almighty God in demonstration of His omnipotence over creation. Such events were often understood to have the ultimate purpose of inspiring *faith* in those who bore witness to them, or subsequently heard stories about them. The "supernatural", then, has for a long time been a *religious domain*.

The association of the term "supernatural" with the direct action of the God of classical theism,[3] coupled with the later idea that such miraculous phenomena were somehow *causally separated* from the rest of the laws governing the natural world, did not appeal to the early members of the Society for Psychical Research (SPR). The SPR was founded in 1882 by the Cambridge scholars F. W. H. Myers (1843–1901), Henry Sidgwick (1838–1900), Eleanor Sidgwick (1845–1936), and Edmund Gurney (1847–1888), specifically with the purpose of investigating similar, seemingly "miraculous", phenomena in the present day (such as visions, apparitions, mediumship, survival after death, poltergeists, telepathy, and psychokinesis), using rational scientific methods (Haynes, 1982; Broughton, 1991; Blum, 2007). It was through the efforts of these psychical researchers to develop a "science of the supernatural" that the term "paranormal" entered the popular lexicon.

"Paranormal" was originally, therefore, a sceptical and scientific term. It represented a scholarly reaction against the "supernatural"—firstly as a specifically religious domain, and secondly as an unscientific, outdated designation for unusual phenomena. Frederic Myers writes in his magnum opus *Human Personality and Its Survival of Bodily Death* (1903) that:

> The word *supernatural* is open to grave objections; it assumes that there is something outside nature, and it has become associated with arbitrary inference with law. Now there is no reason to suppose that the psychical phenomena with which we deal are less a part of nature, or less subject to fixed and definite law, than any other phenomena. (Myers, 1903, as cited by Kripal, 2010, p. 67)

By implementing the neologism "*super*-normal"—later becoming "*para*-normal"—psychical researchers were attempting to bridge René Descartes's (1596–1650) sharp separation of the domains of *science* and *religion*. Indeed, rather than suggesting that supernormal phenomena were unsuitable for scientific investigation, a vestige of Immanuel Kant's (1724–1804) rejection of "non-positive" (extra-sensory/non-empirical/ visionary) knowledge as meaningless—a reference to Swedenborg's visions of the spiritual world (Kant, 1766), Frederic Myers argued that they were simply beyond the scope of *current* scientific understanding (Myers, 1903; Kripal, 2010, p. 66).

---

[3] Traditionally given the attributes of *omnipotence, omniscience, omni-benevolence, immanence,* and *transcendence.*

The prefix "para" suggests phenomena that stand *beyond* the limits of our current explanatory models. *Para*-psychology, for instance, deals with psychological phenomena that are *not adequately explained by dominant psychological theories*. Similarly, a *para*-anthropology might be concerned with human *experiences, abilities, practices,* and *worlds* that are not adequately explained by currently dominant anthropological theories and models. In making this shift of emphasis, psychical researchers were attempting to demonstrate that paranormal occurrences, if real, were as much a part of the *natural* world as anything else: we just require an *expanded* naturalism to see how they fit in. For the psychical researchers paranormal events were equally as amenable to scientific investigation, experimentation, and theorising as any purely physical phenomenon (Hansen, 2001, p. 21).

The term "paranormal", then, although by now associated with a wide range of pop-culture notions (not all of which are positive), *is*, nevertheless, a scholarly and scientific one—implemented in the first place to bring anomalous phenomena *back* into the wider scientific discourse (Strieber & Kripal, 2016, p. 41). It is in this sense that I refer to the practices and experiences of developing trance mediums at the Bristol Spirit Lodge as "paranormal"—because we still don't know what is really going on sociologically, psychologically, neurophysiologically, parapsychologically, theologically, and so on. In Chapter 3, for example, I argue that the dominant anthropological theories of spirit possession and mediumship have been unsuccessful in providing adequate accounts of the phenomenon in its totality. Through employing the term "paranormal" in this context I hope to make it clear that the dominant theories have not yet fully comprehended spirit mediumship (we do not yet have a sufficient theory of it), and aim to emphasise the fact that there is still a lot more to learn about it, some of which *may transcend* the limits of the standard models usually assumed in the social sciences. I feel that the term, to paraphrase Rupert Sheldrake (2012), helps to "free the spirit of scientific enquiry". Admitting the *possibility* of the paranormal is also a necessary first step in developing a new approach to the anomalous and extraordinary

Alternative terminologies: a rose by any name is still a rose

The kinds of experiences reported by the mediums and sitters who frequent the Bristol Spirit Lodge range from communications with ostensibly deceased individuals through to the physical materialisation of spiritual beings, and the dematerialisation of physical objects. Such phenomena most certainly fall into the category of the "paranormal" as classically defined in the psychical research literature. They are events that the dominant materialist framework of Western science currently has no explanation for, and indeed actively dismisses as *impossible*. David Hume's (1711–1776) classic definition of a miracle as "a transgression of a law of nature by a particular volition of the Deity or by the interposition of some invisible agent" (1772, in Hume, 2000, p. 87), which is also an argument against the possibility of miracles in general, forms the basis for this understanding. For Hume natural laws must be *unchanging*, therefore a transgression of a natural law is a logical *impossibility*:

> A miracle is a violation of the laws of nature; and because firm and unalterable experience has established these laws, the case against a miracle is—just because it is a miracle—as complete as any argument from experience can possibly be imagined to be. (2000, p. 86)

Hume's approach to the issue of natural laws has been hugely influential in Western scholarship, which consequently has tended towards a sceptical and reductive attitude toward the non-rational. Yet, in spite of mainstream academia's dismissal of even the *possibility* of the paranormal, such experiences continue to be reported by surprisingly large numbers of the population. Owing to this, biologist and parapsychologist Rupert Sheldrake has argued that the so-called "paranormal" is, in actuality, perfectly *normal*. Sheldrake has also suggested, contrary to Hume's generally accepted view, that the natural laws revealed by the physical sciences *may* be more like *habits* than fixed eternal laws and may change over time—a somewhat more *organic* view of nature than Hume's notion of permanently fixed laws (Sheldrake, 2012, pp. 84–85).

Sheldrake's contention that paranormal experiences are "normal" is bolstered by the extremely widespread belief in, and experience of, phenomena such as telepathy and precognition among the general population. According to a 2001 US Gallup poll, for instance, 54% of respondents reported belief in "Psychic or spiritual healing or the power of the human mind to heal the body", 50% reported belief in "ESP", 38% believed that "Ghosts or that spirits of dead people can come back in certain places and situations", 36% reported belief in "Telepathy, or communication between minds without using the traditional five senses",

28% reported belief "That people can hear from or communicate mentally with someone who has died", and 15% believed in "Channelling", or allowing a "spirit-being" to temporarily assume control of a human body. All of these had seen an increase since the 1990 poll (Newport & Strausberg, 2001).

A more recent survey of 4096 adults conducted in the UK in 2009 by the social research organisation Ipsos Mori found that 24% of respondents reported having experienced precognition, 12.8% reported ESP experiences, 12.4% reported mystical experiences, 11.5% reported telepathic experiences, and 10.4% reported belief in after death communication (Castro, Burrows, & Wooffitt, 2014). These suggest that a surprisingly high proportion of the UK population claim to have experienced phenomena that are supposedly *anomalous* or *abnormal*, and that are "officially" viewed as *impossible*. These findings also support those of earlier sociological research, which suggests that such experiences are far from uncommon among the general population (Greeley, 1975). Sheldrake has, therefore, expressed his preference for what he considers to be the much more neutral term "psychic" (Sheldrake, 2005, p. 12),[4] which does not distinguish such occurrences from other "normal" and "natural" phenomena. For Sheldrake, the term holds open the *possibility* that the paranormal might actually be an everyday occurrence, without postulating that it must be, in some way, *super*-natural, or in defiance of the "laws of nature".

Other scholars, particularly in the humanities and social sciences, have tended to use terms such as "non-ordinary" (Harner, 1990, 2013), or "extraordinary" (Young & Goulet, 1994; Goulet & Miller, 2007; Straight, 2007), when discussing these kinds of experience. These labels attempt to distance their subject matter from the negative connotations of the "paranormal"—a term by now unfortunately associated with notions of irrational thinking and charlatanism—to bring it back into scholarly discourse. Arguing along similar lines, Robert Shanafelt has proposed the term "marvel", which he defines as "an event of extraordinary wonder, thought to have physical consequences, claimed to be the result of ultra-natural forces". He opts for this term because, in his opinion, it "encompasses divine interventions, supernatural wonders, and other

---

[4] Though this term also carries negative connotations in popular culture and the mainstream media.

paranormal phenomena without the implied hierarchy of monotheism or traditional anthropology" (2004, p. 322).

The term "xenonormal" has also been suggested as an alternative label for anomalous experiences and events, and refers to phenomena that *appear* to be paranormal but in fact have much more prosaic explanations.[5] Examples of xenonormal phenomena would include mis-observation, pareidolia, optical and cognitive illusions, and so on. Others prefer the term "anomalous", or "anomalistic", which comes with the implication that such phenomena *will* one day find a place within our scientific understanding of the universe, whether as genuine (objectively verified) occurrences, as simple misinterpretations of otherwise mundane events, or as psychological illusions (Wescott, 1977, pp. 345–346; Holt, Simmonds-Moore, Luke, & French, 2012). They are anomalous *for now*, but will ultimately be explained in scientific terms.

Parapsychologists have labelled these types of experiences and events *psi phenomena*. Social psychologist and parapsychological researcher Daryl Bem, for example, defines "psi" as "anomalous processes of information or energy transfer that are not currently explainable in terms of known physical or biological mechanisms" (2011, p. 407). Psi itself is an umbrella term used in reference to the supposed human faculties of psychokinesis (PK—the influence of mind upon matter) and extrasensory perception (ESP)—which itself encompasses telepathy (mind-to-mind communication), clairvoyance (distant viewing), and precognition (knowing future events before they come to pass). These are the building blocks of the paranormal from the parapsychological perspective—the hypothetical processes by which paranormal events occur. Such phenomena, if real (as the parapsychological literature would appear to suggest), cannot be thought of as somehow *separate* from the natural world, but rather should be conceived as *inherent* and *fundamental* aspects of it—not supernatural, but natural.

There is, however, a significant difference between the kinds of ostensible phenomena designated by the term "psi" and the supposed action of spirits during séances. Parapsychological investigators have historically struggled with the complex problem of distinguishing between spirit action and psi in the context of spirit mediumship demonstrations (Beischel & Rock, 2009; Sudduth, 2013). Given that, in essence, both the survival hypothesis (the argument that mediumistic phenomena are

---

[5] See, for example: www.assap.ac.uk/newsite/articles/Xenonormal.html.

produced by discarnate spirits) and the psi hypothesis (that the phenomena are the product of psi) seem to equally fit the anecdotal and experimental data on spirit mediumship, it is entirely possible that the mediums I encountered during my fieldwork *might actually* have been in contact with deceased spirits. Equally as possible is the idea that they *could* have been employing (or at the very least attempting to employ) some form of psi in their mediumistic demonstrations.

Irrespective of the nomenclature we employ it is clear that we are referring to essentially the same set of experiences and phenomena— whether we call them supernatural, paranormal, extraordinary, ultra-natural, xenonormal, anomalous, psi, or spirit phenomena (Marton, 2010, pp. 11–13). It is all too easy for scholarly discussions to get caught up in tiresome debates over nomenclature and terminology, which in turn diverts attention away from the *experience itself*. For this reason, I have used, and will continue to use, several of these terms interchangeably throughout the course of this book, but I am confident that the reader will "know what I am talking about."

Investigating mediumship

Several researchers over the last thirty years have conducted ethnographic fieldwork in Spiritualist churches and centres (see for instance Richard & Adato, 1980; Biscop, 1985; Gilbert, 2010; D. G. M. Wilson, 2011, 2013; Meintel, 2014), but in that time there have been very few ethnographic investigations of Spiritualist *home-circles* (cf. Skultans, 1974 for a notable earlier exception), and no ethnographic studies of trance and physical mediumship circles specifically (though Fiona Bowie has written an unpublished account of a physical mediumship séance with the medium David Thompson). Photographer Shannon Taggart's recently published photographic study of physical mediumship also gives an insight into the field (Taggart, 2019). In light of the relative scarcity of ethnographic studies of physical mediumship in particular, it is hoped that the research documented in this book will also contribute new ethnographic data concerning this relatively elusive form of spiritualist practice, which is usually hidden from public view, and is often assumed to be extinct in contemporary society.

To this end I have employed an open-ended ethnographic approach, making use of a combination of fieldwork techniques including first-person participant observation in séances and mediumship development sessions, face-to-face interviews (which I recorded in writing, audio, and video), email interviews, and small-scale questionnaire and survey work. My field research was carried out on a part-time basis over the course of five years, between 2009 and 2014. During this period I attended séances as often as I could, and communicated regularly with members of the group both formally through structured and semi-structured interviews, and casually in the context of weekly meetings at the Lodge, as well as through regular email exchanges with members.

The majority of the book makes use of *qualitative data* concerning the *personal experiences* of my informants, as well as my own *subjective* experiences in the field. My own experiences while participating in séances and mediumship development circles lend an auto-ethnographic component to this research project. Jones, Adams, and Ellis (2016) write of auto-ethnography:

> One characteristic that binds all autoethnographies is the use of personal experience to examine and/or critique cultural experience. Autoethnographers do this in work [by] including personal experience within an otherwise traditional social scientific analysis. (p. 22)

In other words, my own experiences of mediumship development, coupled with my experience as a participant in séances, have informed my understanding of the experiences reported by my informants, as well as my understanding of the ongoing theoretical debate over the nature of such experiences and their wider ontological implications. Above all else, I understand my own experiences as providing me with a definite "point of inter-subjective entry" (Jokic, 2008a, p. 36) into the world view, culture, practices, and experiences of my research informants (their *ontological frame*). This is a crucial step in developing the kind of non-reductive approach I consider necessary for grappling with the paranormal in general, and with spirit mediumship in particular. These qualitative and experiential data collection methods have also been supplemented with extensive literature reviews exploring the study's central themes of spirit possession, personhood, and parapsychology, as well as anthropology's historical engagement with the paranormal.

A comparative approach

The discussion that follows takes a broadly comparative approach to the mediumship practices and experiences of my informants (as well as my own auto-ethnographic experiences). Experiences from the Lodge in Bristol are compared with ethnographic accounts of spirit possession from vastly different cultural contexts, such as Brazilian Umbanda and Candomblé, Haitian Vodun, and Malay spirit possession. In doing this I am not suggesting that these traditions and practices are identical in any way, but rather that they might share common processes or characteristics. Through comparison it is hoped that it might be possible to identify "core features", or "core processes", of mediumship that in turn can be used to develop a more nuanced understanding of mediumistic practices in the Western context (Evans, 1987, pp. 11–12; Kripal, 2014).

In his comparative cross-cultural study of afterlife beliefs and near-death experiences in early civilisations, Gregory Shushan (2009) argues that comparative approaches in the academic study of religion have been "out of fashion" in recent decades. In particular he draws attention to the effect of postmodernism's backlash against the grand narratives of Victorian scholars such as James G. Frazer and E. B. Tylor, as well as other "romantic" comparativists of the twentieth century, like Carl Jung and Mircea Eliade. Shushan points out, however, that comparison itself (as a research methodology) need not be equated with the perceived ethnocentric, evolutionist, imperialistic, and universalising tendencies of the early comparativists. Comparison *can* be done without falling into these traps:

> Comparison and the observation of similarities are methods of enquiry, not theories or conclusions. Neither comparison itself nor the observation or interpretation of similarities (or differences) are dependent on any particular theoretical –*ism*. (Shushan, 2009, p. 21)

In making comparisons between different traditions, then, I am not seeking to uncritically, or ethnocentrically superimpose the cultural practices of one group onto another, but rather am attempting to discern *patterns* in the processes by which incorporeal spirits are brought into social reality in different contexts. Examples of such recurring patterns might include, for example, the role of altered states of consciousness, the role of bodily performance, the role of a "circle leader" or "master of ceremonies", the role of dialogue with the spirits, psi processes, and so on. These will be discussed over the course of the following chapters.

Furthermore, it is important to stress that these are not intended as simple comparisons. It is not an effort towards reducing one phenomenon to another, or saying that all mediumistic traditions are the *same*, tapping into the same spiritual reality. As Jeffrey Kripal suggests in his comparison of traditional shamanistic experiences and contemporary UFO abduction narratives:

> ... we will not ... make any kind of simplistic equation ... *in either direction*. Rather, we might "spiral up" and suggest that similar psychological, physiological, erotic and physical processes are behind both traditional shamanistic practices and the modern abduction phenomena. (Strieber & Kripal, 2016, p. 197)

Similarly, then, we will be comparing disparate possession traditions not on the assumption that we are dealing with *identical* phenomena (indeed they may be exceedingly different at face value) but rather because they might share *common features* and similar *underlying processes*, which in turn may be clothed in idiosyncratic layers of cultural elaboration and interpretation.

In addition to the anthropological literature, special emphasis has also been placed on the parapsychological literature, in particular that dealing with spirit mediumship from the nineteenth century to the present day. Parapsychology is the scientific study of "psi phenomena". This literature is of key significance, as while anthropologists have been predominantly concerned with analysing spirit possession and mediumship traditions in non-European contexts, parapsychologists have been actively investigating Western Euro-American mediumship for over 130 years (Gauld, 1982). Perhaps unsurprisingly, however, parapsychologists have generally tended to neglect the wider cross-cultural perspective, just as anthropologists have tended to neglect the Western context (though there are exceptions). The parapsychological literature, therefore, provides a great deal of observational information concerning the practices, beliefs, experiences, and phenomena of Euro-American spirit mediumship that has largely been ignored by anthropologists working on spirit possession in non-Western cultures. The parapsychological literature is ripe for further comparative investigation—to paraphrase Jeffrey Kripal's terminology, we are "putting it back on the table" as valid data for scholarly engagement in anthropology and the social sciences (Strieber & Kripal, 2016, pp. 11–18).

An experience-centred approach

A significant portion of this book is given over to an exploration of the role that experience plays in the development of conceptions of the self, as well as the wider implications of such experiences and beliefs in the formation of distinctive ontological frameworks. These folk ontologies can be thought of in terms of *ethno-metaphysics*—a term coined by the American ethnographer A. Irving Hallowell (1892–1974) in his discussion of North American Ojibwa ontology. He writes of the challenge of studying ethno-metaphysics:

> We are confronted with the philosophical implications of their thought, the nature of the world of being as they conceive it. If we pursue the problem deeply enough we soon come face to face with a relatively unexplored territory—*ethno-metaphysics*. Can we penetrate this realm in other cultures? What kind of evidence is at our disposal? The forms of speech as Benjamin Whorf and the neo-Humboldtians have thought? The manifest content of myth? Observed behavior and attitudes? And what order of reliability can our inferences have? The problem is a complex and difficult one, but this should not preclude its exploration. (2002, p. 20)

This book wades into this "complex and difficult" area of ethno-metaphysics, considering the ways that personal experiences are interpreted, understood, given meaning, and ultimately incorporated into a cohesive (if constantly evolving) world view. This may be thought of as a *constructivist* approach to understanding the development of world view and self concepts—in other words, our world view (including our sense of *self*, or what we *are*) is not something that is simply given to us through cultural socialisation (though parts of it can be), but is something that we learn and build up through *experience* in the world (cf. Piaget, 1964).

This emphasis on the experiential aspects of mediumship—how mediumship is *experienced* and *interpreted* resonates with folklorist

David J. Hufford's *experience-centred approach* (Hufford, 1982, 1995). Hufford explains:

> A major advantage of the experience-centred approach for carrying out this task is that it does not require presuppositions about the ultimate nature of the events investigated, although it can provide some information relevant to investigations of that nature. (1982, p. 256)

Through implementing such a perspective it might be possible to approach the ethno-metaphysics of my fieldwork informants by *taking seriously* their *experiential* claims. By "taking experience seriously" I mean not backing away from the *possible* implications of certain kinds of anomalous experience, and not trying to explain anomalous experiences away in the terms of a reductive materialism (cf. Churchland, 1982) that does not seem to fit the facts, social or otherwise.

Why do people believe in spirits?

This was one of the questions that first initiated my research as an undergraduate. It has been a recurrent theme in the work of anthropologists since the discipline's emergence in the mid-nineteenth century. Sir E. B. Tylor's (1832–1917) pioneering examination of animism—defined as the belief in supernatural beings and as the most basic expression of religiosity—was a major stepping stone for anthropology, and arguably represented one of the discipline's first great theoretical contributions to the study of religion. It was also the start of a long-ranging debate over the nature and function of animism in human societies (Harvey, 2005).

Tylor's theory was an attempt at answering the question of *why* it is that people—across time, cultures, and geography—have almost invariably come to possess some form of *belief* in the existence of invisible spiritual beings. Tylor came to the conclusion that so-called "primitive philosophers" had simply *mistaken* their dreams and trance visions for *real* experiences (1930, pp. 87–109). According to Tylor's theory, belief in spirits is ultimately a symptom of irrationality and faulty reasoning, superseded by Western positivist rationalism. This is the assumption that has dominated anthropology's interactions with the spirit cosmologies of Western and non-Western cultures alike—*there are no spirits only beliefs about spirits*—and that gives rise to the frustration expressed by Edie Turner (1993), as discussed earlier.

The folklorist and psychical researcher Andrew Lang (1844–1912), a contemporary of Tylor, took a slightly different perspective. He suggested that the belief in spirits arose not from misinterpretations of "mundane" experiences (e.g., dreams, etc.) but from *actual* experiences of *real spirits* and genuine paranormal events (Lang, 1900). In these two Victorian scholars we see the emergence of the contemporary debate over the nature of anomalous experience—are anomalous experiences and paranormal beliefs delusional, or do they offer a glimpse of a very real aspect of reality?

And yet, in spite of more than 100 years of anthropological inquiry since Tylor and Lang's first forays into this territory, the question "Why do people *believe* in spirits?" continues to be a moot point in contemporary anthropology (E. Turner, 1993; Glass-Coffin, 2012). Many competing, and occasionally complementary, theoretical approaches (including social and psychological functionalism, psychopathology, etc.) have risen, fallen, been discarded, and reinterpreted, and still there is little in the way of overall consensus opinion (except, perhaps, for a growing emphasis on reductive cognitive explanations, which explain belief in spirits in terms of the ways that human beings process information about the world, cf. Guthrie, 1980, 1993; Boyer, 2001; Pyysiäinen & Anttonen, 2002; Cohen, 2008; Cohen & Barrett, 2011).

The fact of the matter is, however, that despite an alleged tendency towards increasing secularisation in the Western world (Voas & Crockett, 2005, p. 13), and in Western academia in particular (Hansen, 2010), paranormal beliefs of all types—including belief in spiritual beings in all of their varied forms (from ghosts to God, and from faeries to angels)—*continue* to play a very significant role in the lives of a great many people in contemporary Western societies (Berger, 1971; Heathcote-James, 2001; Mackian, 2011, 2012; Castro, Burrows, & Wooffitt, 2014). This poses a challenge to the dominant anthropological theories addressing these issues, because, at least taken as individual theories, their reductive simplicity fails to match up to the complexity of the ethnographic reality. People *do* still believe in spirits—even in societies dominated in the mainstream by positivist rationalism—and one of the overarching reasons many people give for this belief is *personal experience* (Bennett, 1987; Clarke, 1995).

Not why, but how: process and experience

Perhaps one of the reasons for this apparent inability to develop a coherent and satisfactory anthropological theory of spirits is that we are asking the wrong kinds of questions. The question "Why do people believe in spirits?" comes loaded with *a priori* assumptions about the beliefs of others—as well assumptions as about the *believers* themselves—that inevitably skew our understanding of the ethnographic data. For instance, to ask "Why do people believe X?" automatically assumes that there is reason to question the beliefs of others in the first place, as if to suggest that the anthropologist somehow occupies a privileged, intellectually superior position, where what they believe (often, though not always, the materialist foundations of Western academia) does *not* require questioning. Taking inspiration from the alternative (non-anthropological) epistemological systems of thinkers such as Charles Fort and Robert Anton Wilson, amongst others, I aim to suggest that before denying the possibility that the beliefs of our informants have no basis in reality, we must ask how we can be *certain* that *our own beliefs* about the world are well-founded? Why do we believe what *we* believe, and what if the beliefs of others come closer to the "truth" than our own?

Furthermore, "'why questions" assume that there is a *definitive answer* that can be objectively and scientifically understood—preferably an explanation that accords with anthropology's dominant functionalist, psychosocial, and materialist paradigms. This is not necessarily the case. In other words, could there be *something more* going on than the dominant paradigms allow for? Should we really expect *all phenomena*—social or otherwise—to comply with the accepted theories of mainstream academia, or to reduce down to physical causes? Can spirit mediumship practices really be explained in functionalist, psychological, cognitive, or sociological terms alone? In essence I am asking whether the social sciences have really "sorted it all out" yet? Arguing along similar lines, Aaron Joshua Howard writes that:

> Ethnographic methods and anthropological research will continue to be oppressive unless the scholar can take seriously that something, whatever it is, happens within the rituals that tap into gods, spirits, ancestors, that is outside of Freud, Durkheim, or Tylor's ability to explain. Unless anthropologists are willing to open a

discursive space that allows for the transcendent and the supernatural, their research will continue to oppress and demean societies from which we have much to learn. (2013, p. 15)

These are difficult conceptual issues to confront as a researcher working in the field, but the solution proposed here is to ask a slightly different set of questions, namely *how* questions. For example: How do people *communicate* with spirits, and what are the *processes* involved? How do people *experience* spirits? How do people *interpret* their experiences of spirits? These questions avoid the assumptions inherent in the kinds of "why question" that have dominated the scholarly debate by focusing on the processes involved in the experiences and practices of our ethnographic informants.

This approach broadly resonates with the twentieth-century philosopher Alfred North Whitehead's (1861–1947) "process philosophy", which emphasises the fluid *processual* nature of reality, in contrast to the atomistic view of reality that dominates much of the materialist metaphysics underlying contemporary (popular) science, that is, discrete objects occupying physical space. Whitehead calls for a radical shift in perspective and suggests that "… the actual world is a process, and … the process is the becoming of actual entities" (1978, p. 22). This perspective also resonates with Charles Fort's "intermediatist" philosophy (Hunter, 2016b), which is specifically intended as a means to discuss and explore anomalous experiences, observations, and phenomena— "damned facts" in Fort's terminology—in a manner that bypasses the strictures of materialist rationalism. Fort writes:

> … in general metaphysical terms, our expression is that, like a purgatory, all that is commonly called "existence," which we call Intermediateness, is quasi-existence, neither real nor unreal, but the expression of attempt to become real. (2008, p. 15)

In dealing with issues of *process* in mediumship, then, we are concerned with *how* spirits "become real". Anthropologist Aditya Malik (2009, pp. 82–93) makes a similar point in his discussion of central Himalayan spirit possession performances, when he argues in favour of a shift in the analysis of spirit possession away from questions of "belief" towards notions of "embodiment" and "experience" and the *processes* through which spirits are made real in the context of spirit possession practices.

Indeed, processual approaches are also currently gaining traction in the field of parapsychological mediumship studies, which, for some researchers at least, has moved on from the question of whether or not mediums are genuinely making contact with deceased spirits (is it true or false?), to questions of *how* this ostensible communication takes place, and how it is *experienced* by the medium from the first-person perspective (Jahn & Dunne, 1997; Heath, 2000; Rock & Beischel, 2008; Beischel & Rock, 2009; Luke, 2012; Roxburgh & Roe, 2013).

Asking "How do people communicate with spirits?" therefore presents researchers with the opportunity to *engage* with the anomalous without the assumptions inherent in traditional *why* approaches—of bracketing out the question of the reality of spirits—and may pave the way for a non-reductive anthropology of the paranormal. In the words of parapsychological anthropologist Patric Giesler, we can "assume that [spirits] *could exist* and proceed etically on that assumption" (1984, pp. 302–303, emphasis added). In this way we can bypass the "hegemonic dismissal" of alternative ontological systems (Howard, 2013) and get on with the task of investigating the social, cultural, psychological, psi (and more) processes involved in the manifestation of spiritual beings as distinctive social agents.

Secretive communities and the danger of perceived authentication

Spiritualism has had a long history of highly critical investigation by scientific researchers (from parapsychology and psychical research) as well as from sceptical debunkers. The legacy of this history has, naturally, had an impact on my role as an outside researcher in the group. As a representative of the academic community I have at times been seen as an "objective observer" by my informants—as a *scientist*—and as such my own experiences have occasionally been taken as either confirming or denying the reality of certain phenomena produced by mediums in the Lodge.

The primary danger is that what I write about my observations during trance and physical mediumship séances, especially once published, may present problems further down the line in one of two distinct ways: (1) If my writings are read as a favourable account of a particular medium's abilities they may subsequently be used by that medium, the Lodge, or "spiritualists" in general, as validating "proof" of the reality of mediumistic phenomena—as a form of authentication. My writings could then become a part of their own canon of documentary evidence for the reality of mediumship, backed up by the authority of an "academic" (I have already experienced this effect when a phenomenological report written about a physical mediumship séance was used on the medium's website as an endorsement of the reality of the phenomena witnessed. I have also been referred to on spiritualist social media channels as a "practising spiritualist" myself, which is not strictly true). On the other hand, (2) if my account was seen to be critical of the séance, a particular medium, or the phenomena they are purported to produce then I would run the risk of alienating myself from my informants and being branded "just another debunker", which would prevent any future research.

Given this potential feedback effect, there are certain issues associated with the way in which I have had to situate myself as a researcher while participating in the group and its activities. First of all, it has been important to stress that I am *not* assuming the role of a debunker, and to explain to my informants that it is not, and has never been, my intention to question the *validity* of the phenomena being produced, nor to *challenge* their beliefs and experiences in any way. Neither have I set out deliberately to expose the Lodge's mediums as fraudulent—as so many debunkers have historically set out to do in the context of the Spiritualist movement. I have stressed that it is not my place, as an anthropologist, to attempt to *experimentally* verify the claims of mediums at the Lodge (though I do undoubtedly consider the ontological issues in some depth). This book does not, therefore, contain parapsychological *testing* of the claims of mediums, and does not claim to offer *proof* for the reality of spirits (though it may be suggestive in that direction). For example, I do not seek to prove or disprove the reality of ectoplasm—to take samples, for example—or to test the accuracy or veracity of messages received from spiritual beings. Instead my approach has been primarily *descriptive*, *interpretive*, and *theoretical*, focusing on themes that have become apparent through ethnographic and auto-ethnographic observation, namely issues related to *performance,* the *processes* by which spirits participate in social reality, and *experience* and its role in the development of models of the self.

CHAPTER TWO

Spirit mediumship in Bristol

Religion and Spiritualism in Bristol: contemporary and historical

According to census data from 2001 approximately 62% of the population of Bristol described themselves as Christian, and approximately 25% described themselves as non-religious. The remaining 13% of the population consist of Muslims (approx. 2%), Hindus (approx. 0.5%), Buddhists (approx. 0.4%), Sikhs (approx. 0.4%), and Jews (approx. 0.2%). "Any other religion" came in at 0.4%, and "no religion stated" at 9% (Census, 2001). The detail of the census is not accurate enough to give a good idea of the number of nominal Spiritualists living in Bristol, though it is clear that Spiritualists must be a minority religious group. The issue is further complicated by the fact that many Spiritualists would likely also class themselves as Christian, so there is potentially a considerable overlap effect.

The SNU currently lists five registered Spiritualist churches in Bristol, two in Bath, one in Clevedon and another in Weston-super-Mare.[6] It is important to note that these figures do not include *private* spiritualist centres or home-circles, which are independent of the SNU. Of these

---

[6] www.snu.org.uk/community/churches/churches_b.

there are at least three independent Spiritualist centres that I am aware of in Bristol (in addition to the Bristol Spirit Lodge). The Bristol Spirit Lodge itself is a private non-denominational home-circle geared specifically towards the development of trance and physical mediumship, and so is somewhat different to other Spiritualist churches in Bristol.

Records held at the Arthur Findlay College suggest that non-unionised Spiritualist services were being held in Bristol at least as early as 1900, and by 1909 three of these groups had registered themselves with the SNU. It is very difficult to judge the extent of private home-circles and séances *before* 1900, but owing to the general popularity of experimental home séances in the UK at this time (Melechi, 2008) it is not inconceivable to imagine such private practices also taking place in Bristol. There is *some* evidence for this kind of Spiritualist activity in Bristol, though it is admittedly quite sparse. In 1872, for example, a retired Clifton-based photographer by the name of John Beattie decided to conduct his own experiments into spirit photography, after being highly sceptical of purported spirit images he had seen. Arthur Conan Doyle (1859–1930), in his two-volume *History of Spiritualism* (1926), describes how Beattie, with the aid of his colleague Dr G. S. Thompson of Edinburgh:

> ... conducted a series of experiments in 1872 and obtained on the plates first patches of light and, later on, entire extra figures. They found that the extra forms and markings showed up on the plate during development much in advance of the sitter, a peculiarity often observed by other operators. (vol. 2, p. 70)

So influential were the spirit photographs produced by Beattie and his colleagues in Bristol that, as Conan Doyle relates, they were dubbed "valuable and conclusive experiments" by no less an authority than the famed biologist Alfred Russell-Wallace (1823–1913), co-discoverer of the process of natural selection and a prominent Spiritualist himself (a fact that is very often overlooked in accounts of Wallace and his contribution to biology). The authenticity of Beattie's spirit photographs was also vouched for by the famous and very well respected medium and preacher, the Reverend William Stainton Moses (1839–1892). His kind of private "experimental" approach to Spiritualism has been a recurrent feature throughout its history, and the activities of the Bristol Spirit

Lodge certainly seem to be a continuation of this tradition. Historian Georgina Byrne also provides some *suggestive* evidence of both private and public Spiritualist activity in Bristol, noting, for example, that in 1916 "Edmund McClure, an honorary Canon of Bristol, had despaired that spiritualism was widespread and that professional mediums were offering their services in 'all our large towns'" (2010, p. 49).

Newspaper cuttings housed in the Bristol Central Library also seem to suggest that Spiritualist activity was prevalent in the city well into the 1970s and 1980s. In 1978 Bristol was at the heart of a controversy that ran right to the very top of the Spiritualists' National Union. The then SNU president, Gordon Higginson (1918–1993), was accused of fraud following a demonstration of his mediumship at a Bristol Spiritualist church. Members of the church had accused Higginson of using readily available information to embellish his clairvoyant abilities during a public demonstration. It was suggested that Higginson had used names from library lists and healing books stored at the church. The accusation went so far as to end up in court, but Higginson was acquitted. The court was not satisfied that the documents could have provided him with *all* the names and details he had mentioned in his readings. The case was dropped and inadvertently bolstered Higginson's reputation as a medium. In August 2012 I met with Helen Bevan, a long-standing participant in the Bristol Spiritualist scene, at the Bristol Central Library, where she told me:

> Around that time there had been a great to-do centred on Grosvenor Road Church that was in all the papers, local and national. The Secretary of that church had publicly accused Mr Gordon Higginson, the President of the Spiritualists' National Union, of cheating when he had taken a service there … during this time I was present as minute-taker at one of the meetings in the church when Mr Higginson met his accuser. He had come from the North— Stoke-on-Trent I believe—and had been inhospitably left alone for some time in the church prior to the service. His accuser alleged that during that time he had memorised the list of members and their photos, I never saw a church with photos of their members, and had then used this information to give messages at the service. Utter rubbish! In any case, he of all people didn't need to stoop to such depths. (Interview with Helen Bevan, August 2012)

An article in the *Bristol Evening Post*, dated March 1, 1979, details the story of "young Spiritualists" in Bristol searching for a venue in which to "practise their religion". The thirty-two-year-old leader of this drive for a new premises for young Spiritualists (who in fact turned out to be Helen Bevan) explained that "there are lots of psychics in Bristol who aren't able to heal because of lack of facilities" (*Bristol Evening Post*, 1979). The newspaper also followed the story of the "Aquarian United Spiritualist Society" to find a Bristol home for their congregation of "70-plus members" in 1980 (*Bristol Evening Post*, 1980). All of this suggests a long history of spiritualist activity in Bristol going as far back as the craze for Spiritualism in the mid-nineteenth century, right through to the present day.

Belmont road spiritualist centre

My first contact with Spiritualism in Bristol was in the winter of 2008 at one of Bristol's five SNU registered Spiritualist churches. I was attending as part of the preliminary research for my undergraduate dissertation in anthropology (Hunter, 2009). In this instance I found myself standing outside a converted Victorian terraced house in the leafy suburb of St. Andrew's.There was a large black sign outside the building that designated it as the Belmont Road Spiritualist Centre. At the time of my first tentative steps into its world, the centre seemed to have a predominantly (though not entirely) ageing congregation. The overall *feel* of the place was like a cosy bed and breakfast—clean and warm with doilies and *pot pourri*. There was a flat above the church that seemed to have students living in it, and you could hear them coming and going during services.

I attended services at the Belmont Road Spiritualist Centre for six weeks, twice a week—reciting the Lord's Prayer, singing Spiritualist hymns (many of which were pop songs, including "Angels" by Robbie Williams, and ABBA's "I Have a Dream"), taking part in raffles (I won a tin of rice pudding), and receiving some interesting readings when visiting mediums selected me out of the audience. Over the course of this stint I noted that the congregation fluctuated between thirty and fifty individuals per service, all packed into the small repurposed church. This was religious Spiritualism with a capital "S", a syncretic blending of mediumship, supernaturalism, New Age beliefs, and liberal Christianity (Nelson, 1972).

In keeping with this eclectic syncretism I also noted a variety of differing views, opinions, and interpretations among the Belmont Road congregation. As an illustration, on one occasion a reading I received from a visiting medium sparked a little discord in the group. It had involved a discussion about the "Earth's axle [sic]" being "off centre", and how the so-called Indigo Children were superior spirits incarnated on the Earth, and who, although often incorrectly diagnosed as suffering from ADHD and autism, are performing a vital function of transformation for the Earth. The medium spoke of the coming time when Atlantis will rise again, though insisted it would "not be in our lifetime". A member of the congregation seemed to disagree with the idea of Atlantis resurfacing, and called out "It'll never happen!" from the audience. It was good to see that the congregation were unafraid of challenging what they are told by visiting mediums, who—in accordance with the anti-dogmatism of Spiritualism in general—often hold heterodox views.

Most of the services I attended were essentially Christian in nature, and followed much of the standard format of a Church of England service—prayers, followed by hymns and readings—with the added inclusion of the medium's practical demonstration of communication with the spirits of the dead. The room was sparsely decorated with Christian iconography—paintings of Jesus, crosses hanging on some of the walls, though it was not a "Christian Spiritualist" congregation. Interest in other religious traditions was evident in both the conversations of members and the lectures of visiting mediums, who would often incorporate stories or teachings from other traditions (particularly Hinduism and Buddhism) in their sermons. The iconography on display in the church also expressed this syncretism, with symbols from different religious traditions dotted about the centre.

It was clear right from the very outset that spirits—invisible beings—were an essential component of the congregation's world. I recall that on one of my first visits to Belmont Road the church CD player (which was used as an accompaniment to the hymns) was skipping and I overheard a couple sitting behind me half-jokingly chatting about how this was obviously the work of the spirits, making their presence known to the congregation—"This happens all the time," they said. The spirits were not lofty or abstract, but rather were participants in everyday life. This reminds me of Rane Willerslev's (2012) suggestion that, like the Yukaghir of northern Siberia (an admittedly completely different cultural context), we should not take the spirits *too seriously*—they are sometimes tricksy, and don't always bring wisdom from the spirit world. Nevertheless, spirits *seemed* to be everywhere for members of the congregation, making themselves known through mediums and malfunctioning electronics.

At the first service I attended we sang "Lean on Me" by Bill Withers, reading the lyrics from the photocopied *Spirits of Youth Hymn Book*, which was perhaps a little outdated. Our discordant rendition was followed by a prayer reading from the visiting medium and a recital of the Lord's Prayer. I didn't know all the words, and was comforted to see that not everyone was joining in. Following the Lord's Prayer the medium read a short fable, which was praised as "beautiful" by members of the congregation. She then proceeded to give readings to members of the audience, assisted in selecting them out by her spirit guide—a Zulu warrior, whom she called "my Zulu". The medium, a smartly dressed middle-aged woman with cropped white hair, selected individuals from the audience and offered first names ("Can you accept the name … from me?"). For the majority—but not all—of readings the sitter *would* accept the name. The medium then offered personal advice and compliments received from the spirit world ("You done good, girl!"). On the occasions when the participant didn't recognise the name it was recommended that they look out for it in the future. She wouldn't let the names go, explaining that she had "… trust in Spirit …" and that she was just telling us what she saw. She was true to her vision, even if the name was not accepted.

Her descriptions of what she was experiencing ranged from visions of individual spirits—smiling faces and so on, to much more symbolic imagery—for example, rainbows extended over certain people in the audience, or visions of long winding corridors associated with another audience member. She reported seeing the word "Passion" emblazoned across one individual she was reading. Her Zulu spirit guide seemed, occasionally, to offer clues that the medium had to decipher. The meaning contained in the symbols was *usually* personally significant to the individual being read, and meant very little to anyone else. Midway through her readings she would hand out a gift—a small glass model of an angel, a gemstone in a bag, or a fridge magnet—a *gift from spirit*. She then gave a few more messages before moving on to the next individual.

I noted that a great deal of emphasis was placed on compassion at these meetings—"loving thy neighbour" and blessings of "love and light". The medium's messages were positive, optimistic, and reassuring in tone. The spirits seemed to promote a tolerant outlook, though infused with a sentimentality for traditional values. One medium remarked that the spirits even knew when people had been "cussing". During one reading the spirit's message was to love a neighbour that the sitter clearly had an issue with—the intentions of the spirits certainly seemed *pure*. Some members of the audience were quite impressed by the abilities and insights of this particular medium, especially when she appeared to be aware of recent private events in people's lives. The atmosphere of the service was friendly, warm, and surprisingly casual, quite unlike any other church services I have attended.

The psychic development circle

I also attended one of the Belmont Road Centre's psychic development sessions one evening in January 2009. These circles are put on to allow individuals the opportunity to develop their own psychic and mediumistic potentials beyond what is possible during a public church service. During the development session ten participants were guided through a meditation by the circle leader, Cliff—a friendly bearded man in his mid-50s—with the aim of fostering clairvoyance and sharing psychic messages. The development circle took place at the Spiritualist Centre every Friday evening, from 7.30pm until 9.00pm. It was conducted in the same room as the services. Chairs were arranged in a circle in the top half of the room. Cliff sat closest to the altar, where the medium would give their demonstration during services. While people were coming in we sat quietly, listening to relaxing New Age music that reached soothing crescendos of pan pipes and synthesised strings.

When 7.30pm came the doors were locked to prevent any unwanted intrusions (possibly from the students upstairs). The main light was switched off and replaced with a warming red light. The session was based around a guided meditation, led by Cliff, and a period of independent meditation. The whole session was opened with a prayer, then Cliff gently talked to the circle, guiding us towards relaxation. With eyes closed we were told to imagine a "blue flame in the middle of the room" into which we were to send all our negative emotions. Once we were fully relaxed Cliff stopped talking and allowed us to meditate independently for about twenty minutes. The room sat in silence, the sound of deep breathing the only thing I heard as I tried, quite unsuccessfully, to quiet my mind. At times I *was* able to silence my thoughts, stopping the constant chatter of my inner monologue, but these moments did not last long. Nevertheless, it felt good to be sending out *positive vibes*. It almost felt as though we were projecting a column of positive energy upwards from the centre of our circle, out through the roof and into the night sky, like a beacon between worlds. Overall, the experience was quite enjoyable.

Following the twenty minutes of independent meditation, Cliff slowly counted us back into the room from one to five—gradually returning our attention back to the external world. Some people took a little longer to "return" than others ("Welcome back," Cliff would say, smiling, to each returning meditator). The last half hour of the session was spent going around the circle exchanging our subjective insights from the meditation, and passing on any messages that might have been received. Several sitters reported experiencing visions during their meditations, many of which held symbolic meanings for their recipients. Cliff helped us to decipher their meaning. The visions offered to me by one sitter included:

- Someone sowing seeds (indicative of new beginnings/growth)
- Golden light emanating around me (protection)
- An old woman called Ethel (I am not aware of anyone by this name, though the two people sitting next to me could accept the name, so perhaps it was a message for them)
- I was also told that spirit was leading me in my quest for spiritual truth.

I didn't see any visions myself, and nor did I receive any messages during my meditation, but I did feel very relaxed throughout the session. Cliff said that this was to be expected for a beginner like me—developing clairvoyance *takes time*. Following the exchange of stories, and interpretation of meditation experiences, a closing prayer was spoken that thanked the spirits for their revelations. We all joined hands and sang a song—the final words, from the Hindu "Prayer for World Peace", echoed in my mind as I walked home that evening, and further reinforced the idea of spirit beings *inhabiting* and *animating* the space around us—from other planets to other dimensions:

> May all the beings in all the worlds be happy.
> May all the beings in all the worlds be happy.
> May all the beings in all the worlds be happy.
> Om Peace, Peace, Peace.

Although I found the experience revealing, after just over a month's involvement with the centre I had still not managed to initiate any significant or insightful conversations with church members, or to develop a relationship with the congregation. I still felt anonymous—like a stranger—perhaps owing to my relative invisibility in the constantly changing audience, and no doubt also in part due to my own shyness at the time. Because of this, I decided that I needed to find an alternative venue for my research, somewhere a little more intimate—and perhaps a little less formal—where I might stand more of a chance of developing the kind of dialogue I was becoming increasingly interested in— delving deeper into the *experience* of the medium.

It was at this point that I came across the Bristol Spirit Lodge through its website and blog, which advertised the group as a "private non-denominational spiritualist home-circle" devoted to the development of trance and physical mediumship (forms of mediumship quite different to what I encountered at Belmont Road). By fortuitous coincidence (or was it through guidance from spirit, as my message in Cliff's meditation circle had seemed to suggest?) the Lodge was only a twenty-minute walk from where I was living at the time, in student accommodation not far from Bristol's busy Gloucester Road. This new group seemed to provide the ideal opportunity to talk with developing mediums about what mediumship *feels like*—how it is *experienced* and *understood*, and how it is *developed*. I made contact with the founder of the group, Christine, via email to arrange a meeting. She responded quickly and enthusiastically, inviting me to her house for a conversation the next day.

Before we go any further in looking at the beliefs and practices of the Bristol Spirit Lodge, it is important that we take some time to consider the broader social and historical context of the Spiritualist movement.

A brief history of spiritualism: science, spirits, and society

There were many historical precursors to the Western Spiritualist movement. Prominent among them were the expansive writings of the Swedish mystic and scientist Emmanuel Swedenborg (1688–1772) on his interactions with spirits and journeys to spiritual realms in the eighteenth century (see Van Dusen, 1994; Lachman, 2014, pp. 21–34), and the craze for Mesmerism and animal magnetism early in the nineteenth century (Taves, 1999, p. 124; Melechi, 2008). In many ways Swedenborgianism and Mesmerism laid the foundations for the emergence of Spiritualism. There are also the many varieties of "ecstatic" (Lewis, 1971), "shamanistic" (Hutton, 2007), and "animistic" (Harvey, 2005) practices found throughout the world's cultures, which share similarities with Euro-American Spiritualism, and which suggest much deeper roots for the movement in human history and experience.

European and American spirit mediumship practices underwent a *major* resurgence in the mid-nineteenth century. Indeed, it was the emergence of Spiritualism at this time—in the midst of the scientific and industrial revolutions of the nineteenth century—that gave the movement its most distinctive features, in particular its unusual relationship to science and the constant effort to provide *objective*, often even physical, *proof* of spiritual realities.

The movement's official birth date is generally agreed to be March 31, 1848. On this day, in the small town of Hydesville in New York State, the home of the Fox family became the locus of some unusual paranormal activity (Conan Doyle, 1926; Pearsall, 2004, pp. 29–33; Melechi, 2008, p. 161; Byrne, 2010, p. 18). The family was plagued by perplexing bangs and anomalous knocks on the walls and ceiling of their modest wooden house. In an effort to make sense of what was going on the two youngest sisters—there were three: Kate (1837–1892), Margaret (1833–1893), and Leah (1831–1890)—addressed the knocks *as though* they were being produced by an invisible intelligence—giving it the name Mr Splitfoot. Soon, the sisters realised that they could communicate with Mr Splitfoot through a simple code of knocks—one for "Yes" and two for "No"—and in this way discovered that the entity claimed to be the spirit of a peddler by the name of Charles Rosma, who had been murdered in the house some years before the Fox family moved in. Human remains were indeed discovered buried in the basement of the house some years later, which seemed to verify Mr Splitfoot's claims. Already we see

Spiritualism's obsession with *objective* proof of the supernormal begin-ning to emerge (Bednarowski, 1980, p. 213; Gauld, 1982, p. 3; Taves, 1999, p. 166; Pearsall, 2004; Stemman, 2005, p. v; Blum, 2007; Warner, 2008, p. 221; Byrne, 2010; Moreman, 2010, p. 161).

News of the Fox sisters and their apparent ability to communicate with invisible spirits spread rapidly from New York State right through the United States and across the Atlantic to Europe, taking full advan-tage of new developments in communication technologies (telegram, mass print media) and both national and international methods of transportation (railways, steamships). Its rapid spread and huge popu-larity left a trail of individuals discovering their own mediumistic abili-ties in its wake (Nelson, 1969, p. 5).

Eventually the strains of international celebrity status took their toll on the Fox sisters. It is perhaps unsurprising that the constant critiqu-ing of their demonstrations by sceptical audiences (of which there were many) sadly led the sisters down the path of alcoholism and bitter dis-agreements with one another. In 1888 Kate and Margaret publicly con-fessed that the dramatic supernatural phenomena that had propelled them to fame were little more than parlour tricks. The sisters claimed that the enigmatic raps and bangs that had confounded so many over the course of their mediumistic careers were created quite simply by cracking the knuckles in their toes. A year later, however, Margaret fully recanted her confession, claiming that the phenomena *were* genuine, and that she had been forced to confess to trickery by anti-Spiritualist lob-byists. Such toing-and-froing would forever damage the reputation of the sisters, as well as the Spiritualist movement in general, and served to further muddy the waters around the genuineness of their medium-istic phenomena. In spite of their huge popular impact on the latter half of the nineteenth century, the Fox sisters died in relative poverty and obscurity within three years of 1890 (Lehman, 2009, p. 87).

Over time the manifestations of spirit communication claimed by the Spiritualists began to diversify as more and more mediums came for-ward to offer public demonstrations of their own supernormal abilities (Steinmeyer, 2004, pp. 47–70). Mediumistic séances transformed from simple question and answer sessions with knocks (popularised by the public séances of the Fox sisters), through table-tipping experiments, playing with planchettes and ouija boards, right through to automatic writing and full trance communications utilising deep altered states of consciousness—which frequently intermingled with demonstrations of Mesmerism. Spiritualist mediumship arguably reached its apex with the alleged full-body *materialisation* during séances of spirits that could be interacted with, and even touched, by audience members. These materialisations were said to be composed of a mysterious semi-physical substance that would, later in the century, come to be called "ectoplasm" (Moreman, 2010, p. 161). Over the course of this innovative period two distinct forms of mediumship began to emerge. The earliest form, involving objective raps and knocks, the movement of physical objects, and materialisations became what was later called "physical mediumship", while the somewhat more refined forms of clairvoyant and trance mediumship, which are much more subjective, came to be known as "mental mediumship" (Neher, 1990, p. 207).

The rapid rise and spread of Spiritualism was by no means a singular phenomenon in the mid-nineteenth century, however. Sociologist Geoffrey Nelson (1969) has suggested that the widespread cultural acceptance of Spiritualism at the time, and especially in Britain, was aided by several significant social and technological factors including: higher social mobility, extensive geographic mobility, an influx of immigrants with different and conflicting cultural patterns, and the effects of rapid *industrialisation*. According to Nelson's analysis, the rapid process of *modernisation* led to the collapse of traditional social structures and a failure to develop a coherent and integrated pattern of culture, leaving the population ready to embrace supernatural beliefs (Nelson, 1969, p. 69). Indeed, Spiritualism was just one of numerous new religious movements (NRMs) that emerged during the period (cf. L. L. Dawson, 1998). Less than twenty years before the events at Hydesville, in 1830, and also in New York State, for example, Joseph Smith (1805–1844) had established the Church of Jesus Christ of Latter-day Saints (Mormonism). Smith claimed to have discovered—following the instruction of an Angel called Moroni—a new gospel written on golden tablets, which described Jesus Christ's journeys through the Americas in pre-Columbian times (Stark, 1984). Spiritualism was among the first of the truly *globalised* NRMs.

New York State in the mid-nineteenth century was also a hotbed for women's rights activists and other social reform movements (Rosenthal, Fingrutd, Ethier, Karant, & McDonald, 1985). In keeping with this general progressive attitude, Bednarowski (1980) sees the Spiritualist movement as just one in a number of nineteenth-century NRMs—including Shakerism, Christian Science, and Theosophy—that offered women the chance to assume *higher status roles* in religious life than could be found in the more traditional Christian denominations. In Spiritualism the essential role of the medium was thought to be particularly (though not exclusively) well suited to women, who were often thought to be more *sensitive* to subtle influences from the spirit world (Bednarowski, 1980, p. 213). The progressive attitude of the early Spiritualists, and the importance of women in their cosmological scheme, may also go some way towards explaining the movement's rapid uptake in Europe during the latter half of the nineteenth century—it jelled with progressive social attitudes that were gradually beginning to emerge.

When Spiritualism first arrived in the UK it found a social climate particularly ripe for supernatural interactions, and very quickly captured the popular imagination. Indeed, the first Spiritualist mediumship demonstration was given in London by Maria B. Hayden (1826–1883) in 1852, who had come over from Connecticut (Oppenheim, 1985, p. 11), and by 1853, just five years after the movement's birth in New York State, Spiritualism had secured a firm foothold with the establishment of the first Spiritualist church in the small town of Keighley in Yorkshire (Conan Doyle, 1926, p. 84; Nelson, 1969, p. 91). This point really marks the transformation of Spiritualism from a paranormal parlour game into a religion, though it would be some years before a formal governing organisation was established.

In parallel to the emergence of NRMs at this time, rational, scientistic, and anti-religious sentiments were also gaining prominence, especially among the intellectual elite of the day. August Comte's (1798–1857) ideology of *positivism* is perhaps the ultimate expression of this tendency towards the "rational" and "scientific", and away from the !religious", "superstitious", and "supernatural". He explains:

> In the ... positive state, the mind has given over the vain search after Absolute notions, the origin and destination of the universe, and the causes of phenomena, and applies itself to the study of their laws, that is, their invariable relations of succession and resemblance. Reasoning and observation, duly combined, are the means of this knowledge. (Comte, 1976, p. 19)

The positivist world view left little room for spirits. The perceived gulf between religion and science continued to grow following the publication of Charles Darwin's (1809–1882) *On the Origin of Species* in 1859.

For many of his followers, Darwin's theory effectively removed the need for a creative God, replacing Him with a naturalistic explanation for the origin of species—*natural selection*. It is this ontological shift—from a *religious* to a *scientific* world view—that gave rise to what some historians and sociologists have termed "a crisis of faith" in Victorian society (Hansen, 2001, pp. 348–349; Blum, 2007, pp. 34–37; Melechi, 2008, p. 243). R. Laurence Moore, for example, suggests that "Communion with spirits offered comfort to people whirled about in a decade when science and technology undermined traditional social patterns" (Moore, 1972, p. 476). The relatively quick diffusion of Spiritualism into British society could, therefore, be seen as the product of both the *social* and *spiritual* turbulence of the time.

Spiritualism, with its emphasis on *objective proofs* for the existence of the spirits and the non-material world (in the form of messages from the dead and physical séance phenomena), seemed to provide a remedy to this cognitive dissonance by presenting itself as a *science of the supernatural*—legitimating belief in the supernatural as a scientific possibility, and providing an "avenue of safe passage" for religion into the modern, scientific world. Spiritualism effectively bridged what the twentieth-century evolutionary biologist Stephen J. Gould (2007) would later call the "non-overlapping magisteria" of *science* and *religion*. Spiritualists, as well as their Kardecist counterparts in France, mainland Europe, and Brazil, thought of their new movement as a *scientific* one, aimed at providing rigorous experimental proofs for the existence of the spiritual world (Swatos, 1990). Allan Kardec (1804–1869), the French pedagogue responsible for the current popularity of Spiritism in Latin America, reminds us however that spiritual phenomena call for a *different* understanding of science, one that goes beyond the limits of materialism. He writes:

> The positive sciences are based on the properties of matter, which may be experimented upon and manipulated at pleasure; but spiritist phenomena are an effect of the action of intelligences who have wills of their own, and who constantly show us that they are not subjected to ours. The observation of facts, therefore, cannot be carried on in the latter case in the same way as in the former one, for they proceed from another source, and require special conditions; and, consequently, to insist upon submitting them to the same methods of investigation is to insist on assuming the existence of analogies that do not exist. (2006, p. 37)

This sentiment, of a *spiritual science* that extends far beyond the boundaries of materialism, continues to this day among many Spiritists and Spiritualists, who continue to adopt a scientific approach to the spirit world. This is especially evident in the experimental séance practices of the Bristol Spirit Lodge, as we shall see.

The claims of Spiritualists to provide objective proof for the existence of the spirit world also raised the interests of certain scientifically minded researchers. The founding of the Society for Psychical Research (SPR) in 1882, by the Cambridge scholars Henry Sidgwick (1838–1900), Eleanor Sidgwick (1845–1936), F. W. H. Myers (1843–1901), and Edmund Gurney (1847–1888), is perhaps the clearest manifestation of this drive to empirically verify the supernormal. The stated aim of the SPR was to investigate "that large body of debatable phenomena designated by such terms as mesmeric, psychical and spiritualistic in the same spirit of exact and unimpassioned enquiry which has enabled Science to solve so many problems" (Haynes, 1982). It was the first organisation to adopt a truly scientific approach to the supernatural.

After several short-lived attempts at formally organising the movement, first as the British National Spiritualists Federation in 1873 and later as the National Spiritualists' Federation in 1890, the Spiritualists' National Union (SNU) was eventually established in 1901 to protect and promote the interests of Spiritualists and their mediums across the country. This organisation continues to be active today, with its headquarters at Stansted Hall in Essex, now known as the Arthur Findlay College,[7] named after the wealthy businessman Arthur Findlay (1883–1964) who bequeathed Stansted Hall to the Union in 1964. Stansted Hall is now the UK's premier Spiritualist mediumship development centre, running all manner of courses in psychic development and mediumship on a regular basis, usually mental mediumship, though trance and physical mediumship are also sometimes taught at the college. The Bristol Spirit Lodge is not affiliated with the SNU in any way. Nevertheless, the Lodge and its practices do represent a continuation of the spiritualist tradition.

The Bristol Spirit Lodge

My first meeting with Christine took place on the morning of January 30, 2009. I made the twenty-minute walk from my student accommodation

---

[7] www.arthurfindlaycollege.org.

off Gloucester Road to Christine's large semi-detached house in Filton, arriving at a deep-blue door on the kerb of a busy main road. The house was opposite a large sports field. I noticed an unimposing sticker on a window to the left of the door that read "Bristol Spirit Lodge Circle: For the Support and Development of Physical Mediumship". This was the only indication that the house was a centre for the development of mediumship; the neat suburban facade was virtually indistinguishable from all others along the road. The practice of physical mediumship was *hidden in plain sight*.

I was a little apprehensive, unsure of what to expect as I rang the doorbell, but my nervousness dissipated when Christine opened the door and enthusiastically welcomed me into her tidy home, immediately offering me a cup of tea and directing me through into the living room to sit down, as she went into the kitchen to put the kettle on. Christine was bubbly and excited. She was in her sixties with blonde shoulder-length hair and wore a purple skirt with a black shawl, giving off a sort of "witchy" vibe. The living room was immaculately clean, the carpets were plush and there was a wicker hanging chair in the corner filled with sleeping long-haired cats. In the opposite corner was a large flat-screen television. I couldn't see anything in the room that hinted at Christine's preoccupation with mediumship, except, tangentially perhaps, for a couple of miniature dragon sculptures with crystals that suggested what could be called "New Age" concerns (Hanegraaff, 1998; Bartolini, Chris, Mackian, & Pile, 2013). The dragons were displayed on the mantlepiece above an electric fire. She returned to the room with two milky cups of tea, and sat down on the sofa opposite me, and we began to talk. I wrote notes in my notebook as our conversation flowed.

Christine told me that she had established the Lodge in 2005 as a centre for the development of mediumship following a physical séance she attended at Jenny's Sanctuary,[8] a well-known Spiritualist venue in Banbury, Oxfordshire, about seventy miles north-east of Bristol. She had been invited to the séance by a friend as a sort of date and, not knowing what physical mediumship was at that time, decided to go along out of curiosity. Little did she know that this séance would convince her of the reality of "spirit" and change her life forever.

Christine explained how during the séance—conducted in a plain room with about thirty sitters she had never met before—she had seen

---

[8] www.jennyssanctuary.org.uk.

bright lights floating and flashing around the séance room, whirling like fireflies before her eyes. She told me how she had heard several seemingly *disembodied* voices talking with the sitters from unusual locations, as whistles and loud bangs came from all corners of the room. She also reportedly witnessed what she vaguely described as a "partly materialised something" moving about in the room while the medium was apparently still bound with cable ties in the cabinet, gagged and with a pillow case over his head. The peak of the experience came when she heard a voice that she instantly recognised. It is these personal aspects that *really* lend weight to these séance experiences; the unusual physical effects are often of secondary importance. In her short self-published autobiography, *Spirits in a Teacup* (2009), Christine describes the profound effect this séance experience had on her world view. She explains her revelation:

> Then suddenly within the room, clearly, and without doubt, I heard a voice I recognized. I felt my eyes open wide with shock! No way could that person's voice be faked. It was his voice and his personality being presented. This meant nothing much to anyone else, but for me something "clicked into place". I now had no option but to believe that something very serious was happening. I felt sick with the sudden shock. I had suddenly been made aware of Reality ... I knew I couldn't ignore reality ... There are no boundaries. We simply cannot see all that exists. I needed to somehow persuade my mind to accept this fact completely; otherwise I would close my mind, whilst at the same time knowing that my previous belief was incorrect. I had believed that when we died we were dead. I needed to get a grip if I was to learn from the experience that had been offered to me at the séance ... in Banbury (Di Nucci, 2009, pp. 23–25)

Christine is a retired foster parent in her mid-sixties and is a self-described housewife. She has two sons and now lives with her husband Alan (a technician) in a quiet seaside town approximately fifteen miles to the west of Bristol, where she was born in the late 1940s. Christine was keen to highlight to me that before her life-changing séance experience she had been uninterested in religious and spiritual matters. Indeed, she half-jokingly described herself in a questionnaire I asked her to fill out as a "devout atheist". She claims no psychic abilities of her own, and recalls only two possible paranormal experiences from her youth. One of these experiences involved a childhood invisible friend that would keep her company during a period of family disruption. She has since come to understand this experience as little more than the "psychological crutch" of a young child—seeing no reason to consider it a hint at her future interest in spirit mediumship. In other words, she is willing to explain away some elements of her own experience, for example childhood imaginary friends, but not others.

Christine also explained how prior to her interest in Spiritualism she was already a keen follower of developments in modern science, primarily through her reading of popular science books. She had read the bestseller *A Brief History of Time* (Hawking, 1988), and was fascinated by the implications of science journalist Lynne McTaggart's book on quantum physics and consciousness, *The Field* (2001). Christine's own autobiography describes her approach to Spiritualism as a scientific one, explaining how she was attempting to interpret the experiences she had while in the séance room in Banbury through the lens of her interest in science and the scientific method:

> I knew I couldn't ignore reality. Stephen Hawking had touched upon it. Lynne McTaggart had the right idea. The scientific theory suggesting all that is solid is merely vibration, is the reality that proves the reality of all things. (Di Nucci, 2009, p. 25)

Christine has characterised her understanding of science as a "DIY house-wifey awareness of science" (interview with Christine, February 25, 2013). This DIY scientific attitude would go on to form the basis of all activities at the Bristol Spirit Lodge, which she describes as an "open experiment with no fixed agenda" (Di Nucci, 2009, p. 12). The wooden Lodge in her back garden (about which we will hear more soon) is Christine's laboratory. Here we see a novel intersection of science and spirituality, played out from the bottom up in sub-urban Bristol.

Christine now has a *very* great enthusiasm for mediumship, a fact confirmed by the sheer amount of time she spends in her Lodge with developing mediums during the week—by now she has proudly taken part in well over 1,000 séances, both in and out of the Lodge. She explains how this interest is self directed ("I'm doing it for me!") and that she is "not seeking to prove continuing life", or to make contact with the divine. She is simply trying to make sense of that first séance experience in Banbury, attempting to comprehend what was to Christine a *reality shifting* experience ("I just had to know more about it").

Building the Lodge

The first Bristol Spirit Lodge was constructed using £2,000 taken from Christine's savings account. The shed was built according to simple guidelines recommended by Ron Gilkes, the circle leader at Jenny's Sanctuary in Banbury, where Christine had had her first encounter with physical mediumship. It was important to Christine that, from the very outset, the Lodge be built with *love*, and that it be imbued with *positive* emotions. An aura of positive intent was said to be conducive to good séances, so it made sense to Christine to embed this intention in the physical structure of the building. To this end all of the materials used in its construction were blessed, kissed, and treated with great respect. Ideas such as these could express an underlying "panpsychist", "animist", or "relational" ontology in Christine's world view, according to which matter possesses the potential for consciousness, awareness, emotion, and dialogue. Additionally, the blessing of the Lodge served an apotropaic function as a protection against attracting low-level negative spiritual entities to the circle.

The Lodge was also purposefully aligned in space so that the séance cabinet—a curtained-off corner of the room in which the medium sits while in trance (and a direct descendant of the spirit cabinets used by Spiritualist physical mediums in the late nineteenth and early twentieth centuries)—was located in the *north* corner—a position suggested by Gilkes to be conducive to the flow of *subtle energies* necessary for the successful development of physical mediumship. Chairs for sitters were arranged around the edges of the room, and there was a circular area of wooden flooring in the centre of the room. The wooden circle, Christine explained, served as an alarm to indicate any secretive movements during séances, because the wooden boards creaked loudly when stepped on. The wooden circle also functioned as a focal point for activity during séances. Occasionally, Christine would place objects— such as toys, whistles, drums, and bells—in the middle of the wooden circle for the spirits to play with and manipulate. When I first visited, the walls inside the Lodge were decorated with portraits of Native American spirit guides, small notes ostensibly written by spirits on scraps of paper, and photographs of the aftermath of past séances—of toys scattered around the Lodge, for example. They also had on display a collection of weirdly bent-up hooks, screws, and cable ties that had been used to bind mediums during physical séances.

When Christine moved house in 2010 it was the presence of an ideally sized wooden shed in the back garden that ultimately clinched the deal. The new shed was remarkably similar to the Lodge she had purposefully constructed in Bristol. It is slightly larger than its predecessor, but is essentially identical in most respects, which allowed for the continuation of regular séances and development circles almost immediately after moving in. Christine has now extended her home to include a fully functional séance room, further testament to her dedication to mediumship development.

The group: roles and social structure

Although there is no formal hierarchy at the Lodge, its members can be broadly split into four categories: *circle leader, sitters, mediums,* and *spirits.* In the following section I will present snapshots of the members who fulfilled these roles at the Lodge at the time of my fieldwork.

Circle leader

The first key role is that of the circle leader, which naturally is taken by Christine as the founder of the Lodge. It is her job to keep control of the séance proceedings. Christine does not go into trance, nor does she act as a medium during séances—she performs the role of a detached and objective observer. That said, however, Christine does have a spirit guide who occasionally also intervenes. Christine's guide is called Fuzzy Critter (usually referred to simply as FC), so named because when he appears to her it is usually in the form of a fuzzy white blob sensed above her left shoulder. She first became aware of FC at a psychic development circle early on in her exploration of spiritualism. She recalls: "I didn't take it seriously because I just thought it was a social evening, and it didn't matter," but when she heard a distinct voice saying, "I'm here to learn your language," her attention piqued. She was shocked to see that no one else in the circle seemed to have heard the voice and took this as an indication that she and FC would have to learn how to work with each other. FC now regularly assists Christine in the everyday running of the Lodge's many development circles, though he usually operates "behind the scenes" and does not communicate with sitters as other spirits at the Lodge do. At the Bristol Spirit Lodge, the circle leader is also responsible for supervising the smooth running of the séance, ensuring that the medium is safe and comfortable, and maintaining control over what takes place inside the Lodge; she also controls the "musical accompaniment" during séances. Christine explains:

> … management has to come into it. You set the intent, you set some sort of guidelines, and you expect them to work with you. It is a blending thing, you need to get some séance etiquette, or something, you know. You need to get a rapport, you need to get it organised. You sort of make deals between, you know, what is OK and what's not OK, and what behaviour is acceptable around us and what isn't. We've got to be a bit flexible to them too, what they want and what they don't want … so you kind of negotiate your way around. (Interview with Christine, March 23, 2011)

Christine is the main driving force behind the Lodge and its activities. Without her passion and enthusiasm it simply wouldn't exist. Her mediumship development schedule is packed. When she is not hosting séances with visiting sitters she is conducting one-to-one development sessions with mediums on her own—devoting her life to an exploration of mediumship and its implications.

The sitters

The "sitters", who might be described as the "lay" members of the group, do not usually go into trance (though sitters falling into spontaneous trance is *not* an uncommon occurrence at the Lodge). The sitters do not normally play an organising role in the séances (which is Christine's job), they simply come to observe and to ask questions of the spirits. The sitters are, however, essential in providing an audience for the spirit communicators to address.

There was a core group of eleven regular sitters at the time of my fieldwork, five of whom were males aged between twenty-seven and eighty, and six females, aged between thirty and eighty. The Lodge was also attended quite regularly by other visiting sitters—often two or three times a week—who would sit in on one of the regular circles to get a taste for what is going on, and to decide whether they would like to become regulars. They may not return again. More often than not, however, visiting sitters are there because they have an interest in physical mediumship and want to experience it first-hand for themselves, perhaps as a result of hearing about it at Spiritualist churches, or through reading the Spiritualist literature, or by word of mouth from a friend. Visiting sitters sometimes also got in touch with a desire to make contact with a particular deceased loved one (as part of a grieving process), but Christine explained that she tends to avoid inviting these people to attend. She does not think it is possible to guarantee communication with a *specific* individual during a séance, especially someone who is not a member of the medium's spirit team. As already noted, the séances held at the Lodge are framed and understood as *experiments*, and so a desired outcome can *never* be guaranteed—the séance may fail completely, and Christine does not wish to be held responsible for any emotional disturbance that this might cause for the bereaved. She is not a counsellor.

At the time of my most frequent involvement with the Lodge (between 2009 and 2011) the sitters I most often met at séances included Margaret, a retired seventy-four year old who attended most of the séances and development sittings that I participated in, and Lynne, a forty-eight-year-old carer who was also the Lodge's resident baker. She would often bring cakes to meetings, and even baked a wonderful séance themed birthday cake for the Lodge's fourth anniversary, complete with séance cabinet, spirit trumpets, and ghosts crafted from icing. Dave was a retired, very jolly seventy-five year old who described himself as a "religious seeker". He told me that he regularly attended Church of England services, Spiritualist churches, *and* Quaker meetings. He always attended with his eighty-year-old partner Pat.

Both Dave and Pat told me that they were brought up as Methodists, and saw their attendance at the Bristol Spirit Lodge as a part of their wider spiritual development. They both travelled over forty miles to attend séances at the Lodge, showing a considerable dedication to the practice. Dave's wife was at this time suffering from severe Alzheimer's disease. Dave and Pat became an item once Dave's wife could no longer recognise or communicate with her loved ones. Pat was helping to support Dave in caring for his wife. Dave once told me that it was possible to communicate with his wife through trance mediumship. Although she was not "dead", she was closer to the "other side" than this side, and because she could no longer use her own physical body to communicate it was easier for mediums to allow her to talk through them. In this way she let Dave know that she was not suffering, and through the voice of a mediumistic go-between gave permission for Dave and Pat to get together to comfort and support one another.

Geoffrey Nelson's (1975) sociological study of British Spiritualism in the late 1960s suggested four predominant factors leading individuals to become involved in the religion. These included: 1) prior paranormal experience, "composed of individuals who have or seek mystical, psychic or ecstatic experiences", 2) religious disillusionment (a rejection of traditional mainstream religion), 3) curiosity, or a "positive search for meaning", and 4) as part of a grieving process (p. 172). When asked about their reasons for attending, a variety of different responses were offered by members of the Bristol Spirit Lodge. Dave, for example, explained that he was seeking answers to the *big questions*—"Why are we here? Something must go on after death." When I asked if attending had changed his beliefs and opinions in any way, he said: "Sure. We and Spirit need to understand each other better." His partner Pat explained: "My partner already attended and I wanted to be part of his life in all aspects to enable me to be a helpful companion. Since then I have found enlightenment and fulfilment for myself, and enjoy attending for my own advancement." Pat found that her attendance at the Lodge had "not changed, but enhanced and confirmed what I already believed". Margaret told me that: "One of my friends introduced me. I have, for a long time, been interested in all aspects of spirituality—so the mention of physical mediumship and spirit voices re-sparked that interest." Like Pat, Margaret explained that her experiences at the Lodge had not changed her beliefs—"it has only intensified them". None of the sitters at the Bristol Spirit Lodge claimed that they were attending as part of a grieving process, and none of the regular sitters considered the séances to be specifically religious events, preferring to think of them as *scientific*, or *experimental* in nature. Their desire to attend seems, therefore, to be predominantly out of *curiosity*, in Nelson's terms as part of a "positive search for meaning"—to answer the big questions, to make sense of prior anomalous experiences, and as part of a continuing process of personal spiritual development. This positive search for meaning—much as in Evans-Pritchard's (1937) famous account of Azande witchcraft beliefs—is epitomised in the following question posed by

Margaret during a trance session with the spirit Charlie (through Jon's body, see below):

> ... when we're in spirit ... we know the time of our death, but this last week gone there was a teenage girl who was enjoying herself and she had rather an horrific accident. I wonder, do we choose exactly how we are going to die, or is it just a generalisation and then it just happens, like this girl's nasty accident? (As cited in Hunter, 2009, p. 69)

Sitters are concerned with classic questions of meaning, purpose, fate, and destiny, and use mediumistic séances and dialogue with spirits as a means of addressing them and finding answers that help them to make sense of the world and their place within it.

Religious beliefs of Lodge members

The beliefs of Lodge members are quite varied (echoing the wider syncretism of spiritualism). Indeed, Christine states explicitly in her short book, *Spirits in a Teacup* (2009), that the group is a *"non-denominational home-circle"*. Such a stance is also in line with the anti-dogmatism of the Spiritualist movement in general, although Christine does not consider herself to be Spiritualist "with a capital S". In keeping with this non-dogmatic approach, Lodge members do not necessarily share the same interpretations of séance phenomena—each member may have their own explanatory framework or cosmological model—religious or otherwise—for the experiences they have during séances—some may take a more *spiritual* approach, while others prefer a slightly more detached *scientific* approach. Members of the Lodge come from a wide variety of religious backgrounds, ranging from atheist through Church of England, Methodist, Quaker, and Spiritualist perspectives. As already noted, none of the attendant sitters or mediums considered the séances conducted at the Lodge to be *religious* events. Spirit communication is understood to be a *natural fact* (further complicating the "natural/supernatural" dichotomy). Their participation in séances is often seen as a *continuation* of their own *personal* "spiritual journeys", just another stage on the path of learning about *self* and *reality*.

In spite of the non-religious character of spirit communication as practised at the Bristol Spirit Lodge, the behaviours, actions, and experiences of members occasionally suggest a sense of differentiation between the *sacred* space inside the Lodge and the *profane* world outside. The Lodge space is treated with great respect and is often subject to taboos—it is not used for any other mundane activities, for example, and is kept locked at all times when not in use. The séances that take place inside are thought to imbue the building with a *residual energy*. It has even been noted by several members that a distinct "sense of presence" is occasionally felt when alone inside the Lodge, as though it is still attracting spirits, even when there are no séances taking place. So, while the Lodge's practices are not necessarily interpreted as *religious* by Lodge members, they nevertheless appear to partake of at least a *semi*-religious character. Perhaps Rudolf Otto's term *numinous* would be a better designation—referring to the *irreducible, non-dogmatic, non-rational, experiential* aspects of religion—the *essence* of religion (Otto, 1958).

The mediums

The mediums themselves perform the third key role at the Bristol Spirit Lodge. At the time of my research there were six mediums in development at the Lodge, half of whom were female. The role of the medium is to go into trance and thus to provide a means for the expression of the *fourth* category of group members—the spirits. Mediums are respected and highly regarded for their ability to mediate between the spirit world and the physical world, and so have a relatively high social status within the group. After all, without the medium there would be no séances to attend.

The most frequently active mediums during my time with the Bristol Spirit Lodge were Jon, a forty-seven-year-old salesman brought up in the Church of England, Sandy, a forty-nine-year-old nutritional therapist, Syann, a thirty-six-year-old fitness instructor, Emily, a thirty-three-year-old office worker, and Rachael—an artist and crafter in her thirties. Other mediums attended less frequently—sometimes for weeks at a time, sometimes more sporadically. The following extracts from interview sessions with Jon, Emily, and Rachael provide some insight into the motivations behind their mediumship development, how they came to the Lodge, and how their interest in physical mediumship came about.

Jon

Jon is one of the most developed trance mediums at the Lodge, and I sat with him on numerous occasions over the course of my fieldwork.

He told me how he came to the Lodge "originally as a sitter to investigate physical séances". He explained that he had "been to healing and development circles but wanted more objective evidence" of spirit, so ended up (much as I had done) stumbling across the Bristol Spirit Lodge. It soon became clear, after a few sittings with other mediums at the Lodge, that Jon was himself a very able medium, and so he began to sit in his own weekly development circle. The following is an extract from an interview with Jon, describing some of his experiences growing up and leading to the emergence of his interest in mediumship. He also describes some of the stages of the process of mediumship development:

Jack: So, have you had psychic, or spirit experiences throughout your life?

Jon: In retrospect, probably yes! Although at the time I always put them down to something else, or coincidences, or day/night dreams. More so perhaps as a child—I used to be terrified of the man that always came into my room at night when I was in bed. But if I could get the courage up to turn the light on, or open the landing door, there was never anyone there, so I reasoned in the end that it was simply shadows and imagination—which it *may* have been, of course. I remember several instances of finding lost items through dreams, and seeing doorways, staircases, and people that weren't really there. I was very surprised as a young adult that my mum had had the same experience in the same house! That kind of thing—nothing very spectacular I'm afraid.

Jack: When did you first realise you had specifically mediumistic abilities?

Jon: The exact date I'm not sure of, but I do recall the moment. I had become interested in spiritual healing, and had been attending an open circle—more of an open forum on healing and, to some extent, development—that was run by a local man—Bill. Bill had suggested I come to one of his development weekends, which he held once a month on a Sunday. I went along and was having a great time—lots of development exercises to increase sensitivity and awareness. At this time I was only ever interested in the healing aspect. Then, during one exercise, I was asked to step forward, and after *tuning in* as per a healing—which consists of standing behind a person and letting your mind go quiet until you *feel* connected to them—I was asked what I could *see* for them. The information that appeared in my mind seemed to come out of nowhere and the individual I was working with confirmed everything I was telling her—I'd never seen her before that day. I remember walking off to my sandwich straight after feeling dumbfounded, and made a note in my journal to that effect.

I didn't really take it very seriously, but found that soon after Bill was beginning to coach me and make me do more of the "mediumship" work during the fortnightly open circle. Within a year I found myself invited to join a closed development circle, which I stayed in for two years—learning how to do mental mediumship *properly*, and not get sucked into the soft and woolly rubbish so prevalent these days. I never really felt completely comfortable with the process though, as it was such an open loop. I had no control over it and never knew (perhaps trusted) if I was going to be able to give a good reading or not. Sometimes the messages would be crystal clear and spot on, other times confused and vague. So, as a result, I've never really followed it up or made a regular practice of it. Very occasionally someone will want to get a message across to someone and I'm more than happy for them to use me to do it, but I tend to shy away from *offering readings* on a regular basis.

Sandy

Sandy's story about how she came to practise mediumship at the Lodge is similar to Jon's in a number of ways. She explains: "I was firstly encouraged to attend by friends and curiosity. Now because I want to and have a compulsion." Like Jon, what started out as a gentle encouragement by friends to attend a séance ultimately culminated in her developing mediumship herself. Here, Sandy answers questions about how this process played out for her:

Jack: What initially prompted you to begin developing your mediumship?

Sandy: It just happened and I went with the flow. I had attended a circle intermittently a few times out of a vague interest, having chatted to Christine, who I had known as a friend for a few years. Something happened that I did not understand one evening, followed by an intense urge to write down my thoughts, descriptions, and explanations in emails to Christine for several days.

Jack: How old were you at the time?

Sandy: I was forty-seven years old.

Jack: Do you have other mediums in your family?

Sandy: I don't know. There are a few members in my immediate family who have since admitted a knowledge and belief of the existence of Spirit. I know both of my sons are watched over by Spirit, but how this connects with being a medium I do not know.

Jack: Why do you practise mediumship? What benefits does it have?

Sandy: I don't know. I just live it. I do not understand it. Sometimes I give explanations to life that I am, or was, totally unaware of and it makes sense of life. I am a carer and am here to teach others, and that is what it does. It helps me be calm and cope with the trials of life. Spirit are funny and I enjoy their company. They add a dimension to my life I would not otherwise have. I would not be without them, although I have been known to complain about them! Spirit have allowed me to enable healing and to improve the lives (and death of my father) of several of my family. They have guided me with career choices to give me experiences necessary to do this. They are so clever in how they allow the jigsaw puzzle pieces to come together in a combination that works, even when it does not make sense or seem fair. It is fascinating to see and realise how the small, personal jigsaw comes together to be part of the much bigger and wider picture. They have shown and taught me how to have faith.

Jack: How do you perceive your role as a medium?

Sandy: I see it as being part of me. Just something I do, like nursing when I was a nurse, being a mother, sister, daughter.

Jack: How is your mediumship perceived by family and friends?

Sandy: Only close family and friends who attend the circle know. I have never told anyone else. I don't know how to explain it. I have not gone into much detail, particularly since Spirit started to take over out of the séance situation. The right time has never seemed to happen. Those who do know have accepted it. One sister avoids the subject, otherwise sometimes the subject crops up, most of the time it does not. I have felt Spirit talk to them, but I don't think they realised.

Emily

My first meeting with Emily took place on February 11, 2013. Emily had been developing physical mediumship with Christine since October 2012, so by the time of my meeting her she was still in the early stages of development, and yet her mediumship was, according to Christine, quite well advanced. Emily is a mother, and she comes from a small town on the outskirts of Bristol. She first became seriously interested in mediumship after learning of her mother's and grandparents' active involvement in Spiritualism. Emily recalls that, as a child staying at her grandparents' house, she used to sleep in a bedroom above a séance room, complete with séance cabinet for physical mediumship: "My grandparents had a cabinet in their home, but I guess I grew up just thinking that you had one of those if you were a medium and in contact with the spirits in some way." Mediumship, and the idea of being able to communicate with invisible spirits, was clearly an important influence on Emily's life from an early age.

She explained how she had initially thought of mediumship as a single monolithic phenomenon, unaware that there were differences between, for example, mental and physical mediumship, or different forms of clairvoyance. On one occasion, she told me, she had attended a Spiritualist church to enquire about the possibility of joining a mediumship development circle (circles for other forms of psychic development are common at many Spiritualist churches, much like the one I attended in 2009). It was only then that she realised that this form of mediumship was different to that practised by her grandparents. She explained that "cabinet was a kind of buzz-word" among the Spiritualists she met at the Spiritualist church. She was advised that if it was *physical* mediumship she wanted to develop, she would have to seek out a private home-circle to work with. Physical mediumship is not often catered for by Spiritualist churches.

Her search for a physical mediumship group in Bristol led her (again, much like myself) directly to Christine and the Bristol Spirit Lodge. Christine's initial recommendation was for Emily to establish her own home-circle, with her partner and mother as sitters, which she promptly did. It soon became clear, however, that the *energies* in this particular circle were not *right* for Emily's physical development. After a series of email exchanges, Christine invited Emily back to sit in the Lodge in order to focus her efforts on physical mediumship specifically, during one-to-one séances. Emily's home-circle also continues to sit regularly, only now with her mother most frequently taking the role of medium.

Rachael

In the following interview extract, Rachael explains how she came to be involved in physical mediumship development. She told me that her abilities emerged quite quickly over the course of about one year of sitting in development circles with Christine, and were accompanied by an extraordinary burst of creative output in the form of books, artwork, and the construction of her own spirit lodge. It is worth noting that like Emily, Rachael had grown up with family members who also practised mediumship. Unfortunately I was never able to sit in on any of Rachael's séances, but I did manage to speak with her at the Lodge and was able to interview her there with Christine:

Jack: How did you get involved in physical mediumship?

Rachael: I was interested in mental mediumship, I thought that seemed like quite a nice thing to kind of pursue, then a friend of mine that came here [to the Lodge] brought me along, and I just got involved from there really, so just curiosity as much as anything.

Jack: Was your interest in mental mediumship the result of going to Spiritualist churches?

Rachael: No, my great grandmother was a medium, so there's always been kind of something in the family—just a vague interest. So I thought it would be quite nice to be a mental medium, but I never was! I was never very good. So yeah, I kind of gave up pursuing my own development in that area and just came along to see what was going on here.

Jack: How long did it take for you to be able to go into trance?

Christine: It's not a year since you've been here, or is it a year now?

Rachael: Not quite, no.

Christine: Not quite, no. From the very first time she came here it's not quite a year yet.

Jack: So it's taken just under a year for you to develop your abilities?

Rachael: Yeah, kind of …

Christine: To write three books and build a lodge …

Rachael: Yeah, I know. It's crazy isn't it! I don't know what's going on, it's just like time has sort of stood still and I've done all of this stuff—a whole lifetime of stuff, in about six months. It's a bit weird!

Jack: So, do you feel that it is kind of directed from elsewhere, or …?

Rachael: I think so. I think I've been kind of nudged here for a long time, but I've been not wanting to do it for a long time. But eventually they kind of get you here [laughs]. It's just like they keep going *like that* [nagging] and then eventually you get down the path you're supposed to be on. Although I feel kind of like I'm supposed to be here now. It's a completeness which I didn't have before, so I must be doing something right! [Laughs.]

There are a number of common threads running through these short extracts. The first is the importance of an initial curiosity to explore mediumship in the first place—Jon and Rachael both explicitly mentioned this. The second is the role and encouragement of friends in convincing them to attend the Lodge—Jon and Sandy both reported the same thing. The third theme is the role of the family—in the case of Emily and Rachael it was through their relatives that they were first introduced to mediumship. The fourth theme is the role of paranormal experiences that seem to punctuate key moments in their mediumistic development—Jon reported veridical psychic impressions that he could not explain, Sandy felt an extraordinary compulsion to write down messages from spirits, and Rachael described the impression of being "nudged" along the way by invisible forces.

The spirits

Mediums at the Lodge generally work with a set group of spirits known as a "spirit team", which during the time of my involvement usually consisted of up to about sixteen distinctive spirit personalities. The characteristics of the spirits varied considerably, from relatively weak two-dimensional characters (perhaps best described as caricatures, including, for example, Winston Churchill and Louis Armstrong) to highly developed, quite *complex* personalities with equally elaborate metaphysical systems (which they could talk about endlessly). Each spirit being was allocated a particular role in their team, each working towards the development of different types of physical phenomena—levitation, materialisation, dematerialisation, psychic surgery, healing, ectoplasmic manifestations, direct voice, and so on—according to their own particular expertise and specialisms.

In general, the spirits who communicate at the Bristol Spirit Lodge are not famous personalities, but certain mediums do count one or two celebrities among their spirit teams. During my first séance session with Emily, her spirit team included several luminary figures from the history of mediumship research, including the famous mediums Helen Duncan (1897–1956), the last woman to be put on trial under the Witchcraft Act of 1735 for her mediumistic séances during the Second World War, Juliette Bisson (1861–1956), partner of the famed medium Eva Carrière (1886–1943), and Leslie Flint (1911–1994), a well-known trance medium of the 1960s. We were also joined by celebrity entertainers such as the rock singer Freddie Mercury (1946–1991) and the comedian Tommy Cooper (1921–1984).

During this séance with Emily we were also joined at one point by an entity who—so Christine later told me—was also a regular and popular communicator through another well-known physical medium. It seems that mediums can sometimes become quite possessive over their regular spirit teams, and especially over particularly enigmatic or popular spirit personalities, and may become defensive about who else they might communicate through. For the sake of preventing the possibility of a rivalry between Emily and this other medium, the entity in question is only *ever* addressed using the pseudonym "My Favourite Uncle", or sometimes just "Uncle".

The following tables list the names and details (where available) of the spirits that made themselves known through Jon and Sandy, the two most highly developed trance mediums at the Lodge.

Sandy's spirit team

Spirit team member	M/F	Defining features	Rank	Role	Period of origin	Regular
Joseph	M	Native American	Child (12)	Gatekeeper		Yes
John Butler	M		Surgeon	Healer	1797	No
Arethena	F		Nurse			
Craig White	M		Consultant surgeon		1920(d)	
Marcus	M		Medical student	Learning		
Bernard Potter	M			Share knowledge	First World War(d)	
Mike	M		Medium's brother	Visual presentation		
Anne Butt	F					
Becca	F		Child (12)	Physical phenomena		

(Continued)

Spirit team member	M/F	Defining features	Rank	Role	Period of origin	Regular
Kristian	M		Child (10)	Physical phenomena	1850(d)	
Graham	M		Undertaker	Spokesman		Yes
Elf	M		Child	Levitation		Yes
Martin	M			Assist elf		
Edward	M					
Samuel	M		Child (12)			

Of these spirits, I was able to talk with Joseph, Arethena, Graham, and Elf over the course of my fieldwork. Some spirits tend to come through more frequently than others, and consequently become familiar voices at séances. There may be weeks or months between "drop-ins" from some of the less frequently attending spirits. Those spirits who attend most frequently represent a core of well developed spirit personalities.

Jon's spirit team

Spirit team member	M/F	Defining features	Rank	Role	Period of origin	Regular
White Feather	M	Native American		Healer		Yes
Hussan	M	Arabic				Yes
Jeremiah	M		Farmhand	Guide	1736 (d)	
Billy	M		Child (9)			
Sanja	F	Group energy				
Charlie	M	Chinese	Monk	Gatekeeper		Yes

I had the opportunity to communicate with all members of Jon's spirit team over the course of my fieldwork, though the most frequent, sustained, and fully expressed communications came from the spirit going by the name of Charlie.

Charlie

Charlie—the gatekeeper for Jon's spirit team—was especially impressive because of his consistently detailed philosophical musings on a wide range of topics and questions. Charlie first made himself known to the circle in May 2008, when he revealed himself to be Jon's *personal spirit guide*. The spirit explained that in a previous life he had inhabited a monastery with Jon in Tibet, and that his name at that time was Dao Lin. In order to make himself more approachable for sitters, Dao Lin asked to be referred to as Charlie. He explained that he was to be the "project manager" for Jon's spirit team, helping to provide an "overall level of control" during séances. He helps other spirits to come through, and prepares the medium's body during the early stages of trance—balancing energies.

In the months after the completion of my undergraduate degree I spent a great deal of time transcribing many of Charlie's philosophical and spiritual reflections on the nature of reality, along with his carefully reasoned answers to a wide range of everyday questions posed by sitters (Di Nucci & Hunter, 2009). In the following extract from those transcribed conversations I took the opportunity to ask Charlie to explain why it is that spirits choose to return to our world in séances:

Christine: That's the end of my silly questions; would you like some sensible ones if we can think of any?

Charlie: No, silly ones are fine.

Group: Laughter.

Charlie: Sensible ones mean I might have to work.

Group: Laughter.

Christine: That doesn't mean that you're not going to get a sensible question if Jack's got one.

Charlie: He is welcome to ask, I can give no guarantees of a sensible answer.

Jack: I'd like to know why you come to the Earth-plane to talk to us.

Charlie: Hmm, ah, I wonder myself sometimes. I come because I am called, because I desire to work this form. It is an opportunity to give people insight and awareness they might not gain otherwise. To answer questions, but most importantly to give them a *new* platform from which to ask *new* questions. Many people, in this world today, have turned away from matters of spirit and faith and belief, they follow a new master, which is a very inflexible teacher. It allows only one answer to any question, and that answer must always be absolute and irrefutable. More than one answer is simply not accepted by men of today's science. Yet, as now, these men are finding in truth there is more than one answer to many questions. In simple mathematics it is possible to prove two answers to a single question. This is learnt at even school level. And as now they explore deeper into the mysteries that confront them, they are finding that some things have no answer at all until they are observed, and then the act of observation will determine the state of the answer. So, those people who find themselves in this room are often those who are looking for alternative solutions to those [questions] presented by modern thinking. All men, all women have, inside, a yearning that cannot be met by science alone. There is an inbuilt desire to know the truth— the *inner* truth. Some search in their own way, some turn their backs, some meditate, some read others' thoughts and answers and derive their own. Some are hit by a large brick from behind …

Group: Laughter.

Charlie: … and suddenly realise they were on the wrong path. All ways are valid ways, and no path is incorrect; even that of modern science, because there too, unless you follow blindly, you will be required to think and question. To come here is simply an opportunity to look at questions in a different way and provide some room for thought that perhaps there is more to life than meets the eye or can be measured. Does this answer your question, my friend?

Jack: Yes, it does.

Exchanges such as this characterised our conversations with Charlie. He was warm, wise, and encouraged us to think for ourselves. The spirits at the Lodge, then, take on a range of roles—from the trickster-like activities of Sandy's spirit Elf, to the sagacious musings of Charlie.

Fluid hierarchies and psychic potential

Irrespective of the apparent hierarchical social structure at the Lodge—running from *sitter* to *circle leader* to *medium* to *spirits*—the roles of the members of the group are, in actuality, quite *fluid*. Most sitters have the potential to develop as mediums themselves, if they are willing to put in the time to sit in circle. Spontaneous trance among the sitters is also quite a common occurrence during séances, and is often taken as a sign that a particular sitter has latent mediumistic abilities waiting to be developed. When I asked a sample of nine sitters about their own psychic abilities, for example, five responded that they felt they had some form of psychic ability, and four stated that they had had paranormal experiences before attending the Lodge. Mediums may also, on occasion, act as sitters for other mediums in the Lodge, thus further mixing up the usual scheme. Christine's is the only role that remains constant throughout all of the séances—the circle leader is *always* needed, while sitters and mediums may swap and change.

In her study of a Spiritualist home-circle in South Wales in the early 1970s, Vieda Skultans explains how the aim of such development circles is "to develop the latent and nascent mediumistic powers of its members and thus to produce fully fledged mediums". Skultans suggests that this is a "reflection of spiritualist ideology which has as one of its basic tenets the belief that everyone possesses psychic power in a latent if not fully developed form" (1974, pp. 2–3). Skultans further explains that:

> ... spiritualism ... deceptively promises high ritual status to all adherents: spiritualist doctrine recognises the universality of mediumistic or spiritual power in a latent, if not manifest, form ... mediumistic power is the currency in terms of which status within the movement is acquired. (1974, p. 61)

This observation also holds true for the members of the Bristol Spirit Lodge today. Everyone has the *potential* to develop their mediumship, but only very few develop to a significant level.

Trance and possession

All mediums at the Lodge were working towards the manifestation of various physical phenomena including *levitation, transfiguration* (the appearance of spirit faces over the face of the entranced medium), *ectoplasmic materialisation, dematerialisation* of the body, and *psychic surgery* under the direction of their discarnate spirit teams. However, due to the difficulties associated with the production of such unusual and impressive phenomena (which only highly developed mediums are able to produce), the majority of séances held in the Lodge were simply trance sessions, during which the medium would enter into a trance state and allow members of their spirit team to communicate with attendant sitters (Gauld, 1982, p. 29). This emphasis on trance mediumship, or *channelling* (Klimo, 1987; Brown, 1997), locates the practices of the Bristol Spirit Lodge firmly within the remit of the ongoing anthropological debate over the cross-cultural phenomenon known as "spirit possession" (Lewis, 1971; Cardeña, van Duijl, Weiner, & Terhune, 2009; Schmidt & Huskinson, 2010; Dawson, 2010; Hunter & Luke, 2014). In an effort to put the Bristol Spirit Lodge into its wider ethnographic context the next chapter presents an overview of literature on the anthropology, neuroscience, and parapsychology of spirit mediumship and possession.

CHAPTER THREE

Mediumship and spirit possession: A literature review

> The belief in temporary inspiration is worldwide. Certain persons are supposed to be possessed from time to time by a spirit or deity, while the possession lasts, their own personality lies in abeyance; the presence of the spirit is revealed by convulsive shiverings and shakings of the man's whole body, by wild gestures and excited looks, all of which are referred, not to the man himself, but to the spirit which has entered into him; and in this abnormal state all his utterances are accepted as the voice of the god or spirit dwelling in him or speaking through him.
>
> —James Frazer, *The Golden Bough* (1890, p. 108).

Spirit mediumship and possession in the cross-cultural context

The following literature review will present an overview of the contemporary and historical anthropological debate over spirit possession and mediumship in the cross-cultural context. We will survey the dominant explanatory paradigms (models that govern the way that research is done and data interpreted, cf. Kuhn, 1973)—from functionalism to cognitive science—and evaluate their effectiveness as explanatory accounts of spirit possession. Paul Stoller has suggested that anthropological commentaries on spirit possession have tended towards five dominant explanatory frameworks, which include: "functionalist, psychoanalytic, physiological, symbolic (interpretive/textual), and theatrical" frameworks (Stoller, 1994, p. 637). These perspectives, along with others, will be used to structure the following literature review. An overview of the history of parapsychological approaches to spirit mediumship has also been included, as has an overview of the progress of neurophysiological research on mediumistic states of consciousness and their associated brain activity. The chapter concludes with the suggestion that the dominant approaches can only be thought of as *pieces of the puzzle*, rather than as *complete explanations*. An effective model of spirit possession and mediumship would have to take into account such a very wide range of complementary factors that no single approach is able to account for in its totality.

A brief note on terminology: mediumship and possession

There is a great deal of terminological confusion when it comes to the subject of spirit mediumship and spirit possession (Schmidt & Huskinson, 2010, pp. 1–2). Indeed, I have already made use of both terms simultaneously in this book without much attempt to distinguish them. It would seem appropriate, therefore, to address this issue before we progress any further with our literature review.

To begin, a standard parapsychological definition of "spirit medium", taken from the Society for Psychical Research's online glossary, reads: "A person who regularly, and often at will, receives purported communications from the dead ("mental medium") and/or causes physical materializations ("physical medium")".[9] One of the main criticisms of this kind of definition from a mainstream academic perspective is its assumption of the possibility of *genuine* paranormal phenomena—to accept such an interpretation as an anthropologist would essentially be to "go native". It assumes that it is *possible* to receive communications from the dead, and that it is *possible* to produce physical materialisations of discarnate spirits. Social scientific definitions, by contrast, are usually much more reserved in their approach, and are often subject to a form of "ontological bracketing" that perpetuates the dominant underlying materialist view of the social sciences (Northcote, 2004).

---

[9] www.spr.ac.uk/page/glossary-paranormal.

In the ethnographic literature the term "spirit possession" dominates the discourse, even in the context of what parapsychologists would typically call *spirit mediumship*. Anthropologist Vincent Crapanzano's definition serves as a good example of an ethnographic definition of spirit possession. He writes:

> Spirit possession may be broadly defined as any altered or unusual state of consciousness and allied behaviour that is indigenously understood in terms of the influence of an alien spirit, demon, or deity. (2005, p. 8687)

The emphasis here is on the practitioner's *indigenous understanding* of the experience as implying the "influence of an alien spirit, demon, or deity" on the physical body. The ethnographic definition *brackets out* the reality of the possessing entities by focusing on *belief*, while the parapsychological definition focuses on the ostensible phenomena themselves. The term "indigenous understanding" comes with the implicit understanding that the Western scientific tradition (which is not based on belief, but on empirical observation) *really* has the correct interpretation (i.e., it is *not* spirits).

My preference is to operate somewhere *between* the classical ethnographic and parapsychological definitions presented above, remaining open to the *possibility* of genuine paranormal phenomena (informed by parapsychological perspectives), while not necessarily presupposing them, but rather entertaining them as *possible factors* at play. A combination of the two approaches would also lead to a greater emphasis on "indigenous understanding" than the parapsychological definitions have traditionally tended to include. In the ethnographic context, for example, mediumship does not necessarily equate to "communication with the dead" (as the parapsychological definition seems to assume), and may include communication with animal spirits, nature spirits, deities, or any other culturally significant entities. It is my contention that parapsychological understandings, with their *overt* emphasis on the ontological status of the phenomena of mediumship, can in turn serve to *deepen* ethnographic approaches and demonstrate that spirit possession, as traditionally defined by Western anthropologists, is a much more complex phenomenon than it might at first appear, at least from a purely social-functional/cognitive perspective.

A further point to bear in mind is that in the parapsychological literature—as well as among my own informants at the Bristol Spirit Lodge—the term "spirit possession" is *never* used to refer to mediumship, as it carries connotations of *involuntary* and *demonic* possession (often requiring a form of ritual exorcism to remove the evil spirit from the body of the afflicted individual), while mediumship, on the other hand, is usually held to be a *voluntary*, *deliberately initiated*, activity directed towards some purpose—it is *practical*, *does something useful*, and is certainly not pathological. Indeed, sociologist Luc de Heusch (1971) directly contrasted "involuntary possession" requiring exorcism, with voluntary mediumship by proposing the new term *adorcism*, the binary opposite of "exorcism"—a *positive* and *desirable* state that is deliberately induced. Already we see that the anthropological definition lumps together two quite distinct—though undoubtedly related—phenomena that parapsychologists and experiencers have long differentiated.

It is also clear that the parapsychological term "mediumship" refers to a much wider variety of phenomena than the anthropological category of "voluntary spirit possession". Spiritualist mediumship, as we have already seen, can be broadly split into two distinct forms—*mental* and *physical* mediumship. Mental mediumship can itself be split into two further sub-forms: (1) clairvoyant/telepathic/clairaudient/clairsentient mediumship, often also known as "platform mediumship", and (2) trance mediumship, during which the body of the medium is temporarily occupied by an ostensible spirit entity. These are forms of "subjective mediumship". Physical mediumship, by contrast, is a form of mediumship where spirits demonstrate objective physical phenomena through their entranced mediums, including ectoplasmic materialisation, dematerialisation, levitation, various psychokinetic effects, and so on (Gauld, 1982, pp. 1–16). It would be an interesting project to re-examine ethnographic accounts of spirit possession practices in light of these parapsychological distinctions.

As we have already seen in the context of the Belmont Road Spiritualist Centre, the phenomena of *mental mediumship* are predominantly *subjective* (but if accurate *can* be verified objectively). They occur *within* the consciousness of the medium themselves, and usually take the form of audio messages (e.g., voices), visual images (symbols, visions, etc.), and other *qualitative* sensations (moods, emotions, feelings, etc.) that provide *information* about discarnate spirits. Here the medium is a *conscious mediator* between the worlds, interpreting and translating spirit messages to sitters. In *trance mediumship*, the barriers between "internal" and "external" are mediated by the various spirit personalities themselves, who manifest *through* the medium's body. In trance mediumship, then, the medium functions as an *unconscious mediator*. In a sense, this form of mediumship can be seen as a halfway point between mental and physical mediumship.

Physical mediumship, by contrast, represents the *opposite* end of the subjective-objective spectrum, and aims to produce "external", "objective" phenomena that are visible to outside observers. A useful definition of physical mediumship sees it as the "purported ability of the medium to channel unknown energies" to create physical changes in the immediate environment (Klimo, 1987). In this respect physical mediumship shares many similarities with other magico-religious practices that seek to effect change in the physical world by spiritual, magical, or supernatural means—the phenomena of physical mediumship are also similar in many ways to specifically religious phenomena such as *stigmata* (I. Wilson, 1988; Krippner, 2002; Krippner & Kirkwood, 2008), and other phenomena reported in connection with religious ascetics (cf. Littlewood & Bartocci, 2005; Grosso, 2016). Ectoplasm, as it occurs in the Western context, however, is a surprisingly singular phenomenon, with very few cross-cultural parallels, bar the Aboriginal Australian "magic rope", which moves independently of the "clever man" as it is extruded from his mouth, and the phlegm of Ayahuasqueros in the Amazon from which magic darts are materialised and extracted (Haule, 2011, pp. 122–125).

In the context of this book, we are primarily concerned with trance mediumship, midway between mental and physical mediumship (though we will also be touching on physical mediumship). Trance mediumship is the main form of mediumship being developed at the Bristol Spirit Lodge, along with an often unsuccessful attempt to develop physical mediumship phenomena. The development of these particular forms of mediumship, in contrast to the clairvoyant forms of mental mediumship, is one of the main functions for this kind of *private* home-circle. The phenomena and experiences associated with platform mediumship can be found in Spiritualist churches across the country, and training and development in these forms of mediumship can be easily accessed at centres such as the Arthur Findlay College in Stansted and the College of Psychic Studies in London, as well as at Spiritualist churches. Trance and physical mediumship, however, are somewhat more peripheral, taking place in private circles outside established churches and Spiritualist organisations.

Throughout the following literature review, then, the term "spirit possession", in the ethnographic sense, will frequently be employed synonymously with "mediumship" as the bulk of the literature surveyed is concerned with *voluntarily initiated spirit possession*. It is important to remember, however, that practitioners of mediumship would be unlikely to refer to their own practice as "spirit possession", as they are initiating a *deliberate* and *desirable* state of possession.

Spirit mediumship: divisive for secular and Judaeo-Christian traditions

In Western societies, spirit mediumship is often held to be a "suspicious", usually "fraudulent", and occasionally even "dangerous" activity by the dominant culture. The reasons for this are deeply rooted in Western scientific rationalism's struggle to distance itself from *supernaturalism*, the idea that there is a dimension *beyond* the natural/physical (Voss, 2017, pp. 117–118), and to establish *materialist naturalism* as its dominant metaphysical paradigm. The historian of science David C. Lindberg suggests that this divide goes right back to the dawn of Western philosophy in Ancient Greece, where emerging philosophers sought to distance themselves from the superstitions of their forebears through the use of reason and rationality. He writes:

> The world of the philosophers, in short, was an orderly, predictable world in which things behaved according to their natures ... The capricious world of divine intervention was being pushed aside, making room for order and regularity ... A distinction between the natural and supernatural was emerging; and there was wide agreement that causes (if they are to be dealt with philosophically) are to be sought only in the nature of things. (1996, pp. 26–27)

Secularisation, then, is clearly not something new. Equally, many religious traditions (especially the Judaeo-Christian traditions, as a cultural and ontological counterpoint to materialist naturalism) *also* condemn the practice of spirit mediumship (and aspects of the "paranormal" in general), primarily on the grounds that it is specifically prohibited in the Bible—see, for example, the warnings against such practices in *Deuteronomy* 18, 10–12:

> Let no one be found among you ... who practises divination or sorcery, interprets omens, engages in witchcraft, or casts spells, or who is a medium or spiritist or who consults the dead. Anyone who does these things is detestable to the Lord, and because of these detestable practices the Lord your God will drive out those nations before you.

Spirit possession also appears prominently in the New Testament as something that needs to be *cured* through exorcism (Keener, 2010). The notion that possession is *negative* and associated with *illness* has been hugely influential, and there are many theories of spirit possession that reduce it down to pathology and psychopathology. It is also probable, however, that Judaeo-Christian religions condemn spirit mediumship (and other forms of divination and magic) as a means of asserting the primacy of their own particular mode of spiritual communication, that is, through divine revelation, scripture, and the officially sanctioned priesthood. From this perspective, mediums operating in the private sphere are a threat to the established order.

Early approaches

Anthropology has had a long relationship with what it refers to as spirit possession. As early as 1890, for example, Sir James Frazer (1854–1941), in his voluminous exercise in cross-cultural comparison *The Golden Bough*, noted that the belief that "certain persons are supposed to be possessed from time to time by a spirit or deity" is a "worldwide" phenomenon—indicating an awareness of, and a concern for, the near-universality of spirit possession practices and beliefs across human cultures, even at this relatively early stage in the development of the discipline (Frazer, 1890, p. 108).

The interpretive framework employed by early commentators, such as Frazer, however, was fundamentally dismissive of the phenomenon. Frazer, for example, referred to this "temporary inspiration" as an "abnormal state" (1944, p. 152), clearly implying a pejorative attitude towards spirit possession practices and practitioners. According to this perspective, spirit possession practices represented little more than *delusion, folly,* fraud, and, in some cases, *intoxication* (and all the negative implications this term carried in Victorian society). From within Frazer's broader developmentalist paradigm, spirit possession beliefs could never be anything more than this. According to his scheme, such beliefs and practices had already been surpassed by the advances of modern rationalism and empirical science, which has no room for notions of "spirits" or "divine" interaction.

For the earliest theorists of spirit possession then, the phenomenon, to use E. B. Tylor's terminology, is nothing more than a "survival" of *irrational* and *primitive* mentality. Historian of anthropology Marvin Harris (1968) defines a survival as when a "phenomenon originating under a set of causal conditions of a former era perpetuates [itself] into a period during which the original conditions no longer exist" (p. 164). Tylor saw the rise of Spiritualism in Euro-American society as just such a survival. It is worthwhile noting, however, that despite Tylor's public dismissal of Spiritualism as an anachronistic survival, he was nevertheless perplexed by the phenomena he witnessed with some of the Victorian era's greatest Spiritualist mediums, including Daniel Dunglas Home (1833–1886), the Reverend Stainton Moses (1839–1892), and even Kate Fox.

Tylor's private diaries reveal that while participating in séances with these mediums, he had some rather unusual experiences of his own, which challenged his initial assumptions about Spiritualism. After a séance with Home, for example, Tylor wrote that he had "failed to make out how either raps, table levitation or accordion playing were produced". With Stainton Moses he described how "[his] trance seemed real", and concluded that his experience with Kate Fox was "very curious, and her feats are puzzling to me", noting that her phenomena "deserve further looking into". Tylor's experiences with these mediums forced him to admit, in his own words, "a *prima facie* case on evidence" for the abilities of certain mediums, and to conclude that he could not deny the possibility "that there may be a psychic force causing raps, movements, levitations, etc." (Stocking, 1971; see also Hunter, 2011b).

Functionalist interpretations

Functionalist approaches tend to assume a Durkheimian sociological perspective, and suggest that social phenomena—whether we are talking about religion, rituals, kinship systems, politics, or possession—perform their own specific *social functions* that help to maintain the solidarity and cohesion of the social group. The approach has, as its underlying metaphysics, a form of positivist materialism based around the scientific analysis of what Durkheim called "social facts"—held to be objective "social things" out there in the world that can influence human behaviour (Durkheim, 2008).

Social anthropologist I. M. Lewis's (1930–2014) *social-protest theory* is one of the most influential fucntionalist models of spirit possession. It suggests that spirit possession performs an essential social function in allowing women in predominantly male dominated societies (or indeed any other socially peripheral group) to express their discontent in a socially acceptable manner. When in the possessed state, Lewis argues, an individual is free to carry out activities that they would not normally be permitted to do. While in the possessed state they are "totally blameless" for their actions: "responsibility lies not with them, but with the spirits". This interpretation essentially understands mediumship and spirit possession traditions as "thinly disguised protest movements directed against the dominant sex", or group (Lewis, 1971, pp. 31–32).

Functionalist analyses of spirit possession in this vein have been very popular among anthropologists, and have been applied to numerous societies worldwide (Giles, 1987, p. 235). These include accounts of the Zar possession cult of northern Sudan (Boddy, 1988), spirit possession among the Digo in southern Kenya (Gomm, 1975), in the case of spontaneous epidemics of involuntary spirit possession in Malaysian factories (Ong, 1988), and even in a Spiritualist home-circle in 1960s Wales (Skultans, 1974). According to Lewis's model all of these different cultural manifestations can be explained in the same way—spirit possession is a *mode of protest for disenfranchised social groups, and nothing more.*

However, as John Bowker (1973) and Janice Boddy (1988, p. 4) have noted, although the functionalist approach does possess considerable explanatory power, it often ignores both the *significance of subjective experience* for believers, as well as the *possibility* that genuine paranormal phenomena might exist, assuming from the outset that the *objects* of supernatural beliefs are *cultural constructions*, with foundations in misperception, delusion, and fraud (Nelson, 1975, p. 167; E. Turner, 1993; Winkelman, 1982). This underlying functionalist assumption is problematic when it comes to attempting to *take seriously* the beliefs and experiences of our informants, as it automatically rejects and undermines them through the imposition of an etic materialist/natu-ralist ontology.

That said, mediumship, and the ability to incorporate spiritual enti-ties, undoubtedly *can* provide women, and other socially marginalised groups, such as homosexuals (Fry, 1986) and factory workers (Ong, 1988) for instance, with significant social benefits that would not oth-erwise be available to them. Kilson (1971) has written of the transfor-mation in status that spirit mediumship brings about in Ga society in Ghana, for example. At the time of Kilson's fieldwork, the Ga con-sidered women to be innately inferior to men, which when combined with illiteracy, unmarried life, and, potentially, an inability to conceive children, frequently resulted in a low social status. Through becoming spirit mediums women in Ga society were able to achieve a degree of status that could not have been attained under their normal everyday circumstances, primarily because they have now taken on an important *social role* imbued with supernatural authority—the role of the medium.

In her study of a Spiritualist home-circle in a Welsh town in the late 1960s, Vieda Skultans (1974) focused on the therapeutic and supportive elements of Spiritualism as its main attraction for adherents. Skultans interpreted Spiritualist practice and belief as a *coping strategy* for the women of "Welshtown" in light of their traditional "feminine roles" as "housewife, mother and sexual partner". According to this perspec-tive, and in line with Lewis's general hypothesis, Spiritualism provided these women with a means to escape their normal day-to-day circum-stances, at least for the duration of their psychic development circles. She writes:

> Indeed, this is where the contribution of Spiritualism lies. For the weekly repetition of healing activities and the exchange of mes-sages "from spirit" constitute a ritual of reconciliation to a situation which does not permit any radical alternatives to itself. (Skultans, 1974, p. 4)

Peter Wilson, however, perhaps somewhat naïvely disagrees with Lewis's protest hypothesis on the grounds that within "male domi-nated societies", in which males and females often operate in com-pletely different spheres, it is not clear that women necessarily feel peripheral, downtrodden, or neglected. He explains that "deprivation surely implies withholding that which is due, but in what traditionally male dominated society is it ever regarded as a woman's due that she be granted access to the man's domain?" (1967, p. 367). Although Wilson's assumptions about the subjective desires of women in repressive societies are questionable, he nevertheless highlights one potential pitfall in Lewis's theory—that we cannot assume that our own values necessarily apply to other cultures, let alone our ontological assumptions. As another counterbalance to Lewis's model, Susan Rasmussen has highlighted the practice of spirit possession among the Kel Ewey Tuareg of Niger, noting that Tuareg women participate in spirit possession rituals in spite of the fact that they "are not subjugated, but enjoy high status and prestige" (1994, p. 76).

Owing to these obvious discrepancies between Lewis's general theory of spirit possession and the ethnographic reality, Donovan (2000) has argued that although it is applicable to many possession cults, it ought not to be thought of as a *complete theory*, but rather should be supplemented by other approaches. In other words, spirit possession undoubtedly performs a range of specialised social functions, but these functions are not necessarily *all* that is going on. Recent research focusing on the therapeutic potential of mediumship practices for the bereaved, especially in the Western context (cf. Walliss, 2001; Beischel, Mosher, & Boccuzzi, 2014; Osborne & Bacon, 2015), are one example of a way in which Lewis's social-protest theory can be supplemented by other approaches—social protest is not the *only* function performed by mediumship.

Pathological approaches

The association of spirit possession with various pathological conditions has been a persistent theme in both anthropology and psychology (Csordas, 1987; Zingrone, 1994, pp. 102–103; Carrazana et al., 1999; Jilek-Aall, 1999; Emmons, 2008, p. 72). While it is true that in many cultures spirit possession—more specifically "spontaneous" or "pathogenic" possession—*is* associated with illness (see for example, Freed & Freed, 1964; Cohen, 2008), recent neurophysiological research has gone some way towards demonstrating differences between the underlying neurological activity of individuals experiencing spirit possession as a *voluntary* practice (mediumship), on the one hand, and epilepsy and other neurological disorders on the other (Hageman et al., 2010, pp. 103–105; Peres, Moreira-Almeida, Ciaxeta, Leao, & Newberg, 2012). Continuing research in this direction looks set to further differentiate pathological conditions from the trance states associated with spirit possession practices (see for example, Oohashi et al., 2002), and may also point towards neurophysiological differences between specific forms of mediumship, for example differences between psychic readings and communication with discarnate spirits (Delorme et al., 2013). We will return to a more thorough discussion of the neurophysiological correlates of mediumship and possession shortly.

Psychodynamic interpretations and hysteria

As we have already seen, the earliest approaches to the study of spirit possession emphasised the "abnormal state" of the possessed (Frazer, 1890, p. 108), associating it, by virtue of certain behavioural similarities, with the newly identified neurological disorders of the nineteenth century, especially hysteria and epilepsy (Taves, 2006; Maraldi, Machado, & Zangari, 2010, pp. 182–183). The positivist sociologist Herbert Spencer (1820–1903), for example, in the first volume of his *Principles of Sociology* writes:

> … during insensibilities of all kinds, the soul wanders, and, on returning, causes the body to resume its activity—if the soul can thus not only go out of the body but can go into it again; then may not the body be entered by some other soul? The savage thinks it may. Hence the interpretation of epilepsy. The Congo people ascribe epilepsy to demoniac possession … Of Asiatic races may be instanced the Kalmucks: by these nomads epileptics are regarded as persons into whom bad spirits have entered. (1897, p. 227)

In drawing a direct comparison between spirit possession practices and overt pathological conditions, early European scholars were essentially diminishing profound cultural and spiritual practices, reducing them down to the level of illness and disease—something to be *cured*. This could be read as a justification for imperialist expansion and the subjugation of indigenous practices (Somer, 2006). There is a danger with such interpretations, therefore, of perpetuating this by now outdated view of the world—of medicalising cultural phenomena and assuming that practices and beliefs that do not accord with the dominant framework of rationalist materialism are, by necessity, symptomatic of illness or disease (Tobert, 2016).

That said, there are, nevertheless, some striking similarities between spirit possession and certain neurological disorders that possibly suggest underlying (though not necessarily pathological) psycho-physiological processes. In the mid-nineteenth century, for example, the pioneering neurologist Jean-Martin Charcot (1825–1893), at the infamous Salpêtrière hospital in Paris, carefully documented the symptoms of his hysterical patients (usually women), often through the pioneering use of photography as a medical tool—a testament to the highly somatic/performative nature of hysterical symptoms (Hustvedt, 2011). The symptoms of hysteria manifested in a particularly wide variety of ways—ranging from amnesia, blindness, and anaesthesia, through to "hallucinations, excited and inappropriate behaviour … fits and paraly-ses" (Littlewood, 1995, p. 154). Symptoms such as these overlapped so comfortably with the purported experiences and observed behaviours of the possessed in different cultural contexts that it is little wonder ethnographers, anthropologists, and psychologists were so quick to label spirit possession as just another form of hysteria. Freed and Freed (1964), for example, even went as far as suggesting that "almost all who have written on spirit possession regard it as a form of hysteria" (p. 165), and Goff, Brotman, Kindlon, Waites, & Amico, (1991) have suggested a clear *correlation* between belief that one is possessed by another person or spirit and chronic psychosis (hysteria), and schizophrenia (Azaunce, 1995). It is important to remember, however, that correlation does not necessarily imply causation.

The Freudian psychodynamic perspective also understands spirit possession as a form of hysteria—as an "irrational emotional state caused by repressed Oedipal desires in the unconscious" (Castillo, 1994, p. 1). Other psychoanalytic interpretations of spirit possession emphasise "past traumatic and distressful experiences" in the lives of the possessed (Budden, 2003, p. 28), while others have suggested that the behaviours and psychological sensations associated with the possession state are *symbolic symptoms* of the unconscious repression of such experiences, *converted* from the psychological to the physical through a process known as "conversion", or "somatisation" (Freud & Breuer, 1895d, p. 146).

Gananath Obeyesekere's study of ecstatic priests and priestesses in Sri Lanka is perhaps the best-known example of a psychoanalytic

approach to spirit possession. Obeyesekere interpreted possession—
arude, meaning "divine possession" (1984, p. 56)—as a cultural symptom, along with other physical expressions (for example, the matted
hair of the priestesses), as *outward symbols* of repressed (internalised)
negative life experiences. Psychoanalytic interpretations, therefore, consider spirit possession performances to be culturally sanctioned expressions (again echoing Lewis) of underlying pathology. The influence of
culture on the manifestation of hysterical symptoms has been widely
noted in the literature on the subject (cf. Shorter, 1994; Watters, 2011).

The nutrient deficiency hypothesis

Another pathological interpretation of spirit possession that was, until
relatively recently, popular in the anthropological literature is the
"nutrient deficiency hypothesis". This approach essentially suggests
that instances of spirit possession—particularly in women—occur as a
result of, and in direct response to, extended periods of malnourishment (Kehoe & Giletti, 1981; Bourguignon, Bellisari, & McCabe, 1983,
p. 414). Kehoe & Giletti explain that:

> There is a strong correlation between populations subsisting on diets
> poor in calcium, magnesium, niacin, tryptophan, thiamine, and
> vitamin D, and those practising spirit possession; conversely, popu-
> lations reported as having probably adequate intakes of these nutri-
> ents generally lack culturally sanctioned spirit possession. (p. 550)

They go on to suggest that spirit possession cults represent an "institutionalised recognition of class endemic symptoms of nutrient deficiency" (1981, p. 551). Suggesting that spirit possession beliefs and
practices can be explained purely in terms of nutrient deficiency is a
strongly reductive medical-materialist perspective on the phenomenon.
The nutrient deficiency hypothesis has been subject to a lot of criticism,
as it is fairly easy to find instances where it fails to stand up to scrutiny,
for example within the contemporary Euro-American Spiritualist tradition, where nutrient deficiency is unlikely to play a role (but it cannot
be ruled out entirely). Although it is certainly possible that Kehoe and
Giletti's hypothesis may account for *certain* instances of spirit possession (either as a symptom of, or as a sociocultural response to, nutrient
deficiency), it clearly cannot be applied to *all* societies where voluntary

possession is practised. I. M. Lewis (1983) has also criticised Kehoe and Giletti's approach for reducing the culturally rich and complex phenomenon of spirit possession to a single biomedical cause (though his own approach essentially reduces the phenomenon to a single social function). Bourguignon, Bellisari, and McCabe (1983) have also provided several counter arguments to the nutrient deficiency hypothesis, for example they highlight:

> (1) A confusion between possession belief (emic) and possession trance behavior (etic); (2) a confusion between "sumptuary" rules (ideal culture), diets (real culture), nutrient intake (biochemical constituents of foods) and nutritional status; (3) although impressionistic accounts suggest that women often predominate in possession trance cults, the simple equations women=possession trance, is not justified by the available data; and (4) even if a coexistence of women's participation in possession cults, women's nutrient deficiencies, and sumptuary rules were to be established, our understanding of the cultural explanation of trance behavior as possession by spirits would not be advanced. (p. 414)

It is now generally assumed that the nutrient deficiency hypothesis is overly reductive, and fails to take account of a variety of other factors involved in spirit possession practices—especially neurological, cognitive, and experiential factors. The theory is also lacking in its automatic assumption that spirit possession could not be anything other than a symptom of pathology (malnourishment), completely disregarding the *emic* understanding and subjective experience of the phenomenon as something meaningful and practical.

Dissociative identity disorder (DID)

One of the most common comparisons in discussions of spirit possession is with dissociative identity disorder (DID), previously known as multiple personality disorder (MPD). This is a condition that bears several striking similarities to incidences of spirit possession (Braude, 1988; Taves, 2006, p. 123). Psychologist Adam Crabtree, for example, describes DID as "a condition in which two or more personalities manifest themselves in one human being" (1988, p. 60)—much as multiple spirits manifest through a single medium—and psychical researcher David

Scott Rogo (1950–1990) referred to the "infinite boundary" of "spirit possession, madness and multiple personality" (1988)—suggesting a considerable degree of phenomenological and behavioural overlap between possession and DID. The *DSM-IV*'s criteria for the diagnosis of dissociative identity disorder included:

> ... that a person have at least two separate ego states, or alters— different modes of being and feeling and acting that exist inde- pendently of each other and that come forth and are in control at different times ... There are typically two to four alters at the time a diagnosis is made, but over the course of treatment several more often emerge. Gaps in memory are also common and are pro- duced because at least one alter has no contact with the others ... The existence of different alters must also be chronic (long lasting) and severe (causing considerable disruption in one's life); it cannot be a temporary change resulting from the ingestion of a drug, for example. (Davison, Neale, & Kring, 2004, pp. 187–188)

The many voices, characters, or personalities (spirits) that speak through the bodies of entranced spirit mediums find clear parallels in the multiple personalities, referred to in the literature on dissociative states as *alters*, expressed by individuals suffering from DID and related conditions.

A distinction can be made, however, between the *pathological* condi- tion of DID and the highly *controlled* nature of spirit mediumship on the grounds that the presentation of alter personalities in DID is usually associated with *negative consequences* for the lifestyle of the individual (see Keyes, 1995 for a particularly extreme example). Mediumship, how- ever, more often than not, does not impinge on the everyday life of the medium in such an *overtly negative* way. That is not to say that it doesn't occasionally erupt into daily life—in the early stages of mediumship development, as my informant Rachael has recounted—but it is even- tually normalised to become a positive experience for the individual. This could be understood as the result of a "domestication" process, whereby regular séances provide a set time, place, and ritual context for alter personalities to express themselves, thus allowing the medium's primary personality to dominate in everyday circumstances. If, there- fore, we were to consider mediumship and DID to be homologous phe- nomena, structured mediumship development and regular controlled séances could be seen as useful tools for improving the quality of life of the afflicted individual through providing a safe environment and rigid structure in which alter personalities can manifest (Seligman, 2010). This may be yet another therapeutic application of spirit mediumship—admittedly under the assumption that the spirits are psychologically generated alters—which further undermines the suggestion that *all* mediumship/possession is necessarily pathological in nature.

Moreira-Almeida and colleagues have also noted that in a comparative study of Brazilian Spiritist mediums and North American DID sufferers, "mediums differed in having better social adjustment, lower prevalence of mental disorders, lower use of mental health services, no use of anti-psychotics, and lower prevalence to histories of physical or sexual childhood abuse, sleepwalking, secondary features of DID, and symptoms of borderline personality" (Moreira-Almeida, Neto, & Cardeña, 2008, p. 420). Similarly, Roxburgh and Roe, in a study comparing Spiritualist mediums and non-mediums in the UK, concluded that "it does not seem tenable to characterise mediums as psychologically unhealthy or dysfunctional" (2011, p. 294). Indeed, Cardeña, van Duijl, Weiner, and Terhune (2009) have argued that "greater control over one's possession abilities, perhaps gained in part by a more extensive or rigorous training regimen, may characterise non-pathological possession" (p. 178). This is precisely what we see at the Bristol Spirit Lodge—a rigorous regimen of training for mediumship over weeks, months, and years.

Several anthropologists have further challenged the idea that spirit possession is a pathological condition (Budden, 2003; Klass, 2003). Budden, for instance, argues that the prevalence of dissociative possession and possession-trance states across the world, and the extent to which such states are "embedded within historical and cultural contexts", indicates that the phenomenon is far from abnormal, indeed, as we have already seen, in many societies it may be a *desirable* state, with those able to incorporate spiritual entities at will being granted higher social status than would otherwise be attainable. As an illustrative example of an instance in which a clear *indigenous* distinction was made between spirit possession and a pathological state, Thomas Csordas recounts a case where an individual was denied initiation into a Candomblé *terreiro* because the Mae-de-Santo recognised subtle behaviours in his performance that were indicative of pathology rather than ecstasy, indicating a degree of discernment (Csordas, 1987, p. 9). Although only a single example, and drawn from a single cultural context, Csordas's observation does seem to demonstrate an awareness among spirit possession practitioners themselves—as well as those who train and develop them—of essential differences between mediumship and pathological conditions, as well as an ability to *actively* distinguish between them.

Anthropologist Morton Klass suggested that the notion of "patterned dissociative identity" be used to refer to instances of possession trance, in which the personality of the medium is altered or displaced (Klass, 2003, pp. 118–119). Here it is the use of the word "patterned" that distinguishes spirit possession from the pathological condition of dissociative identity disorder. We will see later how it is this *patterning* that reveals whether a medium's trance is pathological or not—that their altered states are structured, useful, and desirable.

So while it is true that spirit possession does bear some surface resemblances to DID and other neurological conditions (which may be indicative of similar *underlying processes*), it does not seem appropriate to consider it a *disorder* in the strict sense of the term, especially when the possession state is actively induced as a culturally meaningful practice—as in most contemporary traditions of spirit mediumship.

Cognitive approaches

The cognitive approach to spirit possession does not necessarily see it as a pathological phenomenon, though it *does* suggest that spirit possession beliefs and experiences ultimately arise from cognitive illusions and category errors (Berlotti & Magnani, 2010).

In her paper "What Is Spirit Possession?", cognitive anthropologist Emma Cohen (2008) suggests that the apparent similarities found in spirit possession practices and beliefs across cultures are the product of *innate cognitive processes*, which human beings employ in making sense of the world. This work draws heavily on the writings of cognitivist scholars of religion such as Pascal Boyer (2001) and Justin Barrett (2000), who argue that religion is best understood as a *by-product* of the way in which the human brain processes and makes sense of the sensory world. Pascal Boyer's book *Religion Explained* (2001), for example, concludes that religion can be explained purely:

> ... in terms of systems that are in all human minds and do all sorts
> of precious and interesting work, but were not really designed to

produce religious concepts or behaviours … religion is portrayed
here as a mere consequence or side-effect of having the brains we
have. (pp. 378–379)

Admittedly, Boyer isn't saying that religion is a *simple* phenomenon that
can be *easily* explained, rather what he is suggesting is that religion is
the result of a "variety of underlying [cognitive] processes" (p. 379).
Nevertheless, Boyer *is* implying that religion can be explained in terms
of basic *cognitive* processes responsible for such mundane (though
essential) things as attention, making sense of other minds, detecting
agents in the environment, and so on. In Boyer's view, it is through
a combination of otherwise normal cognitive processes that religion
ultimately emerges—through misapplying, misunderstanding, and
misinterpreting these processes as evidence of something else (spirits,
gods, telepathy, and so on). To paraphrase the words of materialist philosopher of mind Gilbert Ryle (1900–1976), supernatural belief is the
result of a "category mistake" (2009, p. 6), where we apply a cognitive
tool evolved for one purpose (detecting predators, for example) to an
unrelated context (a cloud) and arrive at a the conclusion that there is a
"spirit" in the cloud (Guthrie, 1993).

  According to Cohen's model, spirit possession is a complex cognitive phenomenon involving multiple cognitive processes, and which
usually takes one of two distinct forms: voluntary, or "executive", possession, and involuntary, or "pathogenic", possession (again reiterating
the distinction between spirit *possession* and spirit *mediumship*). Cohen
suggests that these two distinct forms of possession can be explained in
the following way:

> *Pathogenic* possession concepts result from the operation of cognitive
> tools that deal with the representation of contamination (both posi-
> tive and negative); the presence of the spirit entity is typically (but
> not always) manifested in the form of illness. *Executive* possession
> concepts mobilise cognitive tools that deal with the world of inten-
> tional agents; the spirit entity is typically represented as taking over
> the host's executive control, or replacing the host's "mind" (or inten-
> tional agency), thus assuming control of bodily behaviours. (2008).

According to Cohen, then, spirit possession practices and beliefs are
so widespread primarily because they make *intuitive sense*, owing to

their dependence on otherwise normal, innate cognitive processes. She suggests that "these concepts spread successfully because they are supported by pan-human mental capacities that are employed in the resolution of everyday, common problems". Again, we see here an attempt to explain spirit possession by *reducing* it to very *simple* (everyday) underlying processes, whereby there is no possibility that it might relate to *something more*—the native interpretation is *wrong* and cognitive science has the answers. It is the tendency towards the reduction of social and cultural phenomena down to cognitive (psychological) processes that prompted James Laidlaw to make the following criticisms of the "cognitive science of religion":

1. Cognitive science, like any explanatory method, has blind spots as well as foci.
2. Explanation is intentional, so necessarily plural, and causal explanations in terms of mechanisms of cognitive processing cannot substitute for the contextual interpretation of thought and action, yet the ambition of an integrated "cognitive science of religion" ignores this irreducible plurality.
3. While cognitive science can provide a causal account of some religious phenomena, this is not, as its practitioners claim, an explanation of "religion"; because
4. Much that is distinctive about religious traditions as traditions falls outside the definition of religion used by cognitive scientists; and in any case
5. Religion is not an object, such that "it" can be defined analytically rather than historically, and therefore is not a proper object for the kind of explanations cognitive science can provide.
6. What cognitive science can and to some extent has developed explanations for is what the Enlightenment called Natural Religion, and what both it and many religious authorities have called Superstition.
7. This being the case, the contribution cognitive science can make to any general understanding of religion or to the study of particular religious traditions is necessarily ancillary, and roughly equivalent to the contribution that technical knowledge about materials can make to aesthetics and the history of art.
8. The anti-humanist methodological exclusions on which cognitive science is founded are reflected in the way some if not all cognitive scientists of religion handle the concept of belief, which, even where

this might be against their best intentions, involves implicit denial of the reality of human reason, imagination, and will (Laidlaw, 2007).

Much like the social protest and medical-materialist models, then, the cognitive approach fails to account for the *totality* and *complexity* of the phenomenon it seeks to explain (religion, or in this case, spirit possession), preferring to focus on just one dimension of the phenomenon (the cognitive). In addition, it fails to account for what the *impetus* for the faulty cognitive processing is—what is it that causes the category error, what is the *stimulus* for the cognitive mistake? If it is an experience, what is the experience of? On top of this, the cognitive approach, just like the other approaches discussed so far, certainly does not take into account any of the apparent evidence from the parapsychological literature, which has been neglected in the social sciences.

Spirit possession as performance and the embodiment of history

The performative aspect of spirit possession has been a key area of study within anthropology and the social sciences more generally. Spirit possession rituals exist at the threshold between subjective (internal) trance experience and public (external) performance spectacle. Cross-culturally, spirit possession practices appear to share a distinctively *somatic* component (Pierini, 2016). The body is the *ground of all human experience*, of course, but it also provides the *physical means of expression* for nonphysical entities in mediumistic performances; as such the body must be used in a variety of very specific ways. Methods for recognising the presence of spirits in the bodies of mediums vary across cultures, with each culture having its own traditions of discernment. The performative element of spirit possession may take the form of elaborate *enactments* of cosmic dramas—as in the case of south Indian Theyyam performances (Freeman, 1998)—or elaborate rituals of self-mortification, as found in traditional forms of Taiwanese spirit mediumship (Graham, 2014). Or, at the other end of the spectrum, it may simply take the form of *subtle bodily alterations* to distinguish between personalities, as in spiritualist trance mediumship (Hunter, 2013). We will return to a more thorough examination of the performative aspects of mediumship in Chapter 6.

Paul Stoller has also emphasised the importance of the concept of *embodiment* in understanding spirit possession. He writes, "[T]here can be little doubt that the body is the focus of possession phenomena," and draws attention to the fact that spirit possession often functions as a "commemorative ritual" utilising performative "gestures, sounds, postures and movements" to embody the ancestors (Stoller, 1994, pp. 636–640). Among the Songhay, with whom Stoller conducted extensive fieldwork, possession involves the bodily incorporation of spirits from six different spirit families, each one representing a particular period of Songhay history, who are brought forward to offer advice and guidance.

Similarly, Michael Lambek has noted the use of spirit possession among the Sakalava of Madagascar as a means of retaining and transmitting their history through performance in the absence of textual records. Spirits representing different epochs of Sakalava history possess the bodies of mediums to give advice on contemporary decision-making activities. There are many benefits to discussing such issues with the ancestors, for instance it is possible to produce pragmatic "historically informed" responses to modern situations while also acknowledging the "concerns of earlier generations" (Lambek, 1998, p. 109). Through embodying the spirits, the ancestors can be conversed with and so are able to maintain a central role in contemporary social life ensuring a continuity of tradition. Nils Bubandt (2009) has also made similar observations with regard to the people of North Maluku, Indonesia, for whom ancestral spirits continue to play an important role in contemporary political life when they return *through the bodies* of their entranced mediums to give advice and guidance on matters of politics.

In addition to performing social, historical, and political functions (amongst others), the performative aspect of mediumistic practices may also serve a practical function in the induction of altered states of consciousness, which are often a core feature of mediumistic performances. The anthropologist Felicitas D. Goodman (1914–2005), for example, argued that specific bodily postures and gestures are effective in inducing specific kinds of altered states for particular, state-specific, purposes (1999).

Altered states of consciousness

Altered states of consciousness (ASCs) are central to most mediumship traditions (Bourguignon, 1973; Kelly & Locke, 2009). Erika Bourguignon (1924–2015), in a cross-cultural study of 488 widely distributed societies determined that ninety per cent of her sample employed some form of institutionalised altered state of consciousness (trance), and that seventy per cent of the sample societies associated such states with the notion of spirit possession (Bourguignon, 1973, pp. 9–11; 2007, p. 375). Given the significant role of ASCs in mediumistic traditions it is important that we take a moment to unpack the concept.

Psychologist Charles Tart provides us with a useful starting point through describing ASCs as states 'such that the experiencer feels her consciousness is qualitatively (and often radically) different from the way it functions in the baseline state' (Tart, 2000, p. 259). By using the term baseline state Tart is referring to our "normal" everyday waking consciousness—which admittedly may not even be the same from one person to the next. In Euro-American cultures waking consciousness is usually perceived as the *dominant*, most *practical* form of consciousness. Of course it would be *unreasonable* to suggest that Western culture is entirely *monophasic* (emphasising just one state of consciousness), as contrasted with *polyphasic* cultures (Laughlin, 2013)—think for example of the popularity of alcohol consumption, and even smoking tobacco, which induce culturally meaningful altered states. Nevertheless, it is clear that post-industrial culture places a special significance on one very specific form of consciousness—*normal everyday waking consciousness*—while other forms of consciousness are perceived as inferior, useless, or inhibitive of economic productivity (Haule, 2011, pp. 11–14). This is, again, an expression of our culture's dominant reductionist and materialist attitude—consciousness becomes just another commodity serving economic ends.

The concept of the ASC is, therefore, built upon this foundational perception of a generalised productive waking consciousness. ASCs from this perspective are modes of experiencing the world through forms of consciousness that *differ* from our "everyday waking consciousness", and of course there is an exceedingly wide range of these alternative modes of consciousness, including everything from early morning drowsiness to caffeine rushes and psychedelic states, and from dreams and trances to cosmic ecstasies. Despite this diversity, Michael Winkelman (1986) suggests several common traits of altered states of consciousness:

> ASCs share features in common … alterations of thinking, change in sense of time and body image, loss of control, change in emotional expression, perceptual distortion, change in meaning and

significance, a sense of ineffability, feelings of rejuvenation, and hyper-suggestibility. (p. 175)

Some researchers have expressed doubt as to the usefulness of the concept of ASCs for understanding mediumship and spirit possession. They argue that, although it is clear that an altered state of consciousness is more often than not involved in the mediumship process, it is also clear that the concept of ASCs is so broad as to cover an extremely wide variety of other experiences that are in no way related to mediumship or spirit possession (Levy, Mageo, & Howard, 1996, p. 17). Different states of consciousness may each have their own realms of action.

There is also a danger that the scholarly use of the concept of the ASC lends itself to a reduction of the phenomena of spirit possession to a simple formula: "Spirit possession is *just* an altered state of consciousness, and as such has no basis in reality". This kind of interpretation is inherent in Euro-American culture's general monophasic attitude to consciousness—experiences had in altered states are denigrated as delusional. I would argue, however, that it is perhaps best to think of altered states of consciousness as *preconditions* for the experience of spirit possession, rather than as the cause of the phenomenon. We might say, therefore, that spirit possession involves altered states of consciousness, but is not necessarily synonymous with them.

As we have already seen, mediumship also involves components that are not directly related to ASCs. Levy, Mageo, and Howard write, for example, that "Full possession behaviour is highly skilful. It requires mastery of playing and of subtle, specialized kinds of communally significant communication" (1996, p. 18)—in other words, there are somatic and performative dimensions to spirit possession in addition to ASCs. Arguing along similar lines, Rebecca Seligman (2005) has suggested that altered states of consciousness should not be thought of as the *central feature* of mediumship practices, and instead emphasises the "combination of social conditions and somatic susceptibilities" that cause "certain individuals to identify with the mediumship role". Mediumship cannot, therefore, be understood without reference to these other interrelated components, and might best be understood as something that happens when *both* certain kinds of ASC *and* certain kinds of performance are combined (along with various other factors). To focus *solely* on the role of altered states of consciousness in spirit possession would, therefore, be to ignore a whole range of other equally significant factors. Once again, it is important to emphasise complexity over reductive simplicity—altered states of consciousness occur within deep networks of psychological, social, cultural, and somatic inter-connectedness. With these critiques in mind, however, the concept of altered states of consciousness nevertheless remains a useful concept in the study of mediumship.

Trance

The word "trance" has its origins in the Latin *transire*, meaning "to go across", or to "pass over". The implication here is that trance is a *process* or a *movement*—from one state of consciousness to another, or from one ontological realm to another. Castillo (1995) has suggested that the ability to enter into trance—both pathological and non-pathological—is derived from an ability to narrowly and intensely focus attention onto *inner processes*. Trance and other states of consciousness (sleep, hypnosis, meditation, etc.) represent different "tunings" of the central nervous system, which differ to that of normal waking consciousness (p. 27). It is the *pan-human* capacity of trance states to transport us to other realms of experience that has led to its cross-cultural prevalence in ritual practices that seek to make contact with the invisible world of spirits.

As with "altered states of consciousness", the term "trance" is often used so liberally that it runs the risk of being rendered meaningless without further descriptive detail (Levy, Mageo, & Howard, 1996, p. 17). As we have already noted, while many spirit possession traditions undoubtedly employ some form of altered state of consciousness during their possession rituals, we cannot say that they all employ the *same* alteration of consciousness (Winkelman, 1986, p. 174). How can we be sure, for example, that the form of trance utilised in Haitian Vodun possession rites (cf. Wittkower, Douyon, & Bijou, 1964; Deren, 2004) is the same as that employed by Spiritualist trance mediums in the UK, or that the trance state of the Candomblé medium (Krippner, 2008) is the same as that of the traditional Taiwanese spirit medium (F. Graham, 2014)? We may well find similarities in terms of neurophysiological activity, but the subjective element may vary considerably. It is impor-tant to bear this diversity in mind, and to be aware of the possibility that we are dealing with many *types* of mediumship, and many types of trance, even if they do share *core processes*.

Moreover, and further complicating matters, it is unlikely that *individual* mediums *within* a particular tradition are employing the same form of altered consciousness in each of their trance demonstrations. Mediums often distinguish between different degrees of trance, usually described as ranging from "light" trance to "deep" trance, with many levels in between.[10] So that, on one day, a medium's trance may be particularly deep, while on the next day their trance state may be considered light. Trance is, therefore, a term that refers to a broad *spectrum* of related, but not necessarily identical, states of consciousness. This comes across clearly in scholarly definitions of the term. Historian Brian Inglis, in his book *Trance: A Natural History of Altered States of Mind* (1989), for example, identifies a wide variety of experiences and states of consciousness encompassed by the term:

> At one extreme it is applied to what can loosely be described as possession, in which the individual's normal self seems to be displaced, leaving him rapt, or paralysed, or hysterical, or psychotic, or taken over by another personality. At the other extreme is sleep. Between the two are conditions in which consciousness is maintained, but the subliminal mind makes itself felt, as in light hypnosis or the kind of reverie in which fancy, or fantasy, breaks loose ... (p. 267)

In this extract, Inglis points to both ends of the spectrum—from possession trance (a *displacement of consciousness*) to clairvoyant trance (an *expansion of consciousness*). Judith Becker (1994), on the other hand, defines trance in terms of:

> ... a state of mind characterized by intense focus, the loss of the strong sense of self and access to types of knowledge and experience that are inaccessible in non-trance states. (p. 41)

These definitions encompass a variety of different experiences and bodily states, including meditative states, possession trance, shamanistic trance, communal trance, aesthetic trance, and other moments of transcendence. Similarly, Kelly and Locke (2009) identify a variety of

---

[10] The varying degrees, or stages, of trance are also recognised in other disciplines, for example in hypnotherapy, and in transpersonal psychology.

experiences and behaviours included under the umbrella of "trance", including "hallucinations, obsessive ideas, dissociation, compulsive actions, transient loss of contact with the sensory environment, physiological collapse, and a number of other aspects" (p. 30). They further distinguish between different degrees of trance, ranging from "the visionary experience or journey which opens the sacred realm to the shaman", which the shaman is usually able to recall, to possession trance "in which the central element is the apparent temporary displacement of the ordinary personality by that of a possessing spirit, force, or god", which "generally appears to leave the fully possessed individual amnesic for the period of possession" (pp. 30–31). Again, this emphasises the potential for different types of mediumship with distinctive underlying phenomenology and neurophysiology.

Mircea Eliade also sought to distinguish the altered state of the shaman from that of the possessed by emphasising the shaman's ability to control spirits without "becoming their instrument" (1989, p. 6). Eliade highlighted the difference between the shamanistic and mediumistic trance state with regard to the individual's ability to recall what took place during the trance. According to Eliade, it is essential that the shaman be able to recall what took place during their soul-flight, as they must personally *bring back* information from the spirit worlds. Trance mediums, however, will generally report an inability to recall what took place during their trance state (amnesia), owing primarily to the fact that they were "not present" during the possession—their body was occupied by another entity for the duration of the trance—their consciousness was *displaced*. It is for this reason that trance mediumship demonstrations usually require sitters and a circle leader (master of ceremonies) to interpret and record the spirit communications while the medium is in trance.

More recent research, however, has demonstrated that this classically assumed distinction between the ideal *shaman* as a controller of the spirits, and the ideal *medium* as entirely under the control of the spirits, is very often blurred in the field (Cox, 2008; Jokic, 2008b). David Gordon Wilson has also criticised the distinction between spirit mediumship and shamanism, and has proposed that spirit mediumship, and in particular Euro-American Spiritualist (mental) mediumship—such as I encountered at the Belmont Road Centre—can be thought of as a *variety*, or *form*, of shamanism, with Spiritualist mediumship development seen as a process of shamanistic apprenticeship (2011, 2013). Jon at the Bristol Spirit Lodge, for example, had also spent time in the development of mental mediumship and spiritual healing at Spiritualist churches, and saw his trance and physical mediumship work as a part of a longer process of spiritual development and as an active exploration of different modes of consciousness.

Arnaud Halloy has argued that *possession trance*—as a distinct category of trance—is not itself a single, easy to define, phenomenon but rather represents "a continuum of psycho-biological changes that vary from slight emotional arousal to the ideal possession state" (2010, p. 168). At the Bristol Spirit Lodge, for example, mediumship development is clearly aimed at inducing the "ideal possession state", but in practice mediums at different stages of development often exhibit different degrees of possession, and rarely is the ideal achieved.

It is clear that further research into the phenomenology and neurophysiology of trance states is required in order to clarify precisely what is going on when a medium goes into trance. In the context of spirit mediumship the term "trance" might best be understood as referring to the state of consciousness in which the medium experiences themselves to be "dispossessed by an intruding intelligence" (Gauld, 1982, p. 29), and it is this sense of the term that will be employed for the remainder of this book.

The neurophysiology of mediumship

This section will give an overview of what is currently known about the neurophysiological correlates of mediumistic states of consciousness. It is a far from complete picture, and is riddled with complex issues of interpretation.

Background and early speculation

It was long suspected that mediums might exhibit unusual neurological activity during their trance states. Even before the advent of neuroimaging studies of mediums, American psychologist Julian Jaynes (1920–1997), drawing on his bicameral mind theory, predicted the following neurophysiological correlates of spirit possession:

> We must naturally hypothesize that in possession there is some kind of disturbance of normal hemispheric dominance relations, in

which the right hemisphere is somewhat more active than in the normal state. In other words, if we could have placed electrodes on the scalp of the Delphic oracle in her frenzy, would we have found a relatively faster EEG (and therefore greater activity) over her right hemisphere, correlating with her possession? And in particular over her right temporal lobe? (1976, pp. 342–343)

Jaynes's hypothesis is that the brain's electrical activity (as recorded through EEG electrodes attached to the scalp) would be *increased* during the trance state—indicating a state of *arousal*. Interestingly, however, now that the technology to monitor and record the brain activity of mediums in trance is available, the reverse has recently been found to be true. As we shall see, some of the most interesting recent research on the neurophysiology of mediumship has actually found decreases in activity in the brain during mediumistic trances.

Based on comparisons with neurophysiological studies of other altered states of consciousness, such as meditative states, Michael Winkelman (1986) has argued that a wide variety of trance induction techniques might lead to quite similar neurophysiological states, specifically involving a "parasympathetic dominance in which the frontal cortex is dominated by slow wave patterns". Owing to the apparent similarities between trance mediumship and dissociative identity disorder (DID) discussed above, Williams and Roll (2007) speculated that mediumship and DID might share similar underlying neurophysiological correlates, specifically postulating the involvement of the temporal lobe. Based upon their overviews of the neurophysiological research on dissociative identity disorder, and the few EEG studies of mediumship available at that time, Williams and Roll offered the prediction that future fMRI studies of mediumship would reveal an "activation of the angular gyrus and the areas around the temporal-parietal junction when a medium senses the presence of his or her spirit control".

In a handbook on *Psi and Altered States of Consciousness* first published in 1981, Edward F. Kelly and Raphael Locke suggested there were unfortunate technical and social difficulties associated with attempting such studies in the field at that time. Technical difficulties included the problems inherent in trying to monitor and record brain activity naturalistically in the field setting using cumbersome equipment, while social difficulties include getting spirit mediums, and other practitioners, to agree to participate in such studies in the first place—such is the suspicion many mediums feel towards researchers, owing to the treatment of mediums by debunkers in the nineteenth and early twentieth century (Kelly & Locke, 2009).

Fortunately, since Kelly and Locke first published their research prospectus, technological advances *have* made it possible to measure EEG in the field (see Oohashi et al., 2002, below), though other more accurate forms of neuro-imaging (such as fMRI) still rely on heavy and expensive equipment that is currently impractical for field studies of this nature. Despite these difficulties, however, a small number of studies have been carried out specifically looking at the neurophysiological correlates of mediumistic states of consciousness, mostly in laboratory conditions rather than in naturalistic séance settings.

Neurophysiological studies

Mesulam (1981) suggested that there might be common neurophysiological activity underlying both spirit possession and DID, noting that EEG recordings taken from twelve subjects, seven with DID and five with symptoms of spirit possession, revealed unusual spikes of activity in the temporal lobe (except for in two unclear recordings), very similar to the activity associated with epileptic seizures. The implication here is that epileptic seizures in the temporal lobe are responsible for both spirit possession experiences and dissociative identity disorder. A problem lies, however, in distinguishing between voluntary and involuntary possession in this context. Can the elaborate performances of voluntary spirit possession practitioners be accounted for by the epileptic hypothesis? The behaviours are quite different.

Slightly later, Hughes and Melville (1990) conducted an EEG study on ten trance channellers, five male and five female, in Los Angeles. The channellers were monitored both in and out of trance, and during the trance state their possessing entities were asked a series of questions, so as to create as naturalistic a setting as possible. Based upon their EEG recordings, Hughes and Melville concluded that the channelling state is "characterized by large, statistically significant increases in amount and percentage of *beta*, *alpha* and *theta* brainwave activity", which appears to represent a distinctive psycho-physiological state that can be differentiated from other altered states of consciousness (e.g., forms of meditation and hypnosis), as well as from pathological states such as temporal lobe epilepsy and schizophrenia, which is supportive of the assertion that channelling and possession are *not* pathological in nature, or at least not identical to these recognised disorders.

One of the first studies to use EEG to investigate traditional spirit possession performances in the field (as distinct from laboratory based studies) was conducted by a team of Japanese researchers (Oohashi et al., 2002), using a newly developed portable EEG device to measure the electrical activity of the brain in an individual performing a ritual possession drama in Bali. The team found that the possessed individual exhibited enhanced power in the *theta* and *alpha* frequency bands, again suggesting that the possession trance represents a distinct psycho-phys-iological state different from pathological states such as epilepsy, dissociative identity disorder (DID), and schizophrenia.

A particularly interesting piece of neuro-imaging research conducted by Julio Fernando Peres and colleagues (Peres, Moreira-Almeida, Ciaxeta, Leao, & Newberg, 2012) employed single photon emission computed tomography (SPECT) to record the brain activity of ten automatic writers (five experienced, five less experienced) while in trance. The research findings have been summarised as follows:

> The researchers found that the experienced psychographers showed lower levels of activity in the left hippocampus (limbic system), right superior temporal gyrus, and the frontal lobe regions of the left anterior cingulate and right precentral gyrus during psychography compared to their normal (non-trance) writing. The frontal lobe areas are associated with reasoning, planning, generating language, movement, and problem solving, perhaps reflecting an absence of focus, self-awareness and consciousness during psychography, the researchers hypothesize. Less expert psychographers showed just the opposite—increased levels of CBF in the same frontal areas during psychography compared to normal writing. The difference was significant compared to the experienced mediums. (Thomas Jefferson University, 2012)

The implication here is that during the trance states of the experienced automatic writers, activity is actually *reduced* in those areas of the brain usually associated with reasoning, planning, language, movement, and problem solving (precisely the regions we would expect to be *active* when performing a complex activity like writing), suggesting that the medium's dissociative experience during trance is far from fraudu-lent, though the results could still be due to psychological delusion.

Furthermore, the researchers conducted an analysis of the complexity of the writing and found that, contrary to what would normally be expected, the complexity *increased* as the activity in the areas of the brain usually associated with such complex behaviours was *reduced*. This raises the question of how, if the brain's functioning was reduced, such complex writing was possible. The spiritist interpretation suggests that it was spirits doing the writing while the medium's consciousness was absent, and the data could indeed be read in this way. More cautiously, however, Andrew Newberg has suggested that this research "reveals some exciting data to improve our understanding of the mind and its relationship with the brain" and calls for further research in this area without coming to any significant conclusions about the potential role or reality of spirits (Thomas Jefferson University, 2012).

In 2013 Delorme *et al.* published research on the neurological activity of mental mediums using functional magnetic resonance imaging (fMRI). As has already been mentioned, mental mediumship differs from the types of mediumship practised at the Bristol Spirit Lodge, which might best be labelled as forms of trance mediumship and voluntary possession. The mediums investigated by Delorme et al. did not enter into a trance state during which they surrendered the control of their bodies to discarnate entities. Instead these mediums experienced communication with discarnate entities while in a *lucid state of consciousness*. Because of this difference the results are not directly comparable with the results of the previous studies. They are, however, still important in the context of the broader *spectrum* of mediumistic states of consciousness. EEG recordings with mental mediums revealed a predominance of activity in the gamma frequency band, which is also characteristic of certain meditative states. Perhaps the most interesting finding from this research project was the correlation between the accuracy of the mediumship reading and specific alterations in electro-cortical activity. fMRI scans revealed increased activity in the frontal areas of the brain, similar to fMRI readings for other spiritual states. Decreased frontal midline theta rhythms were also noted, and it was suggested that this might be "consistent with a medium accessing a receptive mental state". Again, the authors conclude that "The experience of communicating with the deceased may be a distinct mental state that is not consistent with brain activity during ordinary thinking or imagination." This lends verifiable support to the subjective claims of mediums that *something* does happen when they go into their trance states—they certainly seem to enter into distinctive psycho-biological states.

Cautious conclusions

At the very least, the neuro-imaging work that has been conducted on mediumship so far appears to support the idea that there is more to mediumship than simple fraud and delusion—something, whatever that something might be, is definitely going on here. But the data are by no means conclusive of anything more than that. The research does seem to indicate a predominance of *alpha*, *beta*, and *theta* waves in trance channelling and possession states, and *gamma* frequencies in mental mediumship. It is unclear, however, how these EEG readings relate to the findings of other studies that suggest a *decrease* in brain function during mediumistic trances. There is also a considerable discrepancy between studies that suggest similarities with pathological conditions such as DID and temporal lobe epilepsy, and those that seem to indicate that mediumship is a distinctive psycho-physiological state. Furthermore, it is unclear how these conditions should give rise to communication with discarnate spirits—what is the role and function of the alteration of consciousness and brain state? What is it about particular neurophysiological tunings that makes mediumship possible?

The truth of the matter is that there are significant difficulties associated with the interpretation of *any* neuro-imaging data (Tallis, 2012). Such studies are, for example, subject to the classic problem of distinguishing between cause and correlation—are these data suggesting that the mediumship experience is *caused* by alterations in brain physiology, or do they show us what happens to the brain *when mediumship takes place*? Do they *explain* mediumship, or do they show us a part of the *processes* of mediumship? These are important questions that only further research can resolve. My inclination, however, is towards the possibility that these states are a part of the *process* of mediumship—necessary *preconditions* (among several others) in the manifestation of spirits in social reality.

Hageman et al. (2010) note several other fundamental problems inherent in the interpretation of neuro-imaging data. They warn against the following tendencies in neurophysiological research:

- Naïvely [accepting] materialist monism (mind as brain product) as an obvious fact, and [rejecting] a fair consideration of other hypotheses for the mind-brain relationship.
- [Basing] work on second-hand descriptions of original findings or writings.

- [Focusing] only on one side of psycho-physiological parallelism, that is, changes in brain function modify mental states.
- [Assuming] that experiences based on superficial similarities are identical.
- [Identifying] a brain region involved with some spiritual experience and [concluding] that this region is the ultimate cause of that experience.
- [Ignoring] the complexity of the body and [refusing] to take a holistic perspective.
- [Focusing] studies on beginners or participants who have not had a full-blown spiritual experience (pp. 87–89).

Only further research, taking into account the difficulties inherent in the interpretation of neurophysiological studies, is likely to help resolve fundamental questions about what is happening in the brain during mediumistic trance states, and this will only take us a small step closer to understanding *how* such alterations of brain states relate to the manifestation of spirits in social contexts. For the time being, however, the research at least indicates that something unusual *is* going on, which demands further attention. Although it has not been possible to conduct neuro-imaging studies on the mediums discussed in this book, based upon the research that has already been conducted with other groups, it is not unreasonable to assume that they *also* experience similar subjective sensations during their trance states, and that underlying these trance experiences are *similar* (though not necessarily identical) neurophysiological alterations to those observed in different cultural contexts.

Research on the neurophysiological correlates of mediumship and possession is a rapidly developing field, with new findings and innovative experiments being published regularly. It is well worth following to keep an eye on developments.

Parapsychology and the history of physical mediumship

In addition to the extensive ethnographic literature on the varied practice and experience of spirit mediumship and spirit possession (see for example Schmidt & Huskinson, 2010; Dawson, 2010; Hunter & Luke, 2014 for concise overviews of various ethnographic accounts), there is also a wealth of experimental and non-experimental data (Braude, 1997, pp. 1–12) going back over a century, which appears to suggest that, with certain mediums at least, there may be some form of information and energy transfer taking place that cannot be accounted for by *normal* means (i.e., material/physical means). This brief survey is by no means exhaustive—there is an enormous wealth of literature out there—rather it is intended to provide an historical overview of some of this research so that it can be put back on the anthropological agenda.

Physical mediumship, psychokinesis, and ectoplasm

As we have already seen, typical phenomena associated with physical mediumship include such things as raps and knocks, table tilting, levitations, apports (objects that appear and disappear during séances), spirit lights, psychic healing, and the materialisation and dematerialisation of ectoplasmic forms. In spite of the apparent outlandishness of these phenomena, however, many highly respected researchers have vouched for their authenticity over the years. As such it would be naïve to dismiss such phenomena as *impossible* without first examining the evidence in favour of their existence, of which there is a considerable amount (see, for example, Braude, 1997, 2003).

Perhaps the most influential innovator in early Spiritualist physical mediumship was the Scottish-born American medium Daniel Dunglas Home (1833–1886), who is famous, unlike many of his mediumistic contemporaries, for never being *definitively* exposed as a fraud—though unsubstantiated accusations were made (Haynes, 1982, p. 115). After an early life allegedly filled with spiritual visions and premonitions, Home conducted his first séance at the age of eighteen and swiftly gained a reputation as a powerful medium, and by 1856 he was conducting séances in Britain. Séances with Home were said to feature a wide range of inexplicable phenomena, from verbal communication with spirits while the medium was in a deep trance state, to levitation and apportations (spontaneous appearance of objects). Home's séances also often featured the alleged materialisation of glowing hands that would mischievously touch the sitters, though, unlike later mediums, he was never said to have produced full-body materialisations—just limbs, hands, and heads (Conan Doyle, 1926, p. 106). In 1868 Home is said to have performed his most famous paranormal feat in front of witnesses—the levitation of his body horizontally out through a third-storey window at Ashley House in London (Conan Doyle, 1926. p. 99; Lamont, 2005, pp. 185–187).

The physicist Sir William Crookes (1832–1919) was arguably the first to conduct a systematic scientific investigation of physical mediumship when, in 1871, he tested Home's alleged abilities in his laboratory. Crookes constructed a specially designed weighing device in order to test Home's claimed capacity to change the weight of physical objects. The device consisted of a delicate spring balance attached to a mahogany board resting upon a table. Crookes relates that when Home's finger was gently placed on the end of the board resting on the table, without applying any pressure (which would clearly be visible to the experimenter), the spring balance registered fluctuations in weight of between 2.5 and 5.5 lbs. (Braude, 1997, pp. 84–85).

These experiments, combined with observations of a variety of other strange anomalous phenomena (including accordions playing themselves, levitation of the medium's body, raps, and materialisations), were enough to convince Crookes of the "existence of a new force, in some unknown manner connected with the human organisation, which for convenience may be called the Psychic Force" (Crookes, 1874, p. 9). So impressive were séances with Home that Arthur Conan Doyle considered him to be something of a *virtuoso* medium in that he was proficient in four of the major phenomena of mediumship: (1) the direct voice (whereby spirits communicate verbally independent of the medium), (2) trance mediumship (whereby spirits communicate verbally through the body of the medium), (3) clairvoyance (the ability to see visions of the spirit world, the future, and distant locations), and (4) physical mediumship (the ability to psychically manipulate physical objects and produce materialisations) (Conan Doyle, 1926, p. 106).

At this early stage in the investigation of physical mediumship we see the emergence of two competing explanations in favour of the anomalous phenomena reported during séances: the *spirit hypothesis*, which suggests that the phenomena were caused by the agency and influence of non-physical spirit beings acting on the physical world, and the "psychic force" hypothesis, which suggests that the phenomena are produced by the mind of the medium, employing some form of macro-PK (large scale psychokinetic, or mind-matter, effect) to affect material objects. The debate between those who favour the spirit hypothesis and those that favour the psi hypothesis continues to this day among parapsychologists.

The term "ectoplasm" (Greek: *ektos* meaning "outside" and *plasma* meaning "something formed or moulded") was coined by the Nobel prize winning physiologist Charles Richet (1850–1935). During séances with a prominent medium of the time, Eva Carrière (1886–c. 1922), Richet observed and documented the ectoplasmic substance on numerous occasions emanating from the medium's mouth, breasts, navel, fingertips, vagina, and scalp (Brower, 2010, p. 85). This substance was described as coalescing into crude limbs, referred to as "pseudo-pods", and human-like heads which would move independently and were particularly sensitive to both light and touch. These materialisations were also observed by other researchers, including Baron Albert von Schrenck-Notzing (1862–1929), who saw them dissolve back into the medium's body (Sommer, 2009, p. 304).

Richet defined ectoplasmic materialisation phenomena as "the formation of divers objects, which in most cases seem to emerge from a human body and take on the semblance of material realities, clothing, veils, and living bodies" (1923, p. 4). For Richet, ectoplasm was a *real* substance, extruded from the bodies of mediums and manipulated psycho-kinetically.

In spite of the conclusions of researchers such as Charles Richet (1923), Albert Von Schrenck-Notzing (1920), and Gustav Geley (2006) in favour of the reality of ectoplasm as a genuine phenomenon, however, there have also been numerous exposures (not *all* of which have been robust or justified) of physical mediums deliberately faking ectoplasm in a variety of different ways. The case of Mina Crandon (1888–1941) is an illustrative example. Dr Walter Franklin Prince (1863–1934), one of the chief investigators of Mina Crandon's mediumship, provides an overview of some of her claimed feats:

> At hundreds of sittings, it is claimed, "ectoplasmic" limbs—extruded from her body and afterwards reabsorbed—have performed various acts, such as touching persons seated nearby in the darkness, shoving, lifting and throwing objects, overturning a small table, ringing the bell in a box activated by contact cover, producing phosphorescent lights, etc. (1926, p. 431)

Mina Crandon's mediumship, however, was very publicly declared fraudulent by the world famous escape artist Harry Houdini (1874–1926) in a pamphlet entitled *Houdini Exposes the Tricks Used by the Boston Medium 'Margery'*, which was first published in 1924. Over the course of his public debunking of the Margery case (as it came to be known, to protect Crandon's anonymity) Houdini employed increasingly tight controls on the medium including, at one point, completely sealing her body within a specially constructed wooden box, with only her head and hands visible in an effort to rule out trickery (Polidoro, 2001, pp. 143–145). This kind of control is just one example of the extremes researchers have gone to in the name of determining the reality of physical mediumship, and, as already mentioned, its effects are still felt today when researching physical mediumship, even as an anthropologist. Physical mediums, and those who gather to assist in their development, are understandably cautious about investigators. In 1925 the Society for Psychical Research sent anthropologist and psychical researcher Eric Dingwall (1890–1986) to investigate Crandon's claimed abilities and discovered that her ectoplasm was apparently composed of "animal lung material" (Polidoro, 2001, p. 155). Dingwall's findings were published in the *Journal of the Society for Psychical Research*. The pioneer parapsychologists J. B. and Louisa Rhine (1927), of whom we will hear more shortly, were also convinced—just as Houdini and Dingwall had been—that they had found incontrovertible evidence of fraudulence during séances with the medium.

Despite such public denunciations of physical mediumship, however, ectoplasmic materialisations of varying degrees of quality continued to be reported in physical mediumship demonstrations right into the 1930s, 40s, and 50s, though they were becoming increasingly rare. This later physical mediumship is perhaps best exemplified by the mediumship of Jack Webber (1907–1940), whose ectoplasmic materialisations were extensively photographed and documented at a private home-circle (Edwards, 1978), and the infamous Helen Duncan (1897–1956), the last woman to be tried and imprisoned under the 1735 Witchcraft Act, during the Second World War (Gaskill, 2001; Hartley, 2007).

The decline of physical mediumship

In comparison with the dramatic, extravagant, and often full-body materialisations described in the earlier literature of psychical research, the ectoplasmic manifestations of the modern world are distinctly lacking—they are just not as well developed. Why could this be? Writing on the history of ectoplasm in volume two of his *The History of*

Spiritualism, Arthur Conan Doyle (1859–1930) noted precisely the same effect with regard to the diminished quality of the physical phenomena of *his* day:

> When we examine the descriptions of the appearance of ectoplasm in Spiritualistic circles forty and fifty years ago, and compare them with those in our own day, we see how much richer were the earlier results. (1926, Vol. II, p. 47)

The explanation Conan Doyle offers for this apparent degradation in the phenomenon was that attitudes towards mediums had changed—in other words there had been a *cultural* change among mediums, sitters, and researchers that led to a diminution of the quality of the manifestations (we will think more on the role of culture in shaping paranormal manifestations later). He writes: "At least ... the early researchers observed one golden rule. They surrounded the medium with an atmosphere of love and sympathy" (ibid.). By the time Conan Doyle was writing his history of the Spiritualist movement, physical mediums were subject to increasingly severe forms of testing, as we have already seen with Houdini's controls in the Margery experiments.

Another example of the obsessively controlled methods of early twentieth-century psychical researchers can be found in the experiments of researcher Harry Price (1881–1948), who employed electrical circuits to ensure that mediumship circles were not broken during séances, so as to rule out deception (Tabori, 1968, p. 90). Price's approach to mediumship research carries all the hallmarks of behaviourist experiments with rats and electric shocks, which were becoming increasingly popular at the time. In addition to this kind of treatment, the popular image of the physical medium gradually came to be associated with notions of fraud and dishonesty, which naturally did not bode well for the way in which mediums were perceived and treated by those who attended their demonstrations.

Robin Foy (2007), founder and key member of the Scole Experimental Group (see discussion below), explains the decline of physical mediumship by suggesting that, in our busy modern world, people no longer have the time or energy to devote themselves to the development of physical mediumship. It takes dedication to sit regularly in séances, and for many this is simply not possible. Foy also agrees with the notion that the harsh ways in which physical mediums had been tested in the laboratory by psychical researchers essentially put people off developing mediumship themselves. He also offers the suggestion that the numerous high-profile exposures of fraudulent mediums had given the profession a bad reputation, which further contributed to its decline.

Another reason might also be found in the shift in the perspective of psychical researchers towards a laboratory-based approach to the investigation of psi—characterised by rigorous experimental controls—inspired by the establishment of Dr J. B. Rhine's (1895–1980) parapsychological laboratory at Duke University, in Durham, North Carolina, in 1930, with its focus directed firmly on the much subtler *mental* psi phenomena of ESP and clairvoyance. When Rhine and his colleagues did investigate physical phenomena, it was on a *much smaller* scale—referred to as micro-PK (small scale psychokinesis)—usually involving experiments into the possibility of consciousness affecting the outcome of dice rolling, or, slightly later, random number generators (Radin, 2006). Such a shift represents the gradual internalisation and subjectification of the paranormal in general in Western society, which has moved paranormal events from the outside, objective world to the interior, subjective realm. Physical mediumship was, by the 1930s, quite simply out of fashion and has never really regained its status as a respectable practice for either mediums or researchers.

The new age of physical mediumship

A reinvigorated interest in physical mediumship developed shortly after the publication of Montague Keen (1926–2004), Arthur Ellison (1920–2000), and David Fontana's (1934–2010) *The Scole Report* (1999) published as a special issue of the *Journal of the Society for Psychical Research*. This was accompanied by a popularised mass-market version, *The Scole Experiment: Scientific Evidence for Life After Death* (1999) by Grant and Jane Solomon, also published in the same year (and which is currently being developed as a feature film). Both *The Scole Report* and *The Scole Experiment* documented a series of séances conducted in a large basement room in the Norfolk village of Scole, during which a wide variety of extraordinary physical phenomena were reportedly produced. Montague Keen (2001), one of the SPR's lead researchers on the case, describes the basic claims made about the Scole experiments:

> Based on two years of regular séances, the Group's chief claims were that they had established contact with a "team" of spirit communicators comprising, or in contact with, a number of former scientists. These had been accessed through … a husband and wife team, both of whom entered swiftly into deep trance, remaining thus throughout the proceedings, of which they retained no conscious recollection. The purported discarnate contacts had facilitated the manifestation of spirit lights, moved furniture, created apports (objects appearing from no known source and by no known means), displayed shadowy figures described as angelic forms, and produced films, allegedly employing a novel form of energy not involving the traditional ectoplasmic extrusions with their enervating and sometimes physically hazardous, and invariably contentious, associations. (pp. 167–168)

One of the chief developments of the Scole group, in terms of the history of physical mediumship, was their claim that their spirit team was employing a new "form of energy" to produce this dizzying array of phenomena. This new energy was understood to be different to the ectoplasm of classical physical mediumship. The Scole group's guiding spirit team felt that ectoplasm was far too volatile and *dangerous*— an idea based on the reports of ectoplasm's tendency to "slap" back into the body medium if exposed to light, causing bruising and internal bleeding. The new energy was deemed to be much safer, and reduced the risk to mediums.

This shift towards the use of a "new energy" has been particularly influential in the development of subsequent physical mediumship circles. Many new groups were inspired to conduct their own experiments after reading descriptions of those carried out at Scole. The Bristol Spirit Lodge is no exception. Occasionally, for example, Christine makes use of a large glass bell-jar for the containment of these "spiritual energies" during séances—a sort of spiritual battery. This practice is directly influenced by theScole group's experiments.

Nevertheless, while many modern physical mediumship circles do claim to employ this "new energy", the manifestation of ectoplasm continues to be a particularly common feature of physical séances, along with other of the traditional physical phenomena—"spirit lights", raps, apports, and so on. Indeed, it was the phenomena of "classical" physical mediumship—ectoplasmic materialisations in particular— that inspired Christine to found the Bristol Spirit Lodge. Reflecting on her very first physical séance, on May 24, 2005 in Banbury, she recalls:

> ... the display of a misty formation that was barely visible within the set red-light conditions. In these conditions I could see the shapes of sitters all seated in their chairs around the room. They were all there. There were no empty chairs ... I could see a haze, of perhaps "something else", some partial materialized "something" near the cabinet. (Di Nucci, 2009, pp. 23–24)

More elaborate descriptions of classical ectoplasmic materialisations produced in private home-circles are now emerging on the internet, which is providing a platform for the new wave of physical mediumship. The Felix Experimental Group in Germany, for example, has in recent years been at the centre of a great deal of interest from the psychical research community. Images, videos, and witness testimony seem to suggest that the Felix Circle and its lead medium Kai Muegge are producing a range of séance phenomena concurrent with those described in the classical literature—ranging from full-form ectoplasmic materialisations to apports of large gemstones and religious figurines. Perhaps unsurprisingly, debates over the authenticity of the Felix Experimental Group's phenomena continue to rage (see Braude, 2014; Nahm, 2014). Other prominent physical mediums in operation today include Stewart Alexander, who sits in a regular circle in Hull, in the north-east of England, Scott Milligan, the Australian physical medium David Thompson, and Warren Caylor, whose physical mediumship séances I have attended.

Perhaps as cultural attitudes towards the practice of physical mediumship slowly begin to change, coupled with the renewed interests of serious psychical researchers (for example Stephen Braude and Michael Nahm's investigations with the Felix Experimental Group), we will also see a return of some of the more elaborate physical phenomena described in the early literature of psychical research.

It is clear from this brief survey that contemporary physical mediumship is, in essence, a continuation of the late nineteenth- and early twentieth-century Spiritualist tradition. The reported phenomena assicated with the practice seem to have degraded quite considerably, likely due to a variety of factors, some of which have just been discussed. When considered from a cross-cultural perspective, the situation is reminiscent of a similar scenario described by the anthropologist Zeljko Jokic (2008b) with regard to the practice of contemporary Buriat shamanism in Siberia. Traditional Buriat shamanism was banned in Buriatiia by the Soviet Russian authorities. Jokic documents the practices of contemporary neo-shamans in Buriatiia, who are striving to *reinvigorate* their traditional forms of shamanism as practised before the Soviet period despite the loss of their traditional knowledge. He describes how the modern neo-shamans are unable to recall their trance journeys (a trait, as we have seen, more common to mediumistic and spirit possession traditions than it is of shamanistic practices) and explains how this is indicative of *lost knowledge* about the techniques of the traditional shamans, who *were* able to remember and describe their trance experiences. Jokic writes:

> The apparently unconscious trance of modern shamans from the Tengeri association is the direct result of the stress and discontinuity that come from the inhibition of the system during the Soviet times, which has left a deep impact on Buriat culture. Fortunately, it appears that the shamans are well on their way to reclaiming the "eternal blue sky" over modern-day Buriatiia. (Jokic, 2008b, p. 45)

Perhaps the decline of physical mediumship could be understood in a similar way. The culture and practice has degraded under a bad reputation, and only with the work of those who are striving to reinvigorate, develop, and promote it will physical mediumship become as dramatic as it was when the pioneers of psychical research described it in the nineteenth century. This is the perceived mission of the Bristol Spirit Lodge and its members: to foster the emergence of a culture that is open to interactions from *spirit*.

Survival vs. super-psi

Due to the increasing association of physical mediumship with fraud, the attentions of psychical researchers gradually shifted towards the investigation of trance and mental mediumship for evidence of survival after death. William James (1842–1910), widely regarded as one of the founders of modern psychology, famously called the trance medium Leonora Piper (1857–1950) his "white crow". Piper's ability to provide accurate information, even under the most scrupulous of controls, seemed to provide James with proof of the veracity of her mediumship. During deep trance states lasting up to about an hour, Piper's body would become host to a spirit control calling himself Phinuit who would provide information to sitters keen to hear from their loved ones in the afterlife (Haynes, 1982, pp. 79–83). James was unconvinced by the Spiritualist hypothesis—that Mrs Piper was in contact with the spirits of the dead—and opted instead for the telepathic hypothesis that the medium is simply receiving information from the minds of still living individuals. Piper would herself later also go on to explain that she thought her abilities were likely the product of telepathy—rather than of communication with discarnate spirits. For Piper the telepathic hypothesis seemed to suit the facts of her experience most comfortably.

Some of the most recent and innovative research into mental mediumship has been conducted by Dr Julie Beischel and colleagues under the banner of the Windbridge Institute,[11] an independent research organisation devoted to the exploration of *hidden human potential*. The Windbridge Institute conducts controlled experiments with mediums who have been through a rigorous eight-step screening process—involving questionnaires, personality tests, interviews, blind readings, and training in the basic methods of mediumship research. Once the candidate has successfully completed this process they become official Windbridge Certified Research Mediums (WCRM) and are then eligible to take part in double-, triple-, and quadruple-blinded controlled studies. Strict protocols are employed to ensure the tightest controls in the experimental set-up, so as to avoid any form of conventional (material) sensory leakage to the medium under investigation. This includes the "blinding" of *all* participants and *all* researchers in the experiment so that there is no way the information could be conventionally accessed from the minds of the researchers, or anyone else participating in the study. Beischel describes a typical Windbridge experiment as follows:

> During a typical quintuple-blind experiment, I contact a certified medium on the phone at a scheduled time with the first name of a

---

[11] www.windbridge.org.

discarnate that another experimenter has provided to me by e-mail. The medium and I are both blinded to any other information about the discarnate or the associated sitter. During the reading, I ask the medium several specific questions about the named discarnate. The sitter does not hear the reading. The medium then performs a second reading at a different time for a second discarnate and sitter. The two readings are then transcribed and formatted to remove references to the discarnates' name, and the two sitters associated with the named discarnates then score each of the two readings for accuracy without knowing which is which. The experimenters who interact with the sitters during their initial training and during the scoring of the readings are blinded to which medium read which discarnates, which reading goes to which name, etc. (2010, p. 10)

Even under these kinds of strictly controlled circumstances certain mediums are apparently able to provide accurate information about their targets. Beischel and Schwartz (2007) refer to this as "anomalous information reception" (AIR). Anthropologists should, therefore, be aware of the fact that similar anomalous exchanges of information *could* be taking place in the context of their ethnographic fieldwork with spirit mediums in different cultural contexts.

In parapsychological experiments, once all normal (sensory) and fraudulent means have been theoretically ruled out, there remain two competing hypotheses regarding the way in which mediums are able to access accurate information about their sitters. One, of course, is the "survival hypothesis", which suggests that mediums are actually making contact with deceased spirits, and the other is the "psi" or "super-psi" hypothesis, which suggests that mediums are employing a heightened form of psi (ESP, remote viewing, psychokinesis, etc.) to access information—either directly from the mind of the sitter, or from some form of universal information repository, sometimes referred to as the Akashic field (Laszlo, 2007). The task for contemporary parapsychological mediumship researchers, then, is to distinguish between evidence for psi and evidence for survival of consciousness. One method currently being employed is to analyse accounts of the subjective experiences of mediums while giving readings in order to see whether mediums have different sensations when using psi to give a reading to when they are ostensibly communicating with discarnate entities. Preliminary research suggests that the experience is qualitatively different, which lends credence to the possibility of two distinctive processes (Beischel & Rock, 2009).

Summary

All of this—the social, the psychological, the performative, the para-psychological, and so on—points towards an understanding of mediumship as a particularly *complex* phenomenon that individual theoretical positions—taken as discrete wholes—are generally incapable of satisfactorily explaining. Each of the dominant approaches outlined above provides an account of mediumship and spirit possession that accords well with the various overarching paradigms of anthropological research, but none of them is able to provide a completely satisfying explanatory model. There is always *something more* that is left out. As I have already explained, for social functionalist approaches the experiential (qualitative) component is very often neglected; cognitive approaches are overly reductive and seem to ignore the wider complexity of the phenomenon (including questions concerning the *objects* about which the proposed cognitive processes are concerned), and the pathological and psychopathological models do not accord well with the ethnographic reality—though there are also interesting parallels which may relate to underlying processes. Psychological models focusing on the concept of "trance" and "altered states of consciousness" often ignore the role of embodiment—to forget that our psychological processes are embedded in the body, which itself is embedded in the world—while performance approaches focus too narrowly on the outward expression of spirit possession and ignore the inner experience of the possessed, and what those experiences imply. As for the neurophysiological approach, the research conducted so far has been generally suggestive that something unusual is going on in the mediumistic trance, but beyond this so far has failed to provide an explanation for whatever that something might ultimately turn out to be. If anything, the neuroimaging work poses more questions than it answers. Furthermore, few of these approaches (if any) pay heed to the findings of the many psychical researchers and parapsychologists who have found evidence of apparently genuine "anomalous information reception" with mediums, as well as apparent evidence of psychokinetic and other physical phenomena, such as ectoplasmic materialisations.

The approach taken in the chapters that follow, therefore, seeks to embrace the complexity of mediumship as a social, experiential, and psycho-physiological phenomenon, while also remaining open to the *possibility* of a genuine "paranormal" (psi or spirits) component, among countless other influencing factors. It does not attempt to reduce mediumship to a single explanatory framework, as such an approach is clearly too narrow, exclusive, and restrictive. All the dominant approaches have *something* to say, but taken as complete explanations in themselves they are all considerably lacking.

CHAPTER FOUR

Physical mediumship

> **Tom**: The new man, the anthropologist! Can I ask *you* a question?
> **Jack**: Yes you can.
> **Tom**: The third hand—where does it come from?
> —Transcribed from séance recording, March 14, 2009.

The following extracts from my field notes describe my own auto-ethnographic observations during a physical mediumship demonstration at the original Lodge in Bristol, with Warren Caylor serving as the visiting medium. Warren is a medium who has attracted a lot of criticism over the course of his mediumistic career.[12] As a physical medium his claims to abilities are far beyond those of many mediums and psychics operating in Spiritualist churches. His séances are also extravagant in comparison to the development circles usually carried out at the Bristol Spirit Lodge.

My first experience of Warren's mediumship abilities occurred on Saturday, March 14, 2009. I didn't know what to expect before going into the séance. Of course I had heard a great deal of talk among the

---

[12]See for example: http://independent.co.uk/extras/sunday-review/features/spirited-away-meet-the-psychics-with-an-uncertain-future-832567.html.

Spirit Lodge members about their own experiences at Warren's séances, but, as with all such things, the actual experience is usually quite different to your imaginings of it based on hearsay. Having attended numerous séances at the Lodge by this time I was accustomed to the idea and experience of channelled communications through mediums in trance, but other spirit phenomena had proved to be much more elusive. At earlier séances I had witnessed, in red light conditions, "face transfiguration" and the odd "spirit light" flashing in the cabinet behind the medium. Over the weeks, these phenomena had become staples: almost an everyday occurrence during séances. Warren's phenomena, on the other hand, are entirely different. While the observations of spirit phenomena during the previous séances I had attended *were* occasionally corroborated by other witnesses (such as with the green monk's face described in the introduction to this book), they nevertheless seemed to be semi-subjective in nature. The things I had seen seemed to exist somewhere between entirely subjective and entirely objective phenomena. Warren's phenomena were fully objective: there is no denying that *something* is happening right before your eyes; something which can be observed and corroborated by multiple individuals, regardless of whether it is a spirit or human creation. It is this that, to my mind, makes Warren's manifestations of spirit phenomena, as well as those of other practising physical mediums, that much more controversial. They go against the understanding of the paranormal as an internal, subjective experience.

The phenomena associated with Warren and his spirit team are so *physical* as to make them seem impossible other than by fraud. The stakes are high with this kind of mediumship. Of course, during the séance and unlike all of those I had previously attended at the Lodge, Warren's proceedings were conducted in full blackout conditions, so it is very difficult to pass judgement on whether fraud is being utilised (despite my own best efforts to inspect the Lodge and to bind the medium inside the cabinet before the evening séance—as a new sitter it was *my* responsibility to check the medium's body for devices and to secure him into the chair with cable ties and rope). The phenomena I observed that evening were so blatantly *real* that I would have be naïve not to be sceptical of them. Nevertheless, what follows are phenomenological accounts of the phenomena witnessed during the first séance with Warren as I experienced them.

Raps, bangs, and whistles

Raps and bangs were heard by some of the sitters while we were sitting in the house talking (although I did not hear them). We were only in the séance room for a very short time before loud knocks were heard coming from inside the cabinet. There were several loud bangs throughout the course of the séance, which were purported to have been created by the attending spirits. On a number of occasions toy slide whistles provided for use by the spirits were blown at extreme volume. The sound was piercing and shrill, and quite unpleasant. The whistles were blown along to the music in a cacophony. On one occasion the whistling was occurring at the same time as a spirit trumpet was floating in the air, which would, perhaps, be a difficult feat for one man to perform.

Extended voice phenomena

The term "extended voice" is used to refer to voices that do not *appear* to be emanating from the voice box of the medium. On several occasions I heard the voices of purported spirits move across the room, getting quieter as they moved further away from me. At one point, when Jon was asked to go up to touch the medium's head, I had the distinct impression that the voice was coming from a location about a foot away from the medium's head—as if from behind the medium. While we were discussing the séance afterwards, Jon told me that he had also thought this while his hand was on top of the medium's head. I had not discussed my experience at the time, and Jon's mention of it served as corroboration for my own experience. The medium made a deep, whooshing, rasping sound before and after different spirit voices spoke, demarcating different individuals.

Séance trumpets and other manipulated objects

Aside from channelled spirit voices, trumpet phenomena were among the first anomalous occurrences to be observed. The trumpet is a lightweight sheet of tin or aluminium bent around and fastened into a cone shape. The trumpet was fitted with two small glow-tabs so that its location could be clearly seen in the darkness of the blackout. The trumpet would be lifted up to the ceiling from the ground, where it was often banged before being dropped to the floor. At one time, the trumpet was paraded around the room presenting to each of the sitters in turn. The trumpet would be moved along to the music as though dancing. Later, the trumpet was used to facilitate communication from a spirit, serving to amplify his faint and rasping voice. In addition to the manipulation of the trumpet the curtains around the cabinet would often appear to be open one minute and closed the next without anyone noticing the sound of the curtains being drawn. The spirits also played with a tambourine and concluded the evening by tying a length of rope to the roof of the cabinet and wrapping it around the neck of the medium—sitting in the chair with his hands tightly strapped to its arms with plastic cable ties—as though it were a noose.

Messages from the spirits

Two messages were written down during the séance. I could hear them being written out with a pencil on paper in the darkness. At one point one of these messages was placed gently on my lap. I did not read what it said, however, and gave it to Christine at the end of the séance (though in retrospect I wish I had taken a look). An emotional message was given to Michelle. She burst into tears when she heard it. I do not know what the message referred to as it was personal to Michelle. Her reaction seemed to confirm that there was meaning to what the spirit was saying. A message also came from a spirit called Edward who said that he had been watching Jon's development with keen interest. A spirit attempted to come through to talk to Chris, but, for some reason, the voice was too quiet and was not clear enough to make sense of.

Spirit lights

As previously mentioned, the spirit lights I saw during the séance with Warren were entirely different to the sort of lights I had observed at other séances in the Lodge. Warren's spirit lights were full and bright. Usually the light was a bright point that would flash. It seemed soft, almost smooth and fluorescent. It wasn't like the light of a torch in that it didn't appear to form a beam—it was localised—though it could have been a torch wrapped in cloth to diffuse the light. At times it was difficult to tell whether this point was in front of, or behind, the curtains of the cabinet. There were times when the light was clearly inside the cabinet: it shone out through the cracks in the top of the cabinet where the curtains were attached and was projected onto the ceiling. For a while, with the curtains of the cabinet open, the light seemed to be focused around the medium's torso, the effect of which was to illuminate the medium's body—it was clear to see that he was still in position in the chair at this time. At other times the light seemed to pulsate slowly, illuminating the cabinet from behind the curtains. At one point, although I was not able to see it for myself because I was sitting directly opposite the cabinet at the time, the light in the medium's lap was used to show the outlines of materialised spirit hands. Jon was asked to come up to the medium, place his hand on the medium's head and look down at his lap; he said that he saw a hand in silhouette over the light in addition to the medium's two hands which were still strapped onto the arms of the chair. Jon described the light as appearing to come from beneath a layer of ectoplasm over the medium's body.

Materialisation of spirit forms

The materialisation of spirit forms is an exceptional occurrence for any medium. Here sitters were touched by hands and were exposed to the sound of heavy footsteps for certain spirits (Luther) and lighter footsteps (Tom) moving across the floor. When Luther materialised there was a distinct sensation of a very large individual standing in the middle of the room, very tall and very heavy. His voice was deep and booming and seemed to be coming from an abnormally high position in the small séance room. His footsteps were heavy thuds (Dave, one of the Lodge's regular sitters, described it as though Luther was "wearing diving boots"). On three occasions I was able to feel the physical nature of the spirit hands for myself: the first time I felt my trousers being flapped playfully from very low down; the second time I felt a very small hand press its fingers into my knee and then a much larger hand pat me on the leg; on the third occasion I was invited over to inspect the empty chair from which the medium had dematerialised. I was asked if I would like to sit in the chair. I consented and sat down. I felt, coming from behind me, and as though through the curtains of the cabinet, the same small hands touching my head. I thought that it could be the medium, and at the same time felt that it was *very strange* indeed. The feeling was very odd on all occasions, almost as though the hands were filled with some sort of energy. One of the most peculiar materialisations was witnessed by Jon during the séance, when the spirit Tom materialised a third hand in the séance cabinet:

  Tom: Jon, long time no see.
   Jon: Hello there.
  Tom: You thought I'd forgotten about you didn't you?
 Group: Laughs.
  Tom: Stand up when I tell you to.
   Jon: Okey Doke.
  Tom: Do you see the light?
   Jon: Yes I can.
  Tom: Move towards the light …
   Jon: Now?
  Tom: Please.
    [Jon moves towards the medium's chair and knocks the trumpet over in the darkness.]
  Tom: Mind the trumpet!
   Jon: I'm sorry. OK?
  Tom: Can you see the hand?
   Jon: Ah, yes I can!
  Tom: Now, you saw the medium tied up didn't you?
   Jon: I did, yes.
  Tom: Can you slowly reach in and place your hands on top of the medium's head?
   Jon: Right, I'll have to come in a little closer.
  Tom: Don't step on his toes!
   Jon: Right, I've got my hand on top of his head.
  Tom: Can you tell if you can see the hand?
   Jon: Yes I can.
  Tom: There's three hands in this cabinet now.
       (Transcribed from séance recording, March 14, 2009.)

Dematerialisation

Because it had been my task to bind and tie the medium into the chair, the spirit called Rachael took great pleasure in teasing me about it:

 Rachael: We want to speak to the man who tied the medium up.
  Group: Jack.

Rachael: What's your name?

Jack: Jack.

Rachael: Jack, hmm. You've done a very good job!

Group: Laughs.

Jack: Thank you.

Rachael: Do you mind if I ask why? Why do you think we should be tied up?

Jack: Just to make sure you, well not you, to make sure Warren's not moving around the room, that's all.

Rachael: Oh, OK. What do you do, Jack?

Jack: I'm an anthropology student.

Rachael: Wooooo!

Group: Laughs.

Rachael: Have you ever heard of dematerisalisation?

Jack: Yes.

Rachael: Do you know what it is?

Jack: I presume it is when something, or a body, *dematerialises.*

Group: Laughs.

Christine: He's a bright one, mind.

Rachael: Shall I dematerialise the rope for you?

Jack: Yeah.

Rachael: His mind's thinking how are they going to do that? Ready, count to three …

Group: One, two, three …

(Transcribed from séance recording, March 14, 2009.)

At the count of three the rope fell onto my lap, apparently having dematerialised from around the medium's legs and rematerialised just above my knees, which came as quite a shock—it was *very* quick. On another occasion the medium was shown to have completely dematerialised from the chair, which was brought out of the cabinet in front of the curtains. The spirit asked Belinda, a visiting sitter, to turn up the red light so that we could all see what was going on. The chair was empty and the medium was not to be seen, although he may have been behind the curtains. I was asked to come up and inspect the wire ties that I had used to bind Warren's arms to the chair; they were intact and still in place. Admittedly Warren is a fairly large man. I could not see how he could have slid his hands out from the wire ties without either stretching them or snapping them (both of which would take a considerable amount of strength).

The medium's exhaustion

At the end of the séance the medium appeared to be visibly flustered, as though he had been engaged in a strenuous ordeal. At this time his hearing was very sensitive, and so we had to be very quiet while leaving the Lodge. He did not look well and it took a fairly long while before he was back to normal following the séance.

Notes from my second séance with Warren

The following events took place at the second Lodge in Clevedon two years later. This was my second physical mediumship séance with Warren. Sandy was kind enough to give me a lift from Bristol to Clevedon to attend the séance:

> When Sandy and I arrived at Christine's new house … Warren was already standing in the shadows just outside the front door having a cigarette. Either he didn't notice us or he wasn't in the mood for conversation. We walked to the door and rang the bell, and soon saw Christine's familiar silhouette in the door's translucent glass as she approached. She was pleased to see us and was clearly excited about the séance (as indeed she *always* is). We weren't the first to arrive. In the living room the table had been laid with glasses and jugs of water. There were eleven seats around the table in front of which were place markers with the names of the various invited sitters written on them. I was at the head of the table with Christine, perhaps because she considered me to be a sort of "objective", "scientific" observer.
>
> On another smaller table was a plate on which sitters were asked to place their donation (£30) for the night's demonstration. Next to the donation plate was a disclaimer form for sitters to sign explaining how the proceedings were purely experimental in nature and that good results could not always be guaranteed. I flicked through the stapled pages and found that I had already signed the form two years earlier. Eventually more people began to arrive, some familiar faces I had seen at the Lodge in the past, and others that I did not recognise—new sitters drawn in by the prospect of witnessing physical phenomena produced by a well known (though not particularly well regarded) physical medium. I, along with two of the

new sitters, was invited out to inspect the Lodge. It felt very much like the old Bristol Lodge inside and was decorated in the same way, with paintings and photographs of spirit guides.

Christine explained how the shed had been a major selling point for the new house when they came to view it. Its dimensions were, she explained, ideal for conducting séances. A new cabinet, complete with specially made black curtains, had been constructed in the north corner of the Lodge. Christine showed us the ropes and cable ties that would be used to bind the medium into the chair, and we all felt certain that there was nothing unusual about them, or about the Lodge itself—everything seemed perfectly normal and quite un-tampered with. (Field notes February 5, 2011)

The format of the physical séances held at the Bristol Spirit Lodge is fairly consistent over time and is not dissimilar to the usual protocol employed with developing mediums, except that a couple of extra precautionary measures are often taken—warnings against making unauthorised recordings or videos and warnings against reaching out during the séance unless given express permission to do so by the spirits, for example. The £30 donation is also a feature not usually found during day-to-day séances with regular mediums at the Lodge, who do not charge (and who are not charged themselves) for mediumship development sittings. Visiting mediums often require payment, however, at least to cover travel expenses, though it inevitably raises suspicions. The evening usually begins with the invited guests sitting around a large table in Christine's living room. There is much more of a party atmosphere at these guest séances—they are a big occasion for Lodge members, and Christine very much looks forward to them.

While sitting around the table making conversation a couple of new sitters were invited out to the Lodge before the start of the séance to inspect the structure of the building (looking for trap doors or secret entrances that could be used for sneaking accomplices in during the demonstration, much as I had done two years previously), and to examine the ropes and cable ties that would be used to bind the medium into his chair at the beginning of the séance, to make sure they are the *real deal*.

As the time for the séance approaches Warren begins to look drowsy and appears agitated or uncomfortable, often shuddering, looking dazed and anxious. He complains of tugging feelings in his solar plexus, an area of the body thought to be, in some way, related to the production of ectoplasm (cf. Edwards, 1940, p. 152 and numerous examples in Edwards, 1978). Regular trance mediums at the Lodge also often claim to experience unusual sensations during the onset of the trance state, described as a feeling of drowsiness or sleepiness that builds as they approach the Lodge. Before moving out into the Lodge, while we were standing about and getting ready, the medium was very clearly showing signs that his trance state was deepening. As he swayed unsteadily with a dizzy expression on his face we heard a couple of deep banging sounds coming from the wall behind him. These sounds were taken as an indication that the séance was going to be a good one—that the spirits were nearby, already beginning to make themselves known to us.[13] This preamble serves to enhance the sense of drama, excitement, and expectancy among participants before we have even set foot in the séance room.

The next extract from my field notes describes the movement of the cohort out from the house, through the garden, and into the Lodge, followed by the binding of the medium with cable ties inside the séance cabinet:

> At 7pm we all went out into the Lodge, where earlier Christine and I had placed name tags on the chairs ... Christine had received communication from her guide FC (as she generally does), regarding where people should be seated during the séance in order to ensure the most effective circulation of necessary energies. When Warren entered the Lodge he consulted his own spirit team about the layout, everything was fine except for two individuals who were asked to swap places. This was to ensure that the right energy was present during the séance. As is customary, the two newest sitters were responsible for binding the medium—his arms were strapped tightly to the chair with plastic cable ties and his legs were bound to the legs of the chair with a long length of cotton rope. Once his bindings were seen to be secure, Chris tied a gag around Warren's mouth and placed a pillow case over his head. He looked like a torture victim, bound and gagged in the dark corner of the room, as we all sat and watched. The curtains of the cabinet were drawn,

---

[13]It is worth noting that this relatively mundane event, before we had even entered the séance room, was more convincing in many ways that the séance itself.

the lights were switched off and the music was played. It wasn't long before bangs were heard from inside the cabinet, and soon we could hear deep, throaty gurgling sounds emanating from the gloom as Warren's spirit team began to make itself known. (Field notes, February 5, 2011)

Warren's regular spirit team consists of an impressive entity know as Luther, two children called Tom and Rachael, the Native American medicine man Yellow Feather, Winston Churchill and Louis Armstrong. While the entities that communicate during these séances *do* claim to have lived lives on the Earth, their aim is not necessarily to prove this during séances (indeed there is very little in the way of "proof" that can be taken away from them). Rather, the goal is to demonstrate physical phenomena.

It is this aspect of physical mediumship—its very physical focus— that leads many commentators to question the supposed "spirituality" of such performances. What is the point of simply producing strange physical phenomena? Where is the higher spiritual purpose in all of this? After attending a physical mediumship séance at the Bristol Spirit Lodge on October 8, 2011 (at which I was also present), psychologist Dr Susan Blackmore, a very prominent sceptical commentator on the paranormal, asked in a lecture at Goldsmith's University:

> … what has this to do with [spirituality]? Well the connection is partly the word "spirit" … So there is a kind of connection. But when they describe it as doing good for people, why is it doing good for people? To go there on a Saturday evening and have chairs fly around and people, whatever they're doing, and strange noises and voices which talk. They don't talk about spiritual things, they just talk about very mundane things, and yet they perceive it as doing good. (2011)

I feel that Blackmore's interpretation is somewhat lacking in *nuance*, though I do understand and appreciate her frustration at the apparent disconnect between crude physical phenomena and *spirituality*. What physical mediumship has to do with spirituality, however, is that it provides an *opportunity* for personal spiritual development. As already suggested, I have come to understand the séance as an experiential experiment where participants (both mediums and sitters) explore and expand their own consciousness and sense of self through exposure to anomalous experiences. There may not be anything inherently *spiritual* in a levitating table, but its broader implications are immense—what it *means,* if true—and participating in this can be a powerful experience. In addition to personal spiritual development, members of the Lodge also see the development of trance and physical mediumship as a vital process of reconnecting with the physical and spiritual worlds. By conducting séances, and inviting spirits into our physical world, the Lodge is performing a positive function for our planet—rebuilding a relationship with the spirits that has been lost through rationalist materialism.

In order to give a sense of the kinds of phenomena demonstrated during these performances, and to give an idea of the atmosphere generated in the séance room, the following extract describes my own *subjective* experiences and thoughts during part of a demonstration of physical mediumship, written up immediately following the séance:

> ... bright lights flashed in the cabinet and shone out through the gap between the roof of the cabinet and the curtain rail. It looked like the light of a torch, perhaps a small LED pocket torch or key-ring torch, flickering inside the cabinet. Whether this is what it was or not, I cannot say for sure as, of course, I couldn't see inside the cabinet, but it is fair to say that these "spirit lights" were nothing like I had seen in previous séances (which seemed subjective), they were definitely *objective*. The rest of the sitters seemed to be suitably impressed by the light display. I did not feel entirely convinced that I was seeing something *paranormal*. Ectoplasm was allegedly produced on a couple of occasions over the duration of the séance. The first time it was displayed on a fluorescent glowing board, and looked very much like a sausage in silhouette. It moved jerkily, as though pulled by a human hand. Occasionally the phosphorescent plaque would be completely obscured as though a sheet were thrown over it, alleged to be a sheet of ectoplasmic material. The second demonstration of ectoplasm production was when a thin strip of the substance was seen apparently protruding out from the cabinet (presumably extruded from the medium within), that was somehow attached to the top of the spirit trumpet (a cone of sheet aluminium) in the middle of the room. This cord took a while to develop in total darkness, and when it was fully materialised the

spirit voice told Christine to turn the red light up very slowly using the dimmer switch. The ectoplasm looked remarkably like a thin strip of silk (on talking to Sandy in the car on the way home she too thought it looked like a piece of silk). The spirit voice asked if we would like to see it move, and we of course replied with a resounding "Yes!" The voice asked for the red light to be switched off again, and when we were told to turn it back on the strip of ectoplasm wagged about a little, quite un-impressively. Some of the sitters were apparently impressed by this demonstration, and cheered and congratulated the entities responsible for its production. (Field notes, February 5, 2011)

As already suggested, many of the phenomena displayed during these séances have parallels in the classical literature of psychical research and parapsychology, and it is clear that they represent a continuous tradition of physical mediumship, even if these modern phenomena are not quite as extravagant, or impressive, as their earlier counterparts. In the next extract I describe some of the reactions of sitters to the phenomena being observed during the séance:

Pat, sitting to my left, exclaimed "Wow, it's amazing, how do they do that?" as a small table, illuminated with glowing sticky pads, whirled mid-air in the middle of the room to the theme music from the Harry Potter films. An attempt was made by the spirit Luther to materialise in the middle of the room, which would indeed have been an impressive feat. He asked us to count slowly to twenty and then to gently increase the red light with the dimmer switch. We did this, but as the light increased we could see no sign of the materialised spirit, just the medium sitting unconscious in the cabinet, we were disappointed but nevertheless congratulated Luther on his gallant effort to materialise visibly.

One of the most unusual episodes during the séance occurred when Jerry (an occasional trainee medium himself) was asked by Luther to inspect the empty chair in which the medium had been sitting just moments earlier. Luther explained how the medium's body was now hovering mid-air above the ground just below the ceiling, and just above the empty chair. Jerry described how he felt the medium's arm dangling down from above, while at the same time he was able to feel both of Luther's materialised hands on his shoulders, and the char remained empty. Sadly, the rest of the sitters could not experience this, as it all took place in total darkness.

Caricature-like versions of Winston Churchill and Louis Armstrong then visited the séance room. At one point Syann was asked to move into the middle of the room where she was tapped on the head by the materialised form of Luther, a seemingly *massive* individual with a deep booming voice. She described the hand as feeling exactly like that of a "real human", only that it was *much* larger. She said that the palm of his hand covered the *whole* of her head. (Field notes, October 8, 2011)

The overall experience of the physical mediumship séance is a very unusual, and quite confusing one (and this may, in fact, be *the point*). On the one hand, the phenomena on show are often so crude as to seem undoubtedly the product of deliberate trickery (that is to say, the effects seemed "too good to be true", and occasionally "too fake to be true"), while at the same time the *sense of presence* associated with the ostensibly materialised spirits is incredibly *tangible,* as is the *numinous* atmosphere that surrounds the performances. In the heat of the moment, the spirits are *very real actors* in the social drama taking place, regardless of their ultimate ontological status. All of this leads me to suspect that the séance is, in a sense, *more than the sum of its parts*. It is also clear that sitters seem to get a great deal out of these demonstrations, in as much as they certainly enjoy them and *feel* that their participation in séances is a positive act for all of humanity—bringing the world of spirits back into contact with our own.

CHAPTER FIVE

Anthropology and the paranormal

The problem of the paranormal

In its popular usage, the *paranormal* is a term that encompasses an extraordinarily wide variety of experiences and phenomena—including everything from ghosts, werewolves, and zombies, to the Loch Ness monster, clairvoyance, psychokinesis, and UFOs (see Cardin, 2015). Indeed, many popular writers on the paranormal have stressed the need to resist the temptation to divide it up into discrete categories of phenomena, because to do so is to ignore the way that the different paranormal experiences overlap (Vallee, 1969; Fort, 2008; Keel, 2013; R. Graham, 2017). This diversity of experiences and phenomena renders the paranormal particularly *difficult*—though by no means *impossible*—for both the "hard" and "social" sciences to tackle: it may simply require an alternative perspective. The paranormal can also be said to possess archetypal "trickster-like" characteristics, which further complicates matters—it cannot be neatly categorised—it is liminal, ephemeral, fluid, and dynamic. Parapsychologist George Hansen (2001) writes:

> Many trickster qualities can be understood in terms of boundaries, structures and transitions. Tricksters are boundary crossers; they

destabilize structures; they govern transitions. They also embody
paradox, contradiction and ambiguity. (p. 46)

The paranormal also manifests these characteristics. Paranormal experiences—much like the physical mediumship experiences recounted
in the previous chapter—are often simultaneously absurd and deeply
meaningful—both ridiculous and highly significant to the experiencer
(Kastrup, 2011; Kripal, 2010, 2011). The paranormal can also be said to
be in *flux*—it is not static. In true liminal fashion it exists somewhere
in the interstices between religion and science, and fluctuates between
them (just as the practices of the Bristol Spirit Lodge do). Jeffrey Kripal
has commented on this feature of the paranormal in his suggestion that
the psychical can best be understood as the "sacred in transit from a traditional religious register into a modern scientific one" (2010, p. 9).

The paranormal is also multidimensional in nature. It operates on
numerous different levels including, but not limited to, social, cultural,
psychological, and physiological levels, and includes spiritual, mythic,
narrative, symbolic, and experiential dimensions. The paranormal, we
can say, is "transpersonal", in that it extends beyond the boundaries of
the individual, and indeed beyond disciplinary and theoretical boundaries as well. The paranormal might also be understood as implying the
existence of other worlds, planes of reality, and realms of consciousness
yet to be fully described, or even recognised, by science. It is *ontologically challenging* and its implications weave weirdly into some of the core
concerns of anthropology's recent ontological turn (Kohn, 2013). Given
the reality-bending implications of paranormal experiences, then, there
are inevitably numerous problems that come with any attempt at making a serious scholarly study of them, not least of which is the academic
taboo against taking the paranormal seriously at all (Cardeña, 2014).

What follows is an attempt at demonstrating that the paranormal
can, and should, be taken seriously as an area of anthropological and
ontological investigation. What this survey reveals is that anthropologists have long been interested in the paranormal, though they have
each approached it in different ways.

Problematic spirits: modernity, ontology, diversity

If mediumship development can be thought of as a kind of folk-
scientific experiment, as was suggested in Chapter 1, then the notion

of the existence of "spirits" might be thought of as one of its major hypotheses—that spirits *exist*. The very same quandaries over the ultimate nature of consciousness (is it a by-product of physiological brain functioning, or something else altogether?) can also be applied to the question of the reality and nature of spirits. Are spirits ontologically distinct entities, "out there" somewhere (non-local consciousness), or are they little more than unusual psychological phenomena—the product of innate cognitive processes, or hallucinations with no form of independent reality (an epiphenomenon of material processes)? The quest to understand the nature of spirits and the quest to understand the nature of consciousness are essentially one and the same thing. Just as we can talk about the so-called "hard problem of consciousness" (Nagel, 1974; Chalmers, 1995), so we can also talk about the "hard problem of the paranormal".

Spirits also pose intellectual challenges for other reasons. At a symposium on "Anthropology and the Paranormal" hosted by the Esalen Institute, in Big Sur, California in October 2013, folklorist David J. Hufford suggested that spirits "mark the modern/non-modern boundary". His paper explored the processes of disenchantment that have gradually encroached on Western academia since the Enlightenment, and highlighted some of the problems that contemporary encounters with ostensible spiritual beings pose for the dominant framework of Western rationalist materialism (which actively constructs itself in *opposition* to the "spiritual"). From the perspective of modern scientific rationalism the existence of spirits is a logical *impossibility*, and those who believe in spirits are thought to be "superstitious" and "irrational": *survivals*—to use Sir E. B. Tylor's Victorian terminology—of pre-modern modes of thought.

The word "spirits" itself is also highly problematic because it is popularly used to refer to a very wide variety of ostensible non-physical entities, ranging from the spirits of the dead (as the majority of the spirits I encountered in the field claimed to be), to nature spirits, ancestors, angels, ghosts, extraterrestrials, faeries, and deities, among numerous other varieties, types, and forms (Evans, 1987; Klass, 2003, pp. 57–60; Harvey, 2005, pp. 121–138). Indeed, in many societies there is nothing intrinsically "spiritual", or even "supernatural" in the Western sense of the terms, about spirits. They may simply be understood as *facts of nature*, just as anything else that exists in consensual reality, or as any human "person" might be. As it happens, this is precisely the way that members of the Bristol Spirit Lodge perceive their spirit communicators—as *spirit friends*.

For this reason, various scholars have proposed alternative terminologies to refer to the spirits, including much more inclusive terms such as "other-than-human persons" and "non-human persons", which may include both empirical (plants, rocks, rivers, jaguars), and non-empirical (spiritual, invisible, and non-physical) beings (Hallowell, 2002; Harvey, 2005; Kohn, 2013; Hunter, 2019). In the context of this book the terms "spirits" and "spiritual beings" will continue to be used in an inclusive way—encompassing this diversity—primarily because many of the same conceptual problems arise whether we are talking about séances with the dead in suburban Bristol, encounters with "luminous entities" in the desert (Escolar, 2012), meetings with "the dragon" in rural Wales (Greenwood, 2015), possession by the *loa* in voodoo rites (Deren, 2004), or conversations with God in Evangelical Christianity (Luhrmann, 2012). That is not to say that we should ignore these overlaps; it is important to be aware of the broadness—and looseness—of this terminology, but for the purpose of this book, the terms "spirits" and "spiritual beings" work quite well, especially as they are also the *emic* terms employed by members of the Bristol Spirit Lodge when they talk about their own encounters with these entities.

Such an interpretation raises important questions for anthropologists working with groups who believe in, and regularly interact with, spiritual beings—are they simply deluding themselves, or is there something more going on that our framework ignores? Furthermore, if we begin to understand practices such as mediumship development as folk-scientific experimentation, what might the "findings" (anomalous experiences) and "theories" (the existence of spirits, mind-body concepts, metaphysical systems, and so on) of such practitioners tell us about the mind-body problem, the nature of consciousness, and about the murky thing that we call reality? What ontological insights might lie waiting in the broad swathe of paranormal phenomena and experiences that is bracketed out by rationalism and materialism? In order to answer these kinds of questions it is necessary to escape from the dominant materialist perspective, with its *a priori* assumption that spirits do not exist, and develop an alternative approach that is not ontologically opposed to their existence, in other words a new way of talking about spirits and a new means of bringing them back into the scholarly discourse.

Naturalising the supernatural

Ethnographic fieldworkers—immersed as they often are in the life-ways of cultures that do not share Western academia's materialist metaphysics—have frequently highlighted the inadequacy of Western distinctions between the "natural" and the "supernatural" when address-ing the beliefs of their informants. Indeed, in many of the world's cul-tures we simply do not find such a distinction. In considering Sudanese Azande witchcraft beliefs, for example, E. E. Evans-Pritchard noted that:

> To us supernatural means very much the same as abnormal or extraordinary. Azande certainly have no such notions of real-ity. They have no conception of "natural" as we understand it, and therefore neither of the "supernatural" as we understand it. Witchcraft is to Azande an ordinary and not an extraordinary, even though it may in some circumstances be an infrequent, event. It is a normal, and not an abnormal happening. (1937, p. 30)

Evans-Pritchard is suggesting here that Western rationalism's usu-ally assumed binary distinction between "natural" and "supernatu-ral" should not be taken as a *universal* feature of human cognition—in actuality it appears to be a distinctly recent, predominantly European cultural construct. Phenomena that would be classified as supernatu-ral, or paranormal, in "modern" Western societies are not necessarily conceived in the same way in other cultural systems and may be under-stood as entirely natural components of everyday life (as witchcraft is for the Azande). It will be argued later that such dichotomies (supernat-ural/natural) also break down in the context of subcultures embedded *within* the dominant Western framework, pointing us in the direction of *ontological*, rather than specifically cultural, relativism—to the idea that there are multiple "worlds" coexisting alongside one another and that "culture" is not the only contributing factor.

Founding sociologist Émile Durkheim made a similar point about the category of the supernatural when he noted that it emerged relatively recently in the history of the development of modern thought—coinciding with the rise of the European Enlightenment and the gradual prolifera-tion of natural science and rational-empiricist philosophy. He writes:

> In order to call certain phenomena supernatural, one must already have the sense that there is a natural order of things, in other words,

that the phenomena of the universe are connected to one another according to certain necessary relationships called laws ... But this notion of universal determinism is very recent ... This idea is a triumph of empirical sciences; it is their basic postulate and has been demonstrated by their progress. Yet as long as this notion was absent or was not firmly established, the most marvellous events never seemed inconceivable. (2008, p. 28)

For Durkheim, then, the category of the supernatural can *only* exist once a natural order has been established—once the unchanging laws of nature have been recognised. Once a society has established a set of unchanging natural laws, anything that appears to contradict them must, by necessity, be *super*-natural—no longer a part of the natural order or reality. In an encyclopaedia entry on the concept of "miracle", Fiona Bowie makes a similar point when she notes that:

[f]or the majority of non-Western people practising a so-called traditional or indigenous religion ... the term 'miracle' has little meaning, as the boundaries between the natural and supernatural, material and immaterial worlds are drawn rather differently. (2015, p. 164)

To a certain extent, then, we can say that what is deemed *possible* is both *limited* and *facilitated* by cultural norms and expectations. Our experience of reality is *shaped* by our cognitive and cultural filters, but is not *created* by them. For those whose world view (which is not necessarily to imply a non-Western world view) *allows* for the possibility of paranormal phenomena, they pose no threat and may manifest more readily, while for those whose world view *rejects* the possibility of such phenomena, they are a very real challenge to established laws and models of nature, and are therefore problematic and so less likely to manifest.

Supernaturalism, materialism, or a middle way?

Although he denied the existence of the varieties of ostensibly paranormal phenomena discussed in the previous section, Gregory Bateson (1904–1980) nevertheless made a salient point—relevant to our inquiry here—concerning the Western cultural dichotomy between "supernaturalism" and "materialism" when he called for a *middle way* in conceptualising the mind and its relation to the body. Since René Descartes

(1596–1650) famously separated mind and body in the seventeenth century with his dualistic model of mind-matter interaction (Descartes, 1968, pp. 164–165), consciousness has often been thought of as somehow distinct from and separate to the rest of the natural world (Randall, 1975, p. 22; Matthews, 2005, p. 9). Philosophers and historians of science now understand Descartes's dualistic model, at least in part, as an intellectual strategy for preserving religion's role as the sole authority on the soul, and of demarcating the boundaries between scientific inquiry and religious insight (Schroll, 2016, pp. 14–15).

Following Descartes's partitioning of mind from matter, and hence religion (the domain of the soul) from science (the domain of matter), theories of consciousness have vacillated between mechanical/materialist and dualist/non-local/spiritual models (Emmons & Emmons, 2012). In response to this ongoing tension, Gregory Bateson called for an understanding of consciousness that is "neither supernatural nor mechanical". He wrote:

> These two species of superstition, these rival epistemologies, the supernatural and the mechanical, feed each other. In our day, the premise of external mind seems to invite charlatanism, promoting a retreat back into materialism which then becomes intolerably narrow. We tell ourselves that we are choosing our philosophy by scientific and logical criteria, but in truth our preferences are determined by a need to change from one posture of discomfort to another. Each theoretical system is a cop-out, tempting us to escape from the opposite fallacy. (Bateson & Bateson, 2005, p. 51)

I agree with Bateson's call for a theory of consciousness (which I also take to include spirits/the paranormal/the sacred—cf. Kripal, 2010) that is *neither* supernatural *nor* mechanical/materialist. There is a need for a middle way, an escape from the narrow and arbitrary dichotomy between two equally uncomfortable, and equally incomplete models of consciousness—what psychonaut scientist John C. Lilly (1915–2001) referred to as the *contained mind hypothesis* and the *un-contained mind hypothesis* (1977, pp. 99–111).

The difficulty with regard to the paranormal and its relation to consciousness more generally lies in developing a model that is able to accommodate the phenomenology of apparently paranormal experiences—such as out-of-body experiences and near-death experiences, as well as countless varieties of mediumship, shamanism, ecstatic flight, astral travel, and remote viewing—all of which seem to suggest that consciousness is not *always* located in the physical body, but can occasionally leave the body and travel to distant locations, or extends out much further into the world than the limits of our physical bodies (Monroe, 1972; Muldoon & Carrington, 1973; Blackmore, 1992; Sinclair, 2001, among numerous others). These are phenomena that seem to point in the direction of the *unconstrained mind hypothesis*—an approach that "does not contain the mind in a central nervous system. The boundaries of the mind, the domains open to the Self, are not limited by the biophysical structure of the brain" (Lilly, 1977, p. 114). I will later refer to this as the *experiential self* in the next chapter.

Further complicating the matter are the apparent veridical aspects of such experiences, which are reported surprisingly frequently, for example in veridical perceptions during out-of-body experiences (OBEs) and near-death experiences (NDEs) (cf. Sartori, Badham, & Fenwick, 2006), or in the abilities of certain mediums to provide accurate information about deceased individuals (cf. Beischel & Schwartz, 2007), or to produce unusual physical phenomena (cf. Maraldi, Zangari, Machado, & Krippner, 2014). Bateson overcomes this problem by choosing to dismiss outright the claims of those who have apparently experienced disembodied consciousness when he writes: "I regard all such accounts as either dreams or hallucinations or as frank fiction" (Bateson & Bateson, 2005, p. 55), but I think this too is—in Bateson's own words—a "cop-out". It simply perpetuates academia's *bracketing out* of that which it deems *impossible* (in much the same way as Charles Fort argued his *Damned Facts* were disregarded by science). What is required, then, is a model and approach that, rather than simply denying, or ignoring, such experiences (as Bateson seems to suggest we do), is able to *accommodate* them in all of their phenomenological complexity, including their apparently veridical components. Such an approach would also necessarily have to overcome the difficulties we have in conceptualising the mind-body relationship—a problem that arose from Descartes's dualistic model of mind and matter as *fundamentally separate* phenomena—and re-conceptualise our understanding of its nature—perhaps through the implementation of Jung's notion of the "psychoid" as a connecting principle between mind and matter (Addison, 2009), the philosophical model of pan-psychism, which sees consciousness as a fundamental property of the universe (Velmans, 2007), animism, which sees the world as consisting of relationships between "persons not all of whom are human" (Harvey, 2005), or models of non-local consciousness, which see mind as ubiquitous in nature (Radin, 2006). This is not the place to elaborate fully on a new model of mind-matter interaction, but it is my hope that over the course of the chapters that follow we will begin to see the emergence of a fruitful non-reductive approach to such issues for anthropology and related disciplines. The next section will show how this non-reductive approach might fit into a longer lineage of anthropological theorising about the paranormal.

Anthropology's engagement with the paranormal

What follows is an historical overview of changing trends in anthropology's theoretical and methodological approaches to anomalous experiences and paranormal phenomena. Such an outline is necessary to lay out the scholarly foundations that support the development of a non-reductive approach to spirit mediumship that is capable of side-stepping prevailing ontological assumptions about the paranormal—that is, without bracketing it out *or* presupposing it—and so allowing researchers to move forward into new arenas of ontological inquiry and understanding.

Pioneers: primitive religion and intellectualism

Widely regarded as anthropology's founding father, Sir E. B. Tylor (1832–1917) held that belief in spiritual beings (a common element of the paranormal, as we have seen), was the very minimum definition of religion. He called this belief *animism*, from the Latin root word *anima* meaning "soul", and suggested that it was from animism that *all religious ideas* ultimately stemmed. In other words, all religions, no matter how complex or developed they may be, are simply reconfigurations of a primitive animism.

Tylor maintained that the *idea* of supernatural beings arose, in the first place, from the *misinterpretation* of otherwise *natural* experiences, such as dreaming and other altered states of consciousness. He argued, for example, that early humans might have mistaken their meetings with deceased acquaintances in their dreams as genuine encounters with the disembodied dead. From such experiences, Tylor hypothesised, early humans posited the existence of an immaterial component of the person that could continue to exist after the death of the physical body—the *spirit*, or *soul*. Tylor further reasoned that primitive humans expanded this idea to include other aspects of the world: attributing spirits to animals, plants, and other natural phenomena such as the wind, lightning, mountains, rivers, and the sun, among many other objects and phenomena which often seem to possess a consciousness of their own. These spirits could then be *petitioned*, *propitiated*, and *worshipped*, so giving rise (through a gradual process of cultural evolution) to specific deities and the emergence of different religious traditions.

Tylor's animistic theory for the origin of religion therefore suggests that supernatural beliefs arise from an attempt to make sense of *unusual* (but certainly *not* supernatural) experiences—dreams and ASCs—and to explain the seemingly conscious activities of animals, plants, and other natural phenomena. Such a view essentially *naturalises* religion by reducing the supernatural to the misinterpretation of normal cognitive processes, an approach that is still widely employed today (Guthrie, 1993). From this perspective, supernatural beliefs represent "survivals" of "primitive", outdated modes of understanding the world, superseded by scientific rationalism—they are little more than "stupid customs" as R. Harris (1968, pp. 168–169) puts it. As we have already noted, however, when Tylor came face-to-face with the *anomalous* himself—while participating in séances with prominent Spiritualist mediums in London—he was not quite so quick to offer reductive explanations (Stocking, 1971).

Like Tylor, James Frazer (1854–1941)—another of the early pioneers of anthropology—also thought of the supernatural as a survival of pre-scientific thought. Frazer held that belief in *magic* was the earliest stage in the development of modern thought, proceeding eventually to *religion* and then finally to *science*. Like Tylor, Frazer imagined that early humans, in an effort to control their environment, developed systems of magical belief that provided *causal explanations* for natural occurrences. For example, by positing the existence of intelligent spirits who controlled the elements of nature—and who might be bargained with and manipulated through ritual and sacrifice—they might achieve a desired goal, such as a plentiful harvest, a successful hunt, or an end to drought.

The next stage in Frazer's scheme was the shift from this magical world view, where spirits could be bargained with, to a religious one, in which the spirits were transformed into more distant deities, epitomised by the God of classical theism. Humans might be able to petition and worship gods like this, but these deities were ultimately in control.

Frazer reasoned that this shift developed as a result of humankind's inability to affect the forces of nature (apparently through noticing that their ritual observances were *never effective*), which had once been thought of as spiritual agencies.

The final stage, the development of truly *scientific* thinking, sees human beings eventually discovering that nature is governed by neither intelligent spirits nor omnipotent gods, and coming to the realisation that the laws of nature *cannot* be bargained with, or pleaded to. Rather, nature is found to adhere to immutable mechanistic rules, like a vast machine, with science, and the scientific method, representing the only means of systematically discovering these laws (R. Harris, 1968, pp. 204–205). This notion goes hand-in-hand with the general nineteenth-century view of culture as moving through distinct cognitive evolutionary stages, ultimately culminating in Victorian rationalism (Spiro, 1986, p. 263). For Frazer, then, supernatural beliefs could not be anything other than a product of *delusion* and *fraud*. Belief in the supernatural could be nothing more than a *wilful reversion to primitive thinking*, in a world revealed by science to be governed by impersonal, unbreakable natural laws (Frazer, 1890).

Comparative psychical research

The need for a *non-reductive* anthropological approach to the paranormal (i.e., an alternative to the *reductive* approaches of Tylor and Frazer) is not a new idea in the history of anthropology, having precedents throughout the history of the discipline (see Schwartz, 2000; Schroll & Schwartz, 2005; Luke, 2010; Laughlin, 2012). It was Andrew Lang (1844–1912), a contemporary of both Tylor and Frazer, who was the first to combine the remits of anthropology and psychical research, and to argue for others to do likewise. He called the emerging discipline "comparative psychical research", a term coined in his 1894 book *Cock Lane and Common Sense*. In the preface to the second edition of the book Lang expresses his opinion that "such things as modern reports of wraiths, ghosts, 'fire-walking,' 'corpse-lights,' 'crystal-gazing,' and so on … are within the province of anthropology" (p. 9). In the book, Lang bemoans the reluctance of anthropologists to take seriously the kinds of contemporary phenomena investigated by the recently established Society for Psychical Research, while simultaneously criticising them for failing to look for comparative data in the anthropological literature. From his own examination of the literature of both fields he discovered distinct similarities in reported experiences and phenomena—across time, space, and culture—which led him to conclude that *something more* than mere "hallucination", "delusion", and "fraud" was going on— they seemed to hint at an underlying reality, a paranormal *common core*. He wrote, for instance, of similarities in descriptions of apparent spirit manifestations cross-culturally, commenting on their core features and historical and cultural pervasiveness:

> ... from the Australians ... in the bush, who hear raps when the spirits come, to ancient Egypt, and thence to Greece, and last, in our own time, in a London suburb, similar experiences, real or imaginary, are explained by the same hypothesis. No "survival" can be more odd and striking, none more illustrative of the permanence, in human nature, of certain elements. (Lang, 1894, p. 19)

Lang considered these cross-cultural correspondences to be particularly important observations for anthropological theorising about folklore and religion (not least because they seemed to provide independent cross-cultural evidence for the reality of certain core paranormal phenomena). Much as his contemporaries Tylor and Frazer had catalogued examples of rites, rituals, and myths to formulate their anthropological grand narratives, so Lang catalogued accounts of ostensible paranormal experiences to form his own parallel approach to the anthropology of religion, appealing to the sheer number of accounts of paranormal phenomena across cultures for the plausibility of his observations, but he was not an ethnographer.

1900–1949: ethnography

Drawing on his fieldwork among the Trobriand islanders of Papua New Guinea during the First World War, Bronislaw Malinowski (1884– 1942) criticised the loftiness and abstraction often ascribed to so-called "primitive" magic and religion by nineteenth-century intellectualist theorists like Tylor and Frazer, pointing to the all-encompassing way in which the belief and practice of magic were embedded in everyday life in Trobriand culture. He writes:

> ... magic and religion are not merely a doctrine or a philosophy, nor merely an intellectual body of opinion, but a special mode of

behaviour, a pragmatic attitude built up of reason, feeling, and will alike. It is a mode of action as well as a system of belief, and a socio-logical phenomenon as well as a personal experience. (1974, p. 8)

Through ethnographic participation, the complexity of "magic" begins to reveal itself—it cannot simply be explained in terms of "belief"—it is a mode of action, a social fact, and a phenomenological experience. For Malinowski, Frazer's evolutionary hierarchy, which positioned belief in magic as the most primitive form of intellectual development, was deeply flawed for the fundamental reason that magical thinking has *not* been "evolved out"—it has not gone away and still performs a function in many of the world's societies (including Western ones).

Malinowski's fieldwork experience in Papua New Guinea suggested that "magical" and "scientific" modes of thought were by no means dis-crete perspectives on reality; indeed, for the Trobriand islanders, they were very much *complementary*. Malinowski observed that where tech-nical knowledge could no longer help, magic was often used to ensure success. This was especially evident in the gardening magic of the Trobriand islanders, which sought to ensure fertility and good crops *in conjunction* with their rational scientific knowledge of gardening tech-niques, and in their fishing magic:

> It is most significant that in the lagoon fishing, where man can rely completely upon his knowledge and skill, magic does not exist, while in the open-sea fishing, full of danger and uncertainty, there is extensive magical ritual to secure safety and good results. (Malinowski, 1974, p. 31)

Magic may, therefore, serve important practical, psychological, and social functions within a society (relieving anxiety in the face of uncer-tainty, for example), and magical thinking need not be thought of as necessarily incompatible with scientific modes of thinking (it is an extension of practical knowledge).

In 1926, E. E. Evans-Pritchard (1902–1973) was commissioned by the British government to discover more about the beliefs and ways of life of the Sudanese Azande. Through a rigorous process of intimate eth-nographic interaction with the Azande over the course of four years, Evans-Pritchard came to an appreciation of the subtleties of Azande cosmology and metaphysics, particularly concerning the way in which the Azande attributed *causality* to occurrences observed in everyday life. In addition, Evans-Pritchard noted that the Azande conceived of witchcraft as an *ever-present force* that connected—and so also explained—unfortunate and unusual occurrences. He famously gives the example of the collapsed granary:

> The Zande knows that the supports were undermined by termites and that people were sitting beneath the granary in order to escape the heat and glare of the sun. But he knows besides why these two events occurred at a precisely similar moment in time and space. It was due to the action of witchcraft ... Witchcraft explains the co-incidence of these two happenings. (1937, p. 23)

In the context of Azande culture, witchcraft may be thought of as a sort of *connecting principle*, linking otherwise unexplainable events (somewhat analogous to Jung's notion of synchronicity, cf. Haule, 2011, only more frequently negative). Evans-Pritchard clearly had a good understanding of Azande metaphysics—he saw the rationality of their belief system, and yet frustratingly he draws back from it when Azande beliefs become experiences. Illustrative of the benefits of participant observation in revealing the paranormal during fieldwork, Evans-Pritchard had an anomalous experience of his own while immersed in the world of the Azande. He writes of an unusual encounter that occurred late one night when he was writing up field notes in his hut:

> About midnight, before retiring, I took a spear and went for my usual nocturnal stroll. I was walking in the garden at the back of the hut, amongst banana trees, when I noticed a bright light passing at the back of my servant's hut towards the homestead of a man called Tupoi. As this seemed worth investigation I followed its passage until a grass screen obscured the view. I ran quickly through my hut to the other side in order to see where the light was going to, but did not regain sight of it. I knew that only one man, a member of my household, had a lamp that might have given off so bright a light, but next morning he told me that he had neither been out late at night nor had he used his lamp. There did not lack ready informants to tell me that what I had seen was witchcraft. Shortly afterwards, on the same morning, an old relative of Tupoi and an inmate of his household died. This fully explained the light I had seen.

I never discovered the real origin, which was probably a handful
of grass lit by someone on his way to defecate, but the coincidence
of the direction along which the light moved and the subsequent
death accorded well with Zande ideas. (1937, p. 11)

To the Azande, the ball of light witnessed by the anthropologist was
witchcraft-substance, a mysterious viscous fluid believed to reside
inside the body of witches, externalised and sent on murderous mid-
night errands (another possible cross-cultural parallel of spiritualist
ectoplasm). In seeking a *normal* (i.e., Western rationalist) explanation
for the mysterious light, Evans-Pritchard makes light of the Azande
interpretation, although he clearly understood the significance of such
experiences within the Zande world view. Later, in his book *Theories
of Primitive Religion* (1965), Evans-Pritchard argued that anthropologists should not be concerned with *reality-testing* the beliefs of their
informants—they should focus only on the *observable* social *effects* and
functions of belief rather than on questions of ontology. This kind of
ontological bracketing would become the standard position for ethnographers who come up against the question of the ontological reality of
the supernatural beliefs they study, but one with increasingly obvious
limitations when it comes to trying to enter into and understand our
informants' *Lebenswelt*.

For ethnographers like Malinowski and Evans-Pritchard, whose
research was based on detailed ethnographic fieldwork with living
peoples, the intellectual evolutionist schemes of nineteenth-century
anthropologists were revealed to be untenable in the light of ethnographic facts. Magic and witchcraft could not simply be thought of as
evolutionarily redundant phenomena because they continue to play an
important role even within contemporary, highly developed, cultures.
In Evans-Pritchard's words: "Belief in witchcraft is not incompatible
with a rational appreciation of nature." Magical beliefs and practices
could no longer be thought of as "primitive" or "irrational", but instead
must be seen to perform deeply embedded social and psychological
functions, with practical importance for the social group. By refusing
to comment on the ontology of the objects of Azande belief, however,
Evans-Pritchard sustains his Western scientific objectivity and denies
the *possibility* that magical beliefs and practices *might* refer to genuine
anomalous phenomena—as Andrew Lang had suggested they might
decades earlier.

The 1950s and 60s: cross-pollination

John Reed Swanton's (1873–1958) "A Letter to Anthropologists", first published in the *Journal of Parapsychology* in 1953 (one wonders how many anthropologists were reading this journal at the time), represents a major step in the progression of the lineage we are tracing. It opens with the declaration that "A significant revolution which concerns us all [anthropologists] is taking place in a related branch of science." This revolution, so Swanton argued, was taking place in the field of parapsychology, and in particular in the work of J. B. Rhine's Parapsychology Laboratory at Duke University, Durham, North Carolina. For Swanton, a well respected member of the anthropological establishment, it was the evidence for telepathy—provided through simple line drawing experiments—that prompted his deeper reading into the literature of parapsychology and psychical research. He was also impressed by the psychical research of psychologist William James and colleagues into the abilities of the American medium Leonora Piper, whom James had called his "white crow". Swanton's 1953 letter calls for anthropologists to take the long neglected data of psychical research seriously, and to consider what implications the evidence for psi phenomena might have for the anthropological enterprise.

Seven years later, Clarence W. Went (1897–1986) took up Swanton's challenge with a paper published in the journal *Manas*, in which he outlined three key aims: (1) to summarise the development of parapsychology, (2) to take note of the influence of parapsychology upon anthropologists, and (3) to point out the desirability of cooperation between parapsychologists and anthropologists (1960, p. 1).

Weiant argued that, for the most part, anthropologists had been fairly reserved in their discussions of paranormal phenomena encountered in the field, generally seeking to ignore or explain them away in terms alien to the interpretations of their host cultures (through reductionism and ontological bracketing). He did note some exceptions in the history of anthropology, however, among them the biologist Alfred Russell Wallace's endorsement of Sir William Barrett's (1844–1925) research on dowsing as anthropologically valid; Andrew Lang's pioneering work on the origins of religion; and the investigations of psychical researcher Ronald Rose (1920–) into the psychic abilities and magical practices of Australian Aborigines (Rose, 1956).

Weiant concludes his paper with the suggestion that "Every anthropologist, whether believer or unbeliever, should acquaint himself with the techniques of parapsychological research and make use of these ... to establish what is real and what is illusion in the so-called paranormal" (a theoretical orientation quite different to Evans-Pritchard's, above). Weiant writes:

> If it should turn out that the believers are right, there will certainly be exciting implications for anthropology. We shall have to re-think Lang's theory of the origin of religion and magic. Students of culture and personality will find their field enormously expanded. The Physical anthropologists ... will have a multitude of new problems. Are there racial differences in ESP ability? Is there a genetic factor? Is it in any manner dependent upon neural organisation? Can it be cultivated? (1960, p. 5)

By the middle of the 1960s, coinciding with the wider social interest in mysticism and altered states, anthropologists finally began to heed Weiant's call to assess the implications of psi phenomena for anthropological theories of magic and religion. Francis Huxley's (1923–2016) short 1967 chapter entitled "Anthropology and ESP", for example, highlights the tendency of anthropological accounts of witchcraft, magic, divination, and shamanism to ignore the possibility that ESP might be a genuine phenomenon. He further suggests that there is a "general anthropological conclusion that tribal diviners—for instance—use quite ordinary methods to achieve their ends". Huxley then points out that despite the apparent rarity of instances of ESP among his Haitian informants, they nevertheless held a strong belief in the existence of such a faculty. He writes: "Wherever one finds divination practised, one finds a belief in ESP." Huxley then observes how a cross-cultural survey of divinatory techniques reveals a fundamental core characteristic: "A profound dissociation has to be provoked, during which the normal connections between consciousness and physical activity are severed." In other words Huxley recognises the crucial role of altered states of consciousness in the mediation of ESP experiences. He suggests that ethnographic observation of practices such as shamanism and spirit mediumship may reveal "a basic process which often seems to bring ESP in its train", and argues that such a process would be "at once psychological and social". We begin to see here the emergence of a *processual* approach to the study of the paranormal, examining the psychosocial processes that are conducive to psi and other paranormal experiences and phenomena (Huxley, 1967).

One of the most controversial—but also influential—anthropological excursions into the paranormal was published in 1968 in the form of Carlos Castaneda's (1925–1998) bestseller *The Teachings of Don Juan: A Yaqui Way of Knowledge*. This book represented something of a benchmark (albeit a particularly contentious one) in the history of anthropology. In the book Castaneda describes his first-hand experiences as an apprentice of Don Juan Matus, a traditional Yaqui *sorcerer* in Arizona (an important point given that many consider Castaneda's books to be about *shamanism*). The enigmatic Don Juan teaches Castaneda about the ritual consumption of various psychoactive plants, including *Datura* and *Peyote*, and about how to use them for magical purposes. Castaneda's book is filled with vivid hallucinatory descriptions of encounters with supernatural beings in various altered states of consciousness. The following extract exemplifies Castaneda's graphic first-person style, which had rarely been seen in standard ethnographic texts:

> At the foot of one boulder I saw a man sitting on the ground, his face turned almost in profile. I approached him until I was perhaps ten feet away; then he turned his head and looked at me. I stopped—his eyes were the water I had just seen! They had the same enormous volume, the sparkling of gold and black. His head was pointed like a strawberry; his skin was green, dotted with innumerable warts. Except for the pointed shape, his head was exactly like the surface of the peyote plant. I couldn't take my eyes away from him. I felt he was deliberately pressing on my chest with the weight of his eyes. I was choking. I lost my balance and fell to the ground. His eyes turned away. I heard him talking to me. At first his voice was like the soft rustle of a light breeze. Then I heard it as music—a melody of voices—and I "knew" it was saying, "What do you want?" (1968, pp. 99–100)

For Castaneda these extraordinary experiences were indicative of the existence of a separate reality, and his descriptions were presented as a factual ethnographic account of his apprenticeship to Don Juan. There is debate as to whether this was actually the case, however, with some researchers claiming to have uncovered inaccuracies in Castaneda's ethnography, along with evidence that certain of his claimed psychedelic experiences matched accounts found in the UCLA library (de Mille, 2000). Despite significant issues over the authenticity of his text, Castaneda's book undoubtedly had a major impact on popular attitudes towards traditional systems of belief, and inspired many to learn more about indigenous consciousness altering techniques in the 1960s and 70s (Schroll & Schwartz, 2005). Regardless of whether or not Castaneda's books are works of fiction or accurate ethnographic descriptions, they represent a turning point for anthropology—a movement towards a more *reflexive* ethnographic method that takes not only the experiences of informants seriously, but also the ethnographer's *own* experiences as valid ethnographic data.

In 1968 a posthumously published book by Italian philosopher and anthropologist Ernesto de Martino (1908–1965), entitled *Magic: Primitive and Modern*, presented a synthesis of the findings of anthropology and parapsychology. De Martino was an early advocate of interdisciplinary collaboration in anthropology, arguing for the need for anthropologists to collaborate with psychologists *and* parapsychologists—especially in magico-religious contexts. Much of de Martino's research into traditional magical beliefs in the South of Italy was funded by grants from the Parapsychology Foundation in New York (Ferrari, 2014, p. 21). One of his most important observations about the paranormal was that laboratory investigations of psi phenomena regularly ignore the emotional, social, and environmental contexts within which ostensible psi experiences *naturally* occur. He wrote that "In the laboratory, the drama of the dying man who appears ... to a relative or friend, is reduced to an oft repeated experiment—one that tries to transmit to the mind of a subject the image of a playing card, chosen at random." This, he suggests, represents "an almost complete reduction of the historical stimulus that is at work in the purely spontaneous occurrence of such phenomena" (de Martino, 1968, p. 46). In other words, the *drama of real life* is ignored in the parapsychological laboratory experiment. It is precisely at this juncture—so de Martino suggests—that anthropology's ethnographic methodology of participant observation succeeds in illuminating the nature of the paranormal as embedded within the wider *interconnected networks* of social, psychological, and cultural life. Specifically, ethnographic accounts can document the social dramas and ecological contexts in which ostensible psi experiences and phenomena manifest in their *most elaborate* forms, that is, the sociocultural-psychological-ecological conditions within which such experiences most frequently occur, as opposed to the sterile conditions of the laboratory.

De Martino's contribution to the development of a non-reductive anthropological approach to the paranormal has often been overlooked by contemporary Anglo-American researchers, primarily because of the scarcity of English translations of his work. It is fair to say, however, that de Martino's work on the paranormal lays a good foundation for the emergence of a *processual* approach to understanding the paranormal.

As a slight aside—it is important to note that in 1969 the famed anthropologist Margaret Mead (1901–1978) became the main driving force behind the incorporation of the Parapsychological Association into the American Academy of Sciences. Mead had taken part in parapsychological laboratory experiments using Zener cards with psychologist Gardner Murphy (1895–1979) in the 1950s, and was particularly interested in understanding what she called the "social and psychological dynamics" of psychic sensitives (see Mead, 1974). With this background, Mead was very keen to see parapsychology taken seriously as a science, and put all of her academic weight behind the push to have parapsychological research recognised as a valid field of scientific inquiry. Like de Martino, Mead saw the potential for research into the sociocultural and psychological *conditions* that give rise to ostensible psi experiences, again emphasising the importance of *process*.

The 1970s: paranormal anthropology

The 1970s was a decade of re-engagement with the paranormal. This "Occult Revival" took place in both scholarly and popular circles (see for example *Time Magazine*, 1972) and gave rise to a boom in paranormally minded anthropology. The year 1973 saw the first international conference specifically concerned with exploring the connections between anthropology and parapsychology. The conference was organised by the Parapsychology Foundation and held in London, and its proceedings were published a year later (Angoff & Barth, 1974). The conference was attended by, among others, social anthropologist I. M. Lewis, known for his functionalist social-protest theory of spirit possession practices (of which we will hear more shortly), and marine biologist Sir Alister Hardy (1896–1985), founder of the Religious Experience Research Unit at Manchester College, Oxford, and now housed at the University of Wales Trinity Saint David, in Lampeter. Diverse topics covered over the course of the conference included: "The Implications of ESP Experiments for Anthropological ESP Research", "The Anthropologists' Encounter with the Supernatural", "Anthropology, Parapsychology and Religion", and "An Investigation of Psi Abilities among the Cuna Indians of Panama"—finally making strides to join the dots.

Another significant contribution to this developing trend in anthropology was collected together by medical anthropologist Joseph K. Long (1937–1999) and published in the book *Extrasensory Ecology* (1974). Long's move towards taking the paranormal seriously as a subject for anthropological investigation was partly inspired by his own unusual experiences in the aftermath of an apparently public apparition of a self-propelled coffin accompanied by a frightful disembodied voice, while he was conducting fieldwork in Jamaica in the 1960s.

Both *Extrasensory Ecology* and the *Proceedings of the First International Conference* brought together papers from leading theorists in both anthropology and parapsychology and were groundbreaking in their presentation of a seriously reasoned anthropological evaluation of the evidence from parapsychology (much as Lang, Swanton, and Weiant had called for). Both books took seriously the implications of the parapsychological data for theory development in anthropology, with contributors from both sides of the paranormal debate (is it real or not?), and were the seeds for what would eventually emerge as the anthropology of consciousness in the 1980s (Schroll & Schwartz, 2005). Indeed, Joseph K. Long served as the first president of the Association for Transpersonal Anthropology (1980–81), and for the Association for the Anthropological Study of Consciousness (1984–86), which immediately preceded the emergence of the anthropology of consciousness as a distinct anthropological sub-discipline (Winkelman, 1999).

Robert van de Castle (1927–2014), in a 1976 chapter entitled "Some Possible Anthropological Contributions to the Study of Parapsychology", suggests that ethnographic fieldwork might provide for parapsychology what Darwin's Galapagos Islands expedition gave to biology. In other words, an anthropological approach to parapsychology might enable researchers to "observe at first hand how psi products can be shaped by environmental and cultural influence". Van de Castle criticises the tendency of parapsychologists to seek demonstrations of psi in the laboratory at the expense of studying spontaneous psi experiences. He also attacks what he considers the prejudice shown by anthropologists who dismiss non-Western magical beliefs and practices as *irrational*, *primitive*, and *fraudulent*—critiquing traditional social functional interpretations of systems of magical belief and practice for ignoring the *experiences* of ethnographic informants. Van de Castle goes on to caution parapsychologists of the need to be culturally sensitive in the development of experimental protocols for testing psi in the field. The paper concludes with an examination of the correspondence between claims to paranormal cognition (clairvoyance, precognition, telepathy, and so on) and the ingestion of psychoactive drugs, thus further highlighting the cross-cultural centrality of altered states of consciousness in the manifestation and experience of psi phenomena (Van de Castle, 1976, 1977).

Although not directly concerned with parapsychology, the work of French anthropologist Jeanne Favret-Saada also has relevance to the anthropology of the paranormal, specifically in relation to the role of immersion and participation in alternative ontologies. In the 1970s Favret-Saada conducted fieldwork in an area of rural France known as the Bocage, which she published as a monograph under the title *Deadly Words* (1977). Favret-Saada found a strong current of belief in witchcraft in the Bocage region, persisting even in the latter half of the twentieth century. The witchcraft beliefs of the rural communities she investigated—similar to those Evans-Pritchard described among the Azande—were intimately entwined with notions of misfortune, especially in the case of an unlikely string of unfortunate events. A single occurrence such as the death of some livestock would not necessarily be interpreted as the result of witchcraft, but if this event occurred coincidentally alongside *other* misfortunes—such as family illnesses, a car crash, and a bad crop yield—then a deliberate act of witchcraft might seem more likely (again we see witchcraft as a connecting principle). Once an individual suspects that they are the victim of witchcraft, they will seek out the assistance of an "un-witcher"—a professional magical practitioner—to perform specific rites to counter the malicious attacks of the supposed witch, who may be a jealous neighbour or other member of the local community. Over the course of her research Favret-Saada was herself identified as an un-witcher and was required to perform that social role. Like Evans-Pritchard's study of Azande witchcraft, Favret-Saada's investigations revealed the social-functional aspect of witchcraft beliefs (serving to express and diffuse social tensions) and offered insight into the *participatory* nature of witchcraft beliefs and magic more generally—witchcraft *becomes real* and *efficacious* by means of *participation* and *immersion* (Favret-Saada, 1977).

The consequences of immersive participation in magico-religious worlds is also explored in Paul Stoller's work. Between 1976 and 1984 Stoller was apprenticed to a sorcerer of the Songhay people in the Republic of Niger. Under the tutelage of the *sorko benya* (sorcerer) Adamu Jenitongo, Stoller "memorized magical incantations, ate the special foods of initiation, and participated indirectly in an attack of sorcery that resulted in the temporary facial paralysis of the sister of the intended victim". The deeper Stoller immersed himself in the world of Songhay sorcery, the more he began to fear the magical attacks of rival sorcerers, until, in 1979, he was forced to return home, fearful for his life, after a terrifying attack by a powerful sorcerer:

> Suddenly I had the strong impression that something had entered the house. I felt its presence and I was frightened. Set to abandon the house to whatever hovered in the darkness, I started to roll off my mat. But my lower body did not budge ... My heart raced. I couldn't flee. What could I do to save myself? Like a *sorko benya*, I began to recite the *genji how*, for Adamu Jenitongo had told me that if I ever felt danger I should recite this incantation until I had conquered my fear ... I began to feel a slight tingling in my hips ... The presence had left the room. (Stoller & Olkes, 1989, p. 148)

Stoller's encounter with sorcery revealed the powerful nature of magical beliefs and practices as *lived experience*. He was exposed—first hand—to the dual nature of magic, sorcery, and witchcraft, as simultaneously fascinating and terrifying—recalling Rudolph Otto's (1958) dissection of the numinous experience into the *mysterium fascinans* and *mysterium tremendum*. Stoller's experience led him to question the responsibility of the ethnographer working in the field, forcing him to ask whether it was ethical for an anthropologist to learn the techniques of the sorcerer, or to participate in magical attacks in the course of ethnographic field-work. In spite of anthropology's generally negative attitude towards the efficacy of magic, it may nevertheless have important social and psychological power within the host culture that should not be taken lightly. His experiences also brought into question the fundamentals of the ethnographic method of participant observation, and in particu-lar the extent to which an ethnographer engaged in such practices can maintain a sense of objective detachment from their research subjects. These are perennial issues in anthropology's engagement with the paranormal.

Writing in 1978, Richard de Mille (1922–2009), who had been one of Carlos Castaneda's chief critics, emphasised the importance when carrying out "anomalistic anthropology" of clarifying our tacit assumptions about the paranormal, especially when presenting ethnographic descriptions of anomalous experiences. He writes:

> ... the anthropologist's assumptions about the paranormal should be made explicit at all stages of work, whether planning, observing, analysing, or reporting. Every anthropologist makes assumptions about the paranormal. Most of these are tacit assumptions. When apparent anomalies are unexpectedly encountered, hidden assumptions bring about sceptical or subscriptive reactions that may not represent the best interpretations the anthropologist is capable of. Either following such an unexpected encounter or before intentional observation, the anthropologist should interrogate himself (includes herself) about all beliefs, feelings, and predispositions toward manifest or alleged paranormal events and make his findings about himself explicit in writing. (1979, p. 70)

Here de Mille is promoting a shift towards a more *reflexive* anthropological method, one that does not attempt to remove the ethnographic observer from his or her account of an experience, event, or situation. This is particularly important in the context of anomalous experiences described in ethnographic writing, and may reveal significant contributing processes, for example the psychological state of the observer, their moods, emotions, beliefs, and so on. Indeed, it may have direct relevance to parapsychological experimentation, which similarly seems to be affected by the involvement of the experimenter in the experiment (Schmeidler, 1943). Again, the clear distinction between the observer and the observed appears to break down in the context of the paranormal.

The importance of understanding the role of the observer as participant is also evident in other ethnographic accounts of the anomalous. In 1983, for example, anthropologist Bruce Grindal (1940–2012) published a very vivid ethnographic description of the apparent re-animation of a corpse during a traditional Sisala death divination in Ghana, witnessed and documented in the 1960s:

> What I saw in those moments was outside the realm of normal per-
> ception. From both the corpse and *goka* [magico-religious practi-
> tioner] came flashes of light so fleeting that I cannot say exactly
> where they originated … A terrible and beautiful sight burst upon
> me. Stretching from the amazingly delicate fingers and mouths of
> the *goka*, strands of fibrous light played upon the head, fingers, and
> toes of the dead man. The corpse, shaken by spasms, then rose to its
> feet, spinning and dancing in a frenzy. (pp. 68–69)

What is so unique about Grindal's account is that his anomalous experience is described as just one social moment in an *ongoing ethnographic
context*—Grindal details not only the social and cultural climate within
which the experience occurred, but also his own psychological and
emotional states leading up to the event. Following the ominously close
deaths of two members of the same village, it was deduced that the
resultant funeral would be a "hot" event "involving ritual danger, or
bomo"—from the outset *expectation* was high. Grindal's account of the
incident included the days leading up to the funeral, during which
the anthropologist's daily routine was significantly disrupted, so that
by the time the "death divination" that necessarily accompanied it
took place he was physically and mentally exhausted (in an altered
state). All of these conditions converged to *produce, mediate,* or *facilitate*
Grindal's paranormal experience, and serve as an illustrative example
of what Ernesto de Martino called the *drama of the real life context* of the
paranormal.

Transpersonalism and the anthropology of consciousness

In 1989 the Society for the Anthropology of Consciousness was finally
incorporated as a member of the American Anthropological Association,
and has subsequently developed its focus and specialisation through
its stated interest in altered states of consciousness and consciousness
studies, shamanistic, religious, and spiritual traditions, psychoactive
substances, philosophical, symbolic, and linguistic studies, and anomalous experiences.[14] It could be argued that the roots of the anthropology
of consciousness go right back to the early pioneering work of scholars

---

[14] www.sacaaa.org.

such as E. B. Tylor and Andrew Lang, whose interests in the experiential origins of supernatural beliefs set a clear precedent for the movement.

The anthropology of consciousness also has roots in slightly more recent trends in intellectual thought—specifically including transpersonal psychology (cf. Lajoie & Shapiro, 1992) and, slightly later, transpersonal anthropology (Schroll & Schwartz, 2005, pp. 6–24)—as well as in the humanistic anthropology of Edith Turner (1921–2016) (cf. E. Turner, 1992, 2012; Schroll, 2016, pp. 177–202). Transpersonal anthropologist Charles Laughlin defines transpersonalism as "a movement in science towards seeing experiences had in life, that somehow go beyond the boundaries of ordinary ego-consciousness, as data" (2012, pp. 70–74). Such experiences may include any number of ostensibly paranormal, mystical, and spiritual experiences, as well as innumerable alterations of consciousness. Encompassed in the category of the transpersonal are also somewhat more common (though not necessarily any less meaningful) experiences such as dreaming (Laughlin, 2013; Young, 2012), *deja vu*, everyday synchronicities, and so on.

Typical methods in the anthropology of consciousness have included active and immersive participation in rituals and other performances, and a deliberate attempt to attain the states of consciousness that are most important to the particular society under investigation. This might include, for example, consuming culturally significant psychoactive substances (cf. Jokic, 2008a), or participating in other forms of consciousness alteration and ritual in order to move towards a comprehension of the "experiential" component of alternative (perhaps parallel) world(view)s. Indeed, Charles Laughlin has defined the transpersonal anthropologist as one who is specifically "capable of participating in transpersonal experience; that is, capable of both attaining whatever extraordinary experiences and phases of consciousness enrich the [sociocultural] system, and relating these experiences to … patterns of symbolism, cognition and practice found in religions and cosmologies all over the planet" (Laughlin, 1997). Laughlin's view of transpersonal anthropology is similar to Lang's notion of comparative psychical research, except that the researcher *participates* in the field, rather than in the library.

Laughlin's broader "biogenetic structuralist" approach has also gone on to inspire other anthropologists with an interest in the paranormal—most notably Michael Winkelman, who has applied similar methodologies to the study of shamanistic practices and experiences (2000).

Winkelman has also put forward the suggestion that the long-standing anthropological debate over the nature and function of magic in human cultures might benefit from parapsychological insights—essentially suggesting the possibility that magical systems around the world might be tapping into (or at least attempting to tap into) psi for their efficacy. Michael Winkelman's (1982) paper "Magic: A Theoretical Reassessment" challenged the dominant anthropological theories of magic as performing purely social and psychological functions by suggesting that efforts to make *practical use of psi* might be inherent in systems of magic, shamanism, witchcraft, divination, and healing. Winkelman notes key correspondences between traditional forms of magic and the research findings of parapsychology, including the central significance of:

1. Altered states of consciousness
2. Visualisation techniques
3. Positive expectation
4. Belief.

Besides being fundamental to traditional magico-religious practices, these factors have also been found to help facilitate psi functioning in experimental laboratory settings (Schmeidler, 1943; Batcheldor, 1984; Hansen, 2001). Winkelman goes on to draw parallels between key concepts in anthropological theories of magic and specific forms of psi. For example, the anthropological notion of *mana*—a term borrowed from the Maori lexicon and used to denote supernatural power—is associated with psi phenomena in general in Winkelman's scheme. *Magic*—understood as the ability to affect change in the physical world—is associated with psychokinesis, and *divination* is associated with psi-mediated information gathering, for example through clairvoyance, telepathy, and precognition. Experimental evidence exists for all of these phenomena, albeit usually on quite a small (though nevertheless statistically significant) scale, reinforcing the suggestion that traditional forms of magic might utilise psi (Winkelman, 1982). The effects, no matter how small, appear to exist, so is it not likely that they have been harnessed in the past—couched in different conceptual and cultural frameworks, which, despite their outward differences, are built on common underlying mechanisms, processes, and phenomena?

Winkelman also offers an approach to the question of the reality and nature of spirits. Although he presents the case for understanding spirits as being shaped by the biological and cognitive structures of the brain and mind, he nevertheless stresses that the possibility of ontologically distinct spiritual beings existing *remains open*. He explains:

> ... the notion that spirits reflect the structures of brain and mind is not to dismiss their ultimate ontological reality. Whatever may be "out there" as a foundation for spirits may exist independently of the brain and mind structure. But what we experience of that ultimate ontological reality is shaped by our brain and mind structures in ways that personify that unknown, rendering it human-like in its qualities. (2004, p. 91)

Unlike the cognitive theorists discussed in Chapter 3, Winkelman suggests that there may well be ontologically distinct spirits out there, but they must also be experienced *through* our biological, cognitive, and cultural filters just like any other sensory experience. Overall, Winkelman's approach seems to blur the boundary between cognitive and parapsychological approaches, and emphasises that our experience of reality (including spiritual reality) is the result of an *interaction* between the external world and our own subjective filters and conceptual models. This is a view that accords well with Henry Corbin's (1964) notion of "active imagination" as a means of perceiving the invisible world of spirits (see discussion below), and F. W. H. Myers's "filter theory" of consciousness (1903), which see the brain and culture as shaping and co-creating our experience of the external world.

Learning to see what the natives see

The ethnographic portions of this research have been greatly influenced by the work of Edith Turner, an ethnographer and anthropologist of consciousness who highlights the importance in the study of religion, ritual, and religious/paranormal experience more generally, for the ethnographer to "learn to see what the Native sees" (1993, p. 11). Following her own paranormal experiences during the *Ihamba* healing ceremony of the Ndembu in Zambia, Turner concluded that it is only through attaining the kinds of experience deemed important by the host culture that the anthropologist can move away from making reductive assumptions about their beliefs and experiences. She sums up the essentials of this position eloquently, laying out guidelines for anthropologists to follow:

> [We should] endorse the experiences of spirits as veracious aspects of the life-world of the peoples with whom we work; that we faithfully attend to our own experiences in order to judge their veracity; that we are not reducing the phenomena of spirits or other extraordinary beings to something more abstract and distant in meaning; and that we accept the fact that spirits are ontologically real for those whom we study. (2010, p. 224)

Through *participating* fully in the life-world of our informants—to the extent of accessing culturally relevant experiences—the ethnographer is able to gain a perspective on a particular culture that could not be attained through any normal means of objective outsider observation. This is what anthropologist Zeljko Jokic calls "a point of intersubjective entry" into another life-world (2008a, p. 36). In order to see what the Natives see, and to make use of transpersonal experiences as ethnographic data, it is necessary to immerse oneself as fully into the life-world under investigation—to essentially *"go native"* for the duration of the research—an act that was, in itself, taboo in the early days of anthropological investigation. A. Irving Hallowell also agrees. Writing decades earlier about Ojibwa belief in "other-than-human-beings", Hallowell emphasised the ethnographic importance of understanding such beliefs from an insider—*emic*—perspective—from the perspective of "world view" or "ontology", rather than "belief":

> ... if, in the world view of a people, "persons" as a class include entities other than human beings, then our objective approach is not adequate for presenting an accurate description of "the way a man, in a particular society, sees himself in relation to all else". A different perspective is required for this purpose. (2002, p. 21)

Once an *emic* (or as *near-emic* as possible) perspective is achieved, it becomes apparent that *etic* (usually reductive materialist) accounts very often miss out on the ontological significance of ideas previously assumed to be *merely beliefs*. Through participation they are revealed to be "experiential realities"—ontologically distinct worlds. An awareness of the fact that the beliefs of our informants are not *just ideas*, but that they are grounded and sustained by experience, better helps us to explain and understand the significance and function of the magico-religious in everyday life and experience. Drawing inspiration from Turner's writings, Frank Salamone (2002) has highlighted the need for a return to holism in anthropology. He writes that this holistic approach must go beyond "a simple return to the *holism* of anthropology's earlier days of somewhat distanced reporting of the Other", adding that the aim is to seek "an experiential union with the Other and not only a respect for the spirituality of the Other but also an acceptance of it". These themes have subsequently been developed by others, as we shall see.

In 2002, sociologists James McClenon and Jennifer Nooney showed just how common anomalous experiences are in the ethnographic literature when they published a short article detailing forty separate anomalous experiences reported by sixteen anthropologists in the field. Comparing the experiences of anthropologists with 1446 anomalous experiences collected from undergraduate students between 1988 and 1996, the authors note distinct similarities in experience and suggest, in line with David J. Hufford's work, that the "experiential source" hypothesis has greater explanatory power than the standard "cultural source" hypothesis. McClenon and Nooney go on to further suggest that scholarly engagement with anomalous experiences can provide novel insights into anthropological theories of religion:

> Field anthropologists, as "professional observers", have a unique position within the social sciences. They undergo special training designed to increase their ability to transcribe their experiences accurately. As a result, their reports have special rhetorical power compared to those of lay people. Published accounts of their anomalous experiences constitute a particularly "worthy" body of data, especially valid for testing social scientific hypotheses pertaining to the origin of religion. (2002, p. 49)

As if to take us a little deeper down the rabbit hole, Joan Koss-Chioino suggests that in discussions of the supernatural belief systems of ethnographic informants the question of "spirit reality cannot be dismissed", especially because "reports of experiences of spirits are ubiquitous in the world, in all cultures" (2010, p. 134). Anthropologists ought, therefore, to take seriously the supernatural beliefs and paranormal experiences of their ethnographic informants because they represent foundational aspects of many of the world's cultures and ontological frameworks.

Fiona Bowie has more recently proposed a methodology—again drawing on Edie Turner's work—with the specific goal of achieving this kind of experiential immersion in ritual, and not to dismiss the question of "spirit reality". She has termed this "cognitive empathetic engagement" (2010, 2012), which is defined as a methodology by which:

> … the observer … approaches the people or topic studied in an open-minded and curious manner, without presuppositions, prepared to entertain the world view and rationale presented and to experience, as far as possible and practical, a different way of thinking and interpreting events. (2010, p. 5)

The ultimate aim of this type of approach, then, is to interpret religious, spiritual, and paranormal beliefs and experiences from a perspective that does not, from the very outset, reduce the *complexity* of the phenomenon, or ignore the significance of *personal, subjective experience*, but rather *embraces* these aspects to playfully engage with the possibilities of alternative ontological systems. Indeed, Deirdre Meintel, in her investigations of contemporary Spiritualist groups in Canada, has specifically noted the usefulness of such open-ended approaches in interpreting and understanding Spiritualist belief and practice in contemporary contexts (2007, p. 125). It therefore seems reasonable to apply this kind of methodology to my own work with spirit mediums in Bristol, as a means of entering into the *life-world* of contemporary trance and physical mediums.

The ontological turn

It would seem to make sense at this juncture to explore how the lineage of paranormal anthropology we have been following intersects with the recent so-called "ontological turn" in social anthropology. The ontological turn in anthropology emerged from the work of several anthropological theorists writing in the 1990s and early 2000s—Eduardo Viveiros de Castro, Morten Pedersen, and Martin Holbraad, though it undeniably had earlier precedents (e.g., Gregory Bateson, Irving Hallowell). In an attempt to summarise the key themes of this loose movement,

Palecek and Risjord (2013) have identified four primary concerns in the writings of the ontological anthropologists:

- In ethnographic analysis, look to the most abstract categories found in a culture: person, relation, power, property, and so on.
- Be prepared to learn theoretical lessons from the concepts used by the groups studied and to adopt (perhaps modified) local concepts into anthropological theory.
- Reject representationalism.
- Adopt the extended mind hypothesis (p. 6)

We could also add into the first key theme notions of magic, religion, the paranormal, consciousness, and so on. The second theme is not uncommon within traditional anthropology; we need only think of key anthropological topics such as "taboo", "fetishism", and so on for examples of where local concepts become cross-cultural theoretical tools. Nevertheless, this idea could be taken a step further, for example in the context of psi and parapsychological phenomena—how might these be incorporated into anthropological theory construction? Can anthropological theory be based upon ontological frameworks other than positivist-rationalist-materialism?

Representationalism, according to the ontological anthropologists, is the philosophical foundation of the Western tradition and the main reason for its failure. According to representationalism we can never truly apprehend reality in itself—our perceptions and ideas about the world are merely *representative* of the true objects that exist in the physical world. This, of course, implies a sharp distinction between experience and reality, a sort of Cartesian divide between the objective world and the subjective experience of it. Willerslev explains that this framework for understanding the world underpins the "world view" approach, which sees cultures as collections of beliefs about the world, and nothing more:

> At the heart of the [world view] approach is a representationalist view of knowledge, according to which people can neither know nor engage with the world directly, but only indirectly through the medium of their cultural representations. (2004, p. 400)

But what if we *can* experience "reality" directly, at least from time to time, in, to use Willerslev's terminology, "the flux of people's everyday, pre-reflexive activities" (2004, p. 401). This notion of accessing *pre*-reflexive—or maybe even *pre*-cultural—experience of the world is reminiscent of Colin Wilson's (1931–2013) concept of *Faculty X*, an innate capacity to experience reality itself, which, although we often fail to realise it, is actually our "natural state" (Lachman, 2017). We could go even further and suggest that we are as much a part of the "real world" as anything else, so that our experience of it *cannot* be separated from the thing in itself. The ontological anthropologists have argued that the traditional reliance of anthropological theory on representationalism has been a major contributive factor in the failure of the discipline's approach to culture in general, and the models and explanations it has thrown up. In other words, representationalism provides an easy escape route for anthropologists confronted with beliefs that contradict Western materialism—they are *just beliefs* and have no bearing on reality.

The fourth key theme, of adopting the extended mind hypothesis, refers to the idea that human cognition is not limited to the brain, but rather that cognition *extends out into the environment*—that we can think *through things*—objects, clothes, tools, etc. An addition to this idea might be that the human mind also makes use of other *forms of cognition*, for example making use of insights from altered states of consciousness, or that cognition might involve interactions with spirits and other non-empirical beings (real or imagined), or that consciousness might *act through* objects, as in psychokinesis, and especially in poltergeist cases (C. Wilson, 1981), and physical mediumship séances. Taken together these ontological themes open up new avenues for engaging the paranormal in the flux of our day-to-day experience of the world.

Eduardo Viveiros de Castro is among the most important contributors to the debate over the ontological turn. In his hugely influential paper "Cosmological Deixis and Amerindian Perspectivism" (2002), Viveiros de Castro calls for a new approach to Amerindian cosmology that moves beyond the standard cultural relativist approach—with its emphasis on *belief*—towards an ontological approach and an appreciation of different *ways* and *worlds* of "being". As an illustration, where animism had once been defined as "the belief in spiritual beings" (Tylor), Viveiros de Castro opts to define animism as a *way of living in, interacting with, and understanding the world*. He defines animism as: "… an ontology which postulates the social character of relations between humans and non-humans: the space between nature and society is itself social" (2002, p. 311). In other words, when dealing with what were once referred to simply as "cultures" (systems of *belief* and *practice*) we are, in effect, dealing with *whole different worlds and ways of being*, that is, much more than *just* a collection of *representational beliefs* about the world. Holbraad, Pedersen, and Viveiros de Castro (2014) give a very useful illustration of the difference between a standard cultural relativist position and the emergent ontological framework to *explain* this subtle difference of approach. They write:

> For example, the relativist reports that in such-and-such an ethnographic context time is "cyclical," with "the past ever returning to become the present." It is an evocative idea, to be sure. But strictly speaking, it makes no sense. To be "past" is precisely not "to return to the present," so a past that does so is properly speaking not a past at all (in the same sense that a married bachelor is not a bachelor). By contrast, like a kind of "relativist-turbo," the ontologically-inclined anthropologist takes this form of e(qui)vocation as a starting-point for an ethnographically-controlled experiment with the concept of time itself, reconceptualizing "past," "present," "being," etc., in ways that make "cyclical time" a real form of existence. In this subjunctive, "could be" experiment, the emphasis is as much on "be" as on "could": "Imagine a cyclical time!" marvels the relativist; "Yes, and here is what it could be!" replies the ontological anthropologist.

In his paper "Who Is Afraid of the Ontological Wolf?" (2014), Eduardo Viveiros de Castro further argues that the anthropologist is confronted with an ontological challenge the moment they encounter the life-worlds of their informants in the field. He writes of how such things as magic, witchcraft, and spirit communication challenge *our own* ontological assumptions—as in those things that *we assume to exist* and to be meaningful in our own life-worlds, as well as those things we assume *certainly do not* exist. He describes the problem faced by anthropologists attempting to make sense of other worlds through the lenses of the Western social sciences that exclude them:

> When a shaman shows you a magic arrow extracted from a sick man, a medium gets possessed by a god, a sorcerer laboriously constructs a voodoo doll, we only see one thing: Society (belief, power, fetishism). In other words, we only see *ourselves* (Viveiros de Castro, 2014, p. 12).

Chief among the methods for dealing with such problems—for overcoming the fact that the dominant approach of the Western social sciences is nothing more than a reflection of its own values (i.e., what it thinks is important)—is to take "seriously the things the people we study tell us" and to "learn *to be able to speak well* to the people you study … to speak *about* them *to* them in ways they do not find offensive or ridiculous" (Viveiros de Castro, 2014). This sentiment resonates harmoniously with Edith Turner's call for anthropologists to "learn to see what the natives see" and Fiona Bowie's notion of "cognitive empathetic engagement", as well as my own approach to engaging with the world of the Bristol Spirit Lodge.

The ontological approach to ethnographic research, then, points us in promising directions for the study of the paranormal. Rather than focusing on questions of belief, or taking a relativist position in which any possible "reality" is a *purely social* one (or a system of *representational beliefs*), the ontological approach allows for an *expansion of perspective* to incorporate areas of inquiry that anthropologists have not traditionally approached (or have at least steered clear of). In the case of this book, for example, the *reality* of spirits and the *processes* involved in mediumship and the manifestation of spirits—not just as culturally relative beliefs and practices, but also as ontologically real "modes of existence" (Latour, 2013).

Paranthropology

The term *paranthropology* was first coined by the linguist Roger Wescott (1977) in Joseph Long's *Extrasensory Ecology*. It refers to an anthropological approach to the paranormal. The label did not stick, however, and was eventually replaced with less problematic terms like "transpersonal anthropology" and the "anthropology of consciousness" (Luke, 2010). In recent years, however, the term has been revived and the idea further refined (cf. L. Wilson, 2011; Hunter, 2012b; Caswell, 2014; Caswell, Hunter, & Tessaro, 2014).

Social anthropologist Fabian Graham, for instance, differentiates paranthropology from more traditional approaches to the anthropology of religion according to the way in which the two approaches interpret the *objects* of religious and paranormal beliefs specifically. The anthropology of religion, Graham argues, focuses primarily on systems of religious *belief* only, and either brackets out the question, or (more often) negates the very possibility, of the ontological status of the *objects* of the beliefs themselves. Paranthropology accepts the *possibility* that the objects of supernatural beliefs *may* have some form of independent ontological reality. He writes that "paranthropology [defines] itself in relation to the phenomena themselves, and not to the belief systems, scientific or religious, that have evolved to support the phenomena" (2011, p. 21). Paranthropology, therefore, sits relatively comfortably within the emergent ontological trend in contemporary anthropology.

Arguing along similar lines, anthropologist Patric Giesler has proposed a step away from the traditional bracketing out of questions of ontology in the majority of phenomenological and social-scientific approaches to the paranormal with his "parapsychological anthropology", which is aimed specifically at attempting to *verify* or *falsify* the reality of paranormal phenomena in the field. Giesler's 1984 paper "Parapsychological Anthropology: Multi-Method Approaches to the Study of Psi in the Field Setting", published in the *Journal of the American Society for Psychical Research*, seeks to improve the one-sided approaches of *both* parapsychology *and* anthropology "by suggesting refinements in each and by proposing combinational and integrated ... approaches to the study of psi processes in their psychosocial contexts". Giesler sees useful potential for applying insights into the nature of psi derived from parapsychology to help interpret the anthropology of magic and religion. Conversely, he argues that parapsychology has failed to "take advantage of the exceedingly rich insights provided by ethnographic fieldwork and cross-cultural research", much as Andrew Lang had done at the beginning of the twentieth century. The paper calls for a *process-oriented* approach to psi, one that takes into account the many ecological variables (ethnographic facts) that correlate with the occurrence of psi phenomena. He argues that insights into the psychosocial contexts within which psi phenomena naturally occur can be synthesised into new models for laboratory testing of psi. The close association between the cultural use of altered states of consciousness and a "deeply instilled belief in the existence of psychical phenomena" is once again reiterated. Giesler's approach marks a significant step away from the traditional bracketing out of questions of ontology in phenomenological and social-scientific approaches to supernatural beliefs and anomalous experiences, proposing instead that experiments be carried out to *test* their reality. He writes that:

> ... one of the purposes of anthropology is to explain the ontology, development, and function of the beliefs, practices, and claims of magico-religious experiencers ... it should assume that psi could exist and then proceed etically on that assumption. (1984)

For example, in an experiment with mediums from the syncretic Afro-Brazilian religious groups Candomblé, Caboclo, and Umbanda, Giesler modified parapsychologist Helmut Schmidt's (1928–2011) classic random number generator psychokinesis (PK) experiments through incorporating the use of culturally meaningful target symbols rather than standard Euro-American Zener card targets (which had little relevance to Giesler's experimental participants). Giesler's results were significantly above chance and were suggestive of PK (mental influence on physical systems), albeit on a small scale (Giesler, 1984). Unlike Giesler's work, however, my own research, as presented in this book, does not attempt to experimentally verify or falsify the claims of mediums, but it does take up his call to "assume that psi *could* exist" as a means to open up a "point of intersubjective entry" into the life-world of our research informants.

In a recent ethnographic account of spirit possession rituals in Indonesia, anthropologist Nils Bubandt has argued in favour of treating spirits as "methodologically real" informants, as to do so allows the anthropologist to "get on with the business of studying the social and political reality of spirits" (Bubandt, 2009, p. 298). To treat the spirits as methodologically real does not require the ethnographer to verify or falsify their existence as ontologically distinct entities, nor is it necessary to attempt to prove that the spirits are who they claim to be, although, as Hufford suggests, such an approach "can provide some information relevant to investigations of that nature" (1982, p. 256). Therefore, rather than attempting to verify the existence of the spirits encountered during my fieldwork, this research will instead deal with the *social, psychological, performative*, and *physiological processes* through which spirits are expressed and interacted with in the context of the séance, as if they are real ethnographic informants, *because they are* (one step further than Bubandt is willing to go).

Building on the foundations laid out by scholars like Edith Turner—coupled with insights from the ontological turn—recent anthropologists have started to open up new avenues for engagement with non-physical realities. In the introduction to their recent edited volume *The Social Life of Spirits* (2013), Ruy Blanes and Diana Espírito Santo recognise the need for anthropologists to try out *new approaches* to investigating the role and nature of invisible spiritual beings. They argue that in order to do this we must move away from the traditional reductive frameworks of social functionalism, pathology, and cognitive science—which have dominated the discourse on spirit possession and mediumship—in favour of *experiential* and *phenomenological* approaches, and an emphasis on the *social effects* of non-physical entities (what they *do*), and the *processes* by which they become social actors (Espírito Santo, 2011; Blanes & Espírito Santo, 2013, p. 7).

Ontological flooding

The epistemological frameworks outlined in the following section pave the way for a destabilisation of ontological certainty, which could, I contend, assist in the development of a more culturally *sensitive* and ontologically *receptive* approach to non-ordinary reality, an approach that does not rely on ontological bracketing as a means of engaging with the paranormal "from a safe distance", and that can enable us to extract ethnographic information from other ontological domains. I have called this approach "ontological flooding", an approach for *engaging the anomalous* head on, with a particular emphasis on process and complexity rather than reduction. Such an approach, combined with the concerns of the ontological turn and Edie Turner's participatory and experiential approach, may open up new avenues for inquiry. These approaches do not derive from the anthropological canon, but occasionally drawing on material from outside the discipline can shed new light on old problems.

Intermediatism

Charles Fort (1874–1932) was famous in the early decades of the twentieth century as a collector of accounts of strange occurrences—from apparent poltergeist activity through to mysterious flying objects and rains of frogs—which he found ample evidence for in newspapers and scientific journals, and which he compiled into four extraordinary books (Fort, 2008). In order to accommodate such unusual phenomena (which he called "damned facts" because of their outright rejection by mainstream science) Fort developed the philosophy of "intermediatism". Fort defined intermediatism as a position in which "nothing is real, but … nothing is unreal … all phenomena are approximations in one way between realness and un-realness" (Fort, 2008, p. 14; Steinmeyer, 2008, p. 170; Kripal, 2014, p. 259). In his characteristically playful way, Fort sought to deconstruct the rigid boundaries between the real and the unreal, and instead placed all phenomena—from the mundane to the extraordinary—on a sliding spectrum where all things fluctuate between the real and the unreal. From this perspective nothing can be said to be entirely "real" or "unreal"—*everything is in flux.* Fort's intermediatism can also be likened to Gregory Bateson's "middle way", though it is a little more inclusive of the weird than Bateson's perspective.

E-Prime and the new agnosticism

Drawing on Alfred Korzybski's (1879–1950) writings on general semantics, and taking inspiration from Benjamin Lee Whorf's (1897–1941) work on language and the construction of reality (1956), the novelist and philosopher Robert Anton Wilson (1932–2007) sought to implement and popularise the use of what he called *E-Prime*, a mode of using the English language that rejects the use of the verb "to be" in all its forms. In this way, E-Prime avoids *definitive* statements of *certainty* in favour of *uncertainty*, and a capacity for *change* (R. A. Wilson, no date). For example, rather than saying "The sky is blue," E-Prime would say "The sky appears blue to me." Wilson also proposes what he calls a "new agnosticism", sometimes also called "model agnosticism" or "creative agnosticism". He writes:

> In this state we "are" model-relativists … and ["are"] actively creative; all perceptions (gambles) are actively known as gambles. We consciously seek to edit less and tune in more, and we look especially for events that do not neatly fit our model, since they will teach us to make a better one tomorrow, and an even better one the day after. We are not dominated by the "Real" Universe. (1987, p. 231)

Like Fort's sliding spectrum between the real and the unreal, Wilson suggests that all perceptions are *probabilities*, and our beliefs about them, and models to explain them, are ultimately gambles too. Wilson's "new agnosticism" is an epistemology of probabilities, uncertainty, and indeterminism that takes its inspiration from the uncertainty of quantum mechanics. *All knowledge is probabilistic.*

Possibilianism

Possibilianism is a recent term coined and popularised by neuroscientist and author David Eagleman. According to Eagleman's *possibilian* philosophy—which seeks to inspire *creativity* and *exploratory wonder* in the scientific enterprise—scientific researchers are encouraged to enter into the "possibility space", a frame of mind in which the researcher celebrates "the vastness of our ignorance [and is] unwilling to commit to any particular made-up story, and take[s] pleasure in entertaining multiple hypotheses' simultaneousness" (Jansen, 2010). Again, this playfulness in considering multiple possibilities is perfectly suited to the study of the multidimensional paranormal, and resonates well with Charles Fort's intermediatist philosophy and Robert Anton Wilson's implementation of E-Prime and the "new agnosticism". According to this perspective, all models are understood as "made up stories" (scientific or otherwise) and all are open to creative and critical exploration, like Wilson's "gambles".

The Western esoteric tradition

In addition to frameworks for destabilising the ontological certainty of mainstream academia, it is also important to note that there exists a lineage of Western scholarship that runs parallel with the mainstream, but that does not share its ontological or metaphysical assumptions—the Western esoteric traditions—lying somewhere in the interstices between science and religion, but accepted by neither. Unlike the positivist attitude of mainstream Western scholarship, which has denigrated the role and power of imagination since the Enlightenment (Harpur, 2002, p. 199), esoteric traditions see the imagination as a gateway to the world of the gods (Voss & Rowlandson, 2013, p. 4). The philosopher and scholar of Islam Henry Corbin (1903–1978), for example, spoke of what he called the *mundus imaginalis*, or the "imaginal world", as an ontologically independent realm that can be accessed through processes of "active imagination", as a form of mediation between the worlds (Corbin, 1964). The implications of Corbin's notion of "active imagination" for our understanding of the paranormal, and medium-ship in particular, are potentially wide-reaching. Angela Voss (2015) illustrates how an approach to the paranormal that begins from an esoteric—as opposed to positivist—perspective, might lead into new areas of engagement and understanding:

> I would like to suggest a way of redeeming the authenticity of visionary experience from both the scepticism of a literalist, physi-calist mentality and the reductionism—or concretisation—of "new age" credulity. As scientific discourse reaches its limits another mode of speaking is required to illuminate realms that lie beyond those limits and to do justice to the lived experience of encounters with other worlds; one which does not attempt to explain or sub-sume them to its own interpretations, but which engages with their ontological ground on its own terms. (p. 153)

A complete examination of the Western esoteric traditions and the role of the imaginal exceeds the limits of this book. It is clear, however, that many of the concepts and approaches of the esoteric tradition—including the *imaginal* and *active imagination*—could be of immense value in the development of a non-reductive anthropology of the para-normal. Indeed, it may even be the first step towards the emergence of what might be called a *metaphysical anthropology* (another step further still than the scope of this book, which lays the groundwork for the next leap forward).

* * *

Although only a very brief sketch of some quite complex ideas, some of these alternative epistemological frameworks mentioned above could be of practical use for the academic and ethnographic study of the marvellously liminal paranormal—allowing us to engage with it *on its own terms* without the need to impose arbitrary ontological brackets, or to attempt to distinguish between what *is* suitable and what *is not* suitable subject matter for social-scientific research. Furthermore, such approaches encourage us to be aware that any conclusions we come to are *never* representative of the *whole truth*. All models are simply *rough approximations* (gambles) of a certain *aspect* of the phenomenon under study, and are never complete.

An ethnographic approach that makes use of tools that destabilise ontological certainty—at least in the context of the ethnographic text, but also experientially in the field—might lead to a more honest appreciation of the "non-ordinary". In a sense, then, what I am suggesting is an approach that is, in many ways, the opposite of the traditional ontological bracketing approaches. Rather than bracketing out questions of ontology for fear that they might lead to truths ("damned facts" in Fort's terminology) that cannot, by their very nature, fit into the established order of Western academia's dominant ontology, I suggest that we essentially *open the flood gates of ontological possibilities*. This places all ontologies on an equal footing, so that while ontological bracketing (as employed in the social sciences) protects and reinforces the mainstream "consensus reality", what we might call *ontological flooding* destabilises it, and opens it up to questioning, exploration, and expansion—in essence such an approach places different ontological systems on an equally questionable footing—each is a gamble—encouraging us to *keep questioning* and to resist the temptation to conclude that we have sorted it all out.

Ontological flooding does not at all mean that we have to be any less critical in our approach, indeed we are encouraged to be *more critical*. Many, if not all, of the same critical themes (gender issues, social functionalism, class struggles, among numerous others) can (and should) continue to be examined and explored from the ontologically flooded perspective just as they always have been. The main difference is that we do not begin our investigation from the position of certainty that *our ontology is the only one that can really be taken seriously*. "We" might have it all wrong. Everything is equally possible, everything is equally questionable, and nothing is certain. This is not a rejection of science or the scientific method, but an expansion of it. What I am calling for is a return to awe and wonder in science.

Summary

To very briefly summarise the ideas presented in the preceding chapters, my research seeks to move away from "why" questions and notions of "belief" towards "how" questions and explorations of the *processes* and *experiences* of spirit mediumship. This emphasis on processes amounts to a rejection of oversimplified explanatory models taken as complete explanations of the phenomenon. In the words of Alfred North White-head, "At best such a system will remain only an approximation to the general truths which are sought" (Whitehead, 1978, p. 13), as it is evident that no single theory is capable of providing a completely satisfactory account of spirit mediumship. Such a shift in perspective also echoes recent developments in academic religious studies, a subject which has sought to move itself away from questions of the reality of religious phenomena (though I consider this a key concern), to the different ways in which people *experience* and *enact* religion (Olson, 2011, pp. 12–13). In addition to this, I aim to employ an experiential approach to my subject matter that focuses on the first-hand experiences of research informants, and to move away from questions of belief towards questions of ontology. This approach does not seek to explain away unusual experiences, but rather examines the processes that give rise to them. In order to achieve this I take a participatory approach that uses my own auto-ethnographic experiences with the group as a point of intersubjective common ground between myself and my informants. This places my research into the sub-disciplinary domains of the anthropology of consciousness, transpersonal anthropology, and paranthropology. The adoption of an ontologically fluid position (ontological flooding) that is simultaneously open to the possibility of genuine paranormal phenomena, but that does not make rigid *a priori* assumptions about the ultimate nature of such phenomena is central to this approach. We must be open to multiple interacting processes.

CHAPTER SIX

Rethinking the séance

The séance *protocol: between ritual and experiment*

The protocol for the séances held at the Bristol Spirit Lodge follows a fairly standard structure which takes direct inspiration from the séance procedures of the Scole Experimental Group (Solomon & Solomon, 1999; Keen, 2001; Foy, 2008), and Jenny's Sanctuary (see Bowie, 2013a for a comparison with the type of séance held at Jenny's Sanctuary).

Following the success of the Scole experiments in the 1990s (Foy, 2008), the group's founders published a set of guidelines for conducting successful physical séances. The guidelines were dictated by the group's communicating spirit team, led by the team's gatekeeper Manu (Solomon & Solomon, 1999, pp. 18–20). The guidebook ultimately took the form of a privately printed pamphlet entitled *A Basic Guide to the Development and Practice of the New Physical Psychic Phenomena* (Scole Group, 1996), which was distributed by members of the Scole group, operating under the banner of the New Spiritual Science Foundation. The pamphlet was given to other groups who wanted to replicate the extraordinary array of phenomena witnessed during the Scole experiments.[15]

To begin, the *Basic Guide* recommends that (1) "All members of the experimental group who seek to develop physical phenomena approach their group sessions with a totally open mind." This attitude of open-minded receptivity—as we shall see later—is thought to be an *essential* component in the manifestation of psi phenomena, and is deliberately fostered by participants at the Bristol Spirit Lodge. The next stage is the so-called (2) "Rainbow Bridge" phase, during which, with the aid of calming music, participants meditate, relax, and try to connect with the group's spirit team. (3) The circle leader must then read the "opening prayer", which sets the intent for the séance. The *Basic Guide* does not prescribe a specific prayer, or draw from any one particular religious tradition, but it does give some ideas about what this prayer should include. The Scole group's spirit team explain through their entranced mediums:

> It is felt that the opening prayer should be very much of a universal nature—in other words, a modern and non-denominational way of prayer that reaches into a universal love which encompasses all faiths, and adds to all faiths, because love knows no barriers and no boundaries. Although the exact form of prayer to be used is a matter for individual choice, it is felt that for the maximum benefit, the prayer should be addressed to the infinite spirit—creative source of all things, and to the spirit friends, helpers and guides of the experimental group.

In addition, it is advised that the opening prayer invite protection from the group's spirit guides, and ask that they assist in the production of physical phenomena. Christine understands this as a "setting of intent" for the séance that follows.

Music is used throughout the séance both as a structuring device—for example to highlight the beginning and end of the séance, or to allow space between different spirit communicators—and as a means of "raising the vibration", that is, producing a friendly and energetic atmosphere in the séance room. The more upbeat the music, the more conducive it is to the manifestation of spirits.

---

[15] The document is now available online, see: http://biofieldimaging.com/uploads/1/1/0/0/11003629/spiritual_science_basic_guide.pdf (accessed April 18, 2020).

The guidebook further suggests that (4) *communication* with spirits (i.e., a *dialogue*) is essential if physical phenomena are to be produced, and that this communication is most easily initiated through the cultivation of altered states of consciousness:

> Communication is therefore the initial aim of every group, and it will come through the altered state of consciousness of one or more of the group members. This is likely to be just a light form of control by the spirit guides and helpers in the first instance, but will move on to a much deeper level as it progresses, so that the person or persons who are used in this way will eventually be totally unaware of any messages, information or advice which is given through them in this way.

(5) Once a firm line of communication with the spirit team has been established—which may take many weeks or months—the guidebook anticipates that physical phenomena will eventually begin to manifest in the séance room (lights, levitations, apports, and so on). Following the demonstration of such physical effects by the spirits, the guidebook next recommends a (6) "healing procedure", whereby the group's guides are asked to use any left-over energy for healing the participants. The healing procedure is then followed by the (7) "closing prayer", which closes down the circle.

The structure of séances at the Bristol Spirit Lodge

In accordance with the procedure outlined above, every séance at the Bristol Spirit Lodge commences with a "non-denominational" prayer addressed to the Heavenly Father. The opening prayer reads as follows:

> Heavenly Father and Spirit Friends. We ask that you draw close to us tonight. We are sitting together in Love and Light, and are working only for the highest good. We invite communication with the spirit world, that is evidential of continuing life and consciousness. We invite physical phenomena that may be witnessed by us all, and be spoken about to others, so that they too may become open towards belief. We thank Spirit for their Love and Protection and ask for a circular canopy to be placed over us all. Thank you, amen.

This prayer serves to provide *protection* for the medium and sitters from the unwanted negative influence of low-level spirit entities—who might otherwise interfere if given the chance—and simultaneously serves to draw down positive entities and spiritual energies closer to the Lodge to participate in the séance. As already mentioned, the prayer is also understood as a means of "setting the intent" for the séance. The line "We invite physical phenomena ...", for example, may be substituted for other desired phenomena—whether for healing, transfiguration, materialisation, etc. The prayer may also be understood as a symbolic separation of the séance from the everyday world of the mundane outside the Lodge, much like the casting of the circle in the practice of ritual magic (L. Hume, 1998). The closing prayer serves the reverse function and *bookends* the séance—that is, it helps to dissipate any remaining spiritual energies, usually asking that they be used for the purpose of healing, as recommended by the Scole guidebook. Every séance is, then, also a healing session:

> We thank Spirit for their Love and Protection. We thank Spirit for all they have achieved. We ask for Spirit to close us down now, and to use any excess energy within this room for the purpose of healing. May Love and Protection remain with us all until we meet again. Thank you, amen.

This represents a symbolic ending to communication with the spirits, and provides a sense of closure to the séance—returning the group to its normal state, ready for participants to re-emerge from the gloom of the Lodge into the garden. Both opening and closing prayers emphasise the importance of "Love", "Light", and "Protection" during and after the séance, and also highlight one of the perceived inherent dangers of mediumship, the danger of attracting negative, or lower-level, entities—known as "spirit attachment".

After the close of the séance mediums and sitters retire to the dining room to drink tea and eat cakes and biscuits, which is just as much a part of the ritual process as anything else. Over tea and cakes, sitters are able to share their experiences and sensations during the séance with the rest of the group, and to try to make sense of what they have witnessed. It provides a space for sitters to discuss their shared experiences in the séance room, and to validate one another's anomalous perceptions. Here, Pat, a regular sitter, describes the sense of community this sharing of experiences engenders in participants:

> … after sitting in the lodge for the séance—round the table, eating everything in sight—I felt like the other sitters and myself were more close—like we had a common affiliation and unity—not just because we have a similar interest. It seemed like more than that. If that makes any sense! (Pat, comments after séance, October 2011)

Like many rituals, the séance can be interpreted through the lens of Arnold van Gennep (1873–1953) and Victor Turner's (1920–1983) famous "structure—anti-structure—structure" scheme. The séance itself is, to borrow Victor Turner's phrase, archetypically *liminal* in nature. The time during which the medium's body is occupied by discarnate entities may be thought of as a period of anti-structure, during which the boundaries between the living and the dead become thinner: the medium is an embodiment of the "betwixt and between". Parapsychologist George Hansen (2001) has suggested that this sense of the liminal is particularly conducive to the manifestation of psi and other paranormal phenomena—when we are *between* worlds and the everyday is turned upside down. Victor Turner describes this ritual structure:

> The first phase (of separation) comprises symbolic behaviour signifying the detachment of the individual or group from an earlier fixed point in the social structure, from a set of cultural conditions (a "state"), or from both. During the intervening "liminal" period, the characteristics of the ritual subject (the "passenger"), are ambiguous; he passes through a cultural realm that has few or none of the attributes of the past or coming state. In the third phase (reaggregation or reincorporation), the passage is consummated. (2002, p. 359)

As Pat's comments above indicate, there is a sense of collective bonding after the séance—a "common affiliation and unity" that arises following the ritual and the experiences that go with it. Indeed, Pat's account almost perfectly captures the essence of Edith Turner's concept of *communitas*—characterised as "togetherness itself" (2012, p. 4)—which often follows in the wake of rituals structured in this way—"not just because we have a similar interest. It seemed like *more than that*" (my italics).

Séance as performance

The séance—as well as other forms of mediumistic demonstration from different cultural traditions—undoubtedly possesses a *performative* element (Lehman, 2009; Natale, 2011). Like an actor on the stage or on the screen, or a magician in the theatre, mediums of different kinds *perform with their bodies* in front of an audience—sometimes on a stage, sometimes from a lectern, or within a circle of sitters, and occasionally even in a designated area called a "cabinet". In calling the séance a performance, however, it is not my intention to suggest that it is all "make-believe". Performance theorist Richard Schechner defines the term "performance" broadly:

> Performance is an inclusive term. Theater is only one node on a continuum that reaches from the ritualizations of animals (including humans) through performances in everyday life—greetings, displays of emotion, family scenes, professional roles, and so on—through to play, sports, theater, dance, ceremonies, rites and performances of great magnitude. (1988, p. xii)

The séance, then, is a very particular kind of performance with a very particular purpose. During the séance *all eyes are on the medium*. They are the locus of attention in the séance room—the conduit between the worlds. Jim Steinmeyer, an historian of stage magic and illusions, has highlighted the significance of the medium as a "conductor of experience" during the séance. He uses the following scenario to illustrate his point:

> This evening, if a painting were to fall off your wall, you might think nothing of it—a frayed wire or a loose nail. You might repair it tomorrow and forget that it ever happened. But, if a medium were holding a séance in that room at the precise moment that the picture fell, that single incident could change your life. The only difference is the medium, who directs your attention and provides the interpretations. When the painting falls, it is a special effect. It is the presentation of a séance that makes it magic. (2004, p. 180)

As the centre of attention during a séance the medium is able to influence—if not entirely hand to us—the interpretation of the events we are witnessing, in much the same way as a stage magician performing tricks can—they become a *conductor of consciousness*. The medium, after all, tells us *what* we should expect to experience in the séance, and explains to us the nature of the phenomena (the usual interpretation being that they are produced by non-physical entities). *They* tell us that they will go into a trance state to allow the spirits to manifest through their bodies. Despite the parallels that exist between mediums and stage magicians, however, it is important to point out that professional magicians are not *always* able to reproduce the types of phenomena produced by mediums, especially under the kinds of control conditions so many mediums have historically been subjected to. I am not suggesting, therefore, that stage magic and spirit mediumship are the same thing, or that the phenomena of physical mediumship are *necessarily* tricks or illusions, just that they share illuminating similarities and may make use of similar *processes of consciousness modulation*.

From this perspective, the only difference between a medium and a stage magician is that the medium is alleged to be able to produce *genuine parapsychological phenomena*, while the magician performs self-confessed tricks, which are often "impressions" of paranormal phenomena (Burger, 2012). This is a part of the stage magician's charm and charisma; they do not necessarily intend to *convince* the audience that the effects being produced are genuinely paranormal (though a good trick may give the illusion of a genuine paranormal phenomenon) as there is an implicit understanding that the magician is performing illusions *intended to deceive* the audience. We go to see a magician precisely because we *want* to be tricked. This is not the case with a medium—we *do not* want to be tricked.

Peter Lamont and Richard Wiseman, in discussing the similarities and differences between stage magicians and those they term "pseudo-psychics" (which clearly suggests an unwillingness to entertain the *possibility* that *some* mediums and psychics may well be genuine), point out the importance of understanding the way in which a particular performance is *framed*. They suggest that:

> … rather than making a sharp distinction between magician and pseudo-psychic, it might be more appropriate to think of a spectrum along which individual performers may be placed, according to how their performances are framed … differences between what the magician does and what the pseudo-psychic does may be

identified in terms of how the effect is presented, how the effect is framed by the spectator, and how the method is executed. (1999, pp. 104–105)

Using this interpretive framework, then, much as Steinmeyer suggests, mediumship performances are framed *as though the medium is able to produce genuine paranormal phenomena*, while the performances of stage magicians come with an implicit understanding that the effects witnessed are the product of non-paranormal tricks, which although they may appear real are in actuality the result of carefully designed illusions.

The equivocation of stage magicians and mediums makes perfect sense if we are to assume that there is no possibility of the medium actually being able to manifest paranormal phenomena (as Lamont and Wiseman evidently believe). From this perspective, all mediums *must*, by necessity, be "pseudo-psychics"—magicians framing themselves as if they are the *real thing*. But, as we have seen in previous chapters, this automatic blanket dismissal of the *possibility* of the paranormal does not lend itself particularly well to gaining a deeper anthropological understanding of mediumship practices and experiences, nor of the world view that they are expressions of. For example, the anthropologist John Beattie has highlighted precisely the dangers of applying these sorts of *etic* ontological assumptions to the mediumistic performances of other societies around the world. He writes in particular of his initial assumptions when faced for the first time with Bunyoro possession performances in Uganda:

> The first of these [assumptions] was that a medium had to be either in a state of possession, a genuine trance, or in a condition of normal everyday awareness. This too sharp disjunction allowed for no intermediate conditions; that there might perhaps be degrees of dissociation. And the second false assumption ... was that if "possession" was in some sense and in some degree an "act" consciously performed, it followed that the whole thing was therefore fraudulent, a mere trick and not to be taken seriously. It did not take me very long to realise that this view was naïve and superficial. (1977, p. 2)

Here Beattie suggests that we should avoid making the overly simplistic assumption that during mediumistic performances the medium is *either genuinely experiencing* an altered state of consciousness or *faking it*—of assuming that it is a simple case of one or the other. Instead, so Beattie argues, there must be room in our interpretive framework for the *possibility* that, for instance, a medium may experience genuine ASCs on some occasions while on others he or she may experience a different state of consciousness, while on further occasions the medium may not experience an ASC at all, and consequently will have to "pretend" to be in trance in order to keep up appearances. This does not, of course, detract from the reality of their previous ASCs, or even from the efficacy of their performance in that particular instance. In other words, a mediumistic performance may be one thing on one day, and another thing on the next day, but this is not evidence of "fraud", at least not in the sense of the word as employed by debunkers and sceptics of the paranormal.

The cultural perspective dominant in Euro-American societies that performance is essentially "only role playing", or that performance is just "pretending" (Foley, 1985, p. 27), does not necessarily apply to the performances of other societies (or, indeed, to sub-cultural systems within dominant Euro-American culture), where such clear-cut categories of distinction may not exist at all. Elaborating on these themes and ideas Richard Schechner writes:

> When, in western theatre, we speak of an actor "portraying a role," using a metaphor from painting where the artist studies a subject and produces an image of that subject, we slide away from the main fact of performance: that the "portrayal" is a transformation of the performer's body/mind—"the canvas" or "material" is the performer. (1988, p. 175)

Here Schechner opens up the possibility that performance—and acting in particular—can be more than mere "pretending". Indeed, Schechner argues that the process of performing a particular role can be understood as an actual *transformation* from one state to another. From this perspective the medium does not "pretend" to embody a spirit, but actually *becomes* one through the process of bodily performance. Here Schechner, like the later ontological anthropologists, is trying to move *beyond representationalism* and *symbolism*—beyond the limitations of Western academic ontology—to embrace an alternative ontological position. Performance is not simply "representational" or "symbolic", but is also an *actual transformation*.

Schechner further addresses these issues in his discussion of what he calls the "efficacy-entertainment braid", which he defines as a hypothetical continuum along which performances may be classified according to whether their function is for *efficacy* (to affect transformation in the world) or simply for *entertainment*. This is identified as a continuum, rather than as discrete categories, because a performance can never be *absolutely* either one or the other. A performance may, however, be situated closer to one side of the spectrum than another. Schechner considers spirit possession performances, for instance, to lean more towards the efficacy end of the spectrum, because the performance is geared towards the *transformation* of the medium through the *embodiment* of spiritual beings for *communally significant purposes*. Nevertheless, the performance will still, unavoidably, possess many of the characteristics of an entertainment spectacle—something unusual to be seen, a drama to be watched (Schechner, 1988, p. 120). A physical mediumship séance is a particularly good example of this idea in practice. While simultaneously being a performance in which spirits are incorporated—to demonstrate the survival of consciousness after death, or to seek the advice of the spirits—the séance is *also* an entertaining and exotic spectacle. Sitters may, then, equally attend for *both* spiritual *and* entertainment purposes (we could also add folk-scientific purposes here as well). This is certainly the impression I have received from my experience attending séances at the Bristol Spirit Lodge—it is *fun* and *serious* at the same time.

What we observe in the mediumistic performance should not, therefore, be dismissed as *simply* "role playing", "trickery", or "entertainment" (as enticing as the option might seem at times). We must try to get beyond our own cultural hang-ups about what a performance actually *is, and engage with an alternative perspective*. As critical observers we should attempt to understand the performance as it is understood within its own cultural and ontological matrix. The séance *must* be understood from the perspective that when the medium enters into their trance state and speaks, dances, or sings as a discarnate entity, they *become* that entity, because this is the perspective of believers and practitioners themselves, and it is the only perspective through which such practices make sense to them. This is a sentiment echoed in Eduardo Viveiros de Castro's seminal paper on "Amerindian Perspectivism", in which he explains that during Amerindian shamanistic performances in the Amazon the "performer" actually *transforms* and *becomes* the animal or spirit they are enacting:

> It is not so much that the body is a clothing but rather that clothing is a body. We are dealing with societies which inscribe efficacious meanings onto the skin, and which use animal masks ... endowed with the power metaphysically to transform the identities of those who wear them, if used in the appropriate ritual context. To put on mask-clothing is not so much to conceal a human essence beneath an animal appearance, but rather to activate the powers of a different body. The animal clothes that shamans use to travel the cosmos are not fantasies but instruments: they are akin to diving equipment, or space suits, and not to carnival masks. (2002, p. 482)

We *could*, therefore, understand the performances of trance and physical mediums in a similar way, though in a slightly different cultural and ontological context—not as "fantasy role-play", but as *instruments* designed to produce specific effects both in the medium and in those participating in the séance. Performance is a *technique* for transformation and consciousness alteration.

Trickery and efficacy

Spirit mediumship, then, is almost certainly a form of performance, but, as we have seen, this does not detract from the *possibility* that *something* more profound might *also* be taking place. Firth (1967), for instance, has suggested that mediumistic performances may have a considerable therapeutic effect for those involved, an idea that is famously exemplified by the case of the Kwakiutl healer Quesalid (see below). Sociologist James McClenon (1993) has also argued that shamanistic performances operate in a similar fashion, utilising subconscious cues and what he calls "wondrous events" (demonstrations of supernormal abilities, such as fire-walking, body skewering, or the handling and eating of hot coals) to provide experiential proofs of the reality of the shaman's abilities, which in turn leads to genuine physiological healing in the patient through processes of psychoneuroimmunological suggestion (Ray, 2004). Through performing "wondrous events" the shamanistic healer demonstrates their power, which in turn convinces the patient that they *can* be healed. This can be likened to the efficacy of placebos in medical trials, and very likely involves complex psychoneuroimmunological processes (Winkelman, 2000, p. 209). This section will deal with the implications of trickery as an efficacious feature of shamanistic and spirit possession traditions, and its implications for ethnographic interpretation.

Claude Lévi-Strauss's (1908–2009) famous retelling of the story of Quesalid, a Kwakiutl medicine man, is a useful account to highlight the relationship between trickery and efficacy in shamanistic healing. Quesalid, who was interviewed by the ethnologist Franz Boas (1858–1942) in the 1920s, was a shaman who did not believe in the power of his teachers. He understood their practices to be little more than charlatanry aimed at fooling sick and vulnerable patients. Nevertheless, as a precondition of being initiated into the secrets of his teachers, Quesalid was required to learn their traditional healing techniques, which Lévi-Strauss describes as:

> ... a curious mixture of pantomime, prestidigitation, and empirical knowledge, including the art of simulating fainting and nervous fits, the learning of sacred songs, the technique for inducing vomiting ... precise notions of auscultation and obstetrics, and the use of "dreamers", that is, spies who listen to private conversations and secretly convey to the shaman bits of information concerning the origins and symptoms of the ills suffered by different people. (1986, p. 175)

Before he had a chance to leave his apprenticeship, however, Quesalid was summoned to treat a sick person who had dreamed of him as their healer. The inclusion of this dream-calling element adds another interesting layer of paranormality to the account, but a discussion of paranormal dreams exceeds the limitations of this book. Despite his doubts about the efficacy of the techniques he had learned as part of his traditional training, Quesalid had no choice but to use them to treat his patient. To his great surprise, Quesalid's treatment was successful and the sick person was soon healed. Eventually Quesalid came to be widely regarded as a powerful healer, and even came to consider the methods he had learned from his own traditional teachers as superior in their ability to heal to those of other shamans from different tribal groups (Lévi-Strauss, 1986, pp. 176–178). His performances—despite consisting of very deliberate acts of deception (prestidigitation, simulated fainting, induced vomiting, "dreamer" spies)—were entirely *effective* cures of illness. Such accounts go a long way towards demonstrating the complex relationship between performance, belief, consciousness, and the body.

Although Quesalid was essentially performing tricks, and so deliberately deceiving his patients, his cures were ultimately effective, and as such surely cannot be interpreted as *fraudulent*. In this context, then, acts of deception (such as simulating fainting and prestidigitation), are perhaps best understood as a *deliberate manipulation of perceived reality for the purpose of affecting change in the world*, beginning first at the level of conscious perception, and then at the physiological level of healing.

Altered and magical consciousness

In the liminal darkness (or red light) of the spirit lodge, sitters immerse themselves in an atmosphere of what Rudolf Otto (1958) called the *numinous*—a sense of uncanny awe at a much wider, and hitherto hidden, perspective on a vastly mysterious reality. For Otto, the numinous is the pure essence of religion, its "non-rational" aspect—an irreducible "feeling response" that lies at the *core* of religious experience. This feeling response, in the context of the Bristol Spirit Lodge, seems to be facilitated through a combination of stimuli—environmental, symbolic, performative, and ritualistic—aimed at the induction of altered states of consciousness, through which might be glimpsed hints of that wider world of spirit. These cues would include:

1. Entering the sacred space of the Lodge and leaving the "everyday" mundane world behind.
2. Prayers clearly denoting entrance into a liminal zone in which spirit interaction becomes   possible, setting the necessary intent, mindset, and desire for something to occur.
3. The medium as a halfway point between the realm of human life and spirit, effectively   blurring the distinction between the living and the dead, and dissolving binary oppositions (a hallmark of liminality).
4. Darkness (or partial darkness in red light) and its effect on perception. Noll (1985), for example, has suggested that many shamanistic practices are specifically concerned with cultivating the vividness of

mental imagery and improving control over the way it unfolds, very often using darkness to induce such perceptions (see also Storm & Rock, 2009).

5. The use of music within this context as a means of both inducing and modulating the trance state. Edith Turner has characterised music as a "fail-safe bearer of communitas, significantly because it is the genre that is by its very nature most ephemeral" (2012, p. 4).

The combination of these factors, in addition to the general positive atmosphere of relaxation and meditation among the sitters, likely assists in the induction of "magical consciousness" in participants, characterised by a form of "creative thinking that goes beyond the immediately apparent" (Greenwood, 2013). According to Susan Greenwood's reframing of magical consciousness, such states result in an *increase* in sensitivity to coincidence, and the emergence of a frame of mind in which "meaning" becomes a central aspect of experience. Such a state of consciousness may be efficacious in facilitating the manifestation of séance phenomena, as well as in assisting the medium in the development of his or her trance state. Magical consciousness may explain how a séance is able to become more than the sum of its parts—moving, in Schroll and Krippner's (2016) terms, from *event* to *experience*. In this context, the séance performance/ritual constitutes the *event*, and the subjective first-person perceptions of the sitters constitute the *experience*—including the *meaning* the sitters derive from the event. Magical thinking, therefore, is not *just* a cognitive state, but also gives rise to real psycho-physiological effects.

Sidney Greenfield made a similar observation with regard to the altered states of the patients in his analysis of Spiritist surgery in Brazil in the 1990s, suggesting that patients, as well as the mediums treating them, must be in altered states of consciousness during their surgical procedures. He writes of the patients:

> All displayed the same "body language," regardless of age, gender or social status. They were perfectly calm, almost motionless unless instructed to move, with faces whose expressions can best be described as placid, perhaps even serene. This demeanor did not change when they were stabbed, sliced, or punctured during a treatment procedure ... they were in fact participating in the therapeutic ritual interacting as a patient or an observer. (2008, pp. 89–90)

Although sitters at the Bristol Spirit Lodge rarely enter trance states as deep as those described by Greenfield (though occasionally they might), alterations of consciousness in sitters—whether *light* or *deep*—nevertheless play an important role in the unfolding of the séance performance. This perspective, therefore, suggests that mediumship and its associated phenomena are *collectively manifested*, as part of a wider socio-psychological process involving *both* mediums and sitters—a collective performance accentuated by magical thinking and altered states of consciousness. Indeed, this notion is attested to by the spirits communicating at the Lodge. When asked about the nature of facial transfiguration phenomena, for example, Charlie, Jon's main spirit control, stated that what we observe in the séance is the product of multiple interacting causal factors:

> The energy around the [medium's] body is changing and being manipulated. This causes your perception to not see what it is used to seeing. At the same time you are within the same building in close proximity to this energy ... your perception is also being changed ... It is a combination which results in what you perceive, but it is not reliant totally upon you ... (Transcribed from a séance recorded February 18, 2009)

The séance might best be understood, then, as a *complex system of symbols, ritual acts, and performances that seek to cultivate altered and magical states of consciousness in participants. These psycho-physiological states in turn facilitate the manifestation of spirits and psi effects through processes of performance and social interaction* (dialogue).

Dual nature: both/and

In her discussion of the Ihamba healing ritual of the Ndembu in Zambia, Edith Turner considers the role of trickery when she comments on the "spirit tooth" extracted from the back of the patient at the heart of the ceremony. Turner describes the tooth as "the material prize gained from the long morning of ritual" (2002, p. 169; 1992). She notes that this material object was thought of by the Ndembu as *one-and-the-same-thing* as the spirit-form that had been witnessed at the ritual's climax (1992, 1993). Turner argues that the spirit tooth possesses a "dual nature", at the same time as being a normal, everyday, physical human tooth (that may or may not have been used in a manner we would class as *trickery*, such as palming, or prestidigitation); it was *also* the material receptacle for the immaterial Ihamba spirit—an expression of the spirit itself. The mundane tooth was considered to contain a very real power, or energy, requiring careful ritual treatment—including feeding the tooth/spirit with blood (1992, pp. 156–157). In the context of the ritual, the tooth and the spirit become one. The Ndembu did not see a contradiction in the idea that a mundane physical object can have a dual nature, *both sacred and profane* simultaneously. I would suggest that performance—and especially mediumistic performance—can also partake of such a dual nature—blurring the boundaries between the sacred and the profane in the body of the medium. Turner writes:

> … Meru's affliction by a human tooth looks impossible; in the West the only words for such a process are "trickery," "sleight of hand," and the like. But these terms derive from a quite different world from the scene at Mulandu farm. (1992, p. 169)

A similar theme emerges in the annals of psychical research, where the presence of trickery does not *always* imply the non-existence of genuine paranormal séance phenomena. The case of the Italian medium Eusapia Palladino (1854–1918), for example, provides a particularly good illustration of this dual nature in action (Hansen, 1990, p. 30; Alvarado, 1993). Palladino was rigorously investigated over the course of her long mediumistic career, and had successfully convinced several eminent scientists that her supernormal abilities were indeed genuine. The psychical researcher and physiologist Charles Richet (1850–1935), for example, is reported to have exclaimed that "All the men of science, without exception, who experimented with her were in the end convinced that she produced genuine phenomena" (cited in Johnson, 1955, p. 91; see also Tabori, 1968, pp. 142–163).

Regular features of Palladino's séances included trance communications from ostensible spirit entities, the levitation of tables and other items of furniture, the appearance of spirit lights, raps and bangs, the materialisation of ectoplasmic limbs and the production of anomalous winds and breezes (Alvarado, 2011, p. 79). On numerous occasions, however, Palladino was caught red-handed in the act of performing tricks—freeing her hands from the researchers' controls to manually lift and move objects, for example (Conan Doyle, 1926, p. 9; Johnson, 1955,

p. 91; Braude, 1997, p. 95). Further complicating matters, Palladino once told the Italian physiologist, criminologist, and psychical researcher Cesare Lombroso (1835–1909), "Watch me! You must watch me all the time—or I'll cheat. John King makes me do it!" (Tabori, 1968, p. 150). The spirit John King was Eusapia's primary control—apparently even her spirits were trickster-like. Despite the detection of such crude and self-confessed tricks, however, researchers continued to experience phenomena which could not, so they honestly thought, have been produced by fraudulent means (Alvarado, 2011, p. 78). As the philosopher and parapsychologist Stephen Braude suggests in reference to the Palladino investigations:

> The fact that a person cheats in some cases does not show that he cheats in all cases. The issue is not whether there are instances in which the medium apparently cheated, but whether there are instances in which the indications are strong that cheating did not occur. Besides, lapses in honesty may make good sense when one takes account of the psychodynamics of the person's life (e.g. the strong pressure to produce phenomena when the "power" is not forthcoming. (1997, p. 95)

Psychologist R. C. Johnson (1901–1987), in his book *Psychical Research* (1955), suggests a further explanation for Eusapia Palladino's trickery. He reminds us that "When a medium is in trance we should not necessarily expect the same standard of conduct as would be anticipated in the normal state," and suggests that there is evidence to indicate that "In a trance a medium is sometimes very suggestible, and that if there are suspicions of fraud in the minds of investigators, they may be communicated to deeper levels of the medium's mind and productive of this very thing" (p. 91). We could perhaps call this "unconscious fraud" (Frazer, 1890, pp. 52–53). Interestingly, this notion is echoed in the following quote from Billy, a member of Jon's spirit team at the Bristol Spirit Lodge, who gave the following perspective when asked about the practice of physical mediumship:

> … you have to remember it's not him [the medium]. It's easy to think just because he's got a name and a physical body that he's doing it. He's not doing anything! He's just sitting there going for a sleep, and that's where a lot of people get upset, because they think

it's him, and they get all angry with him because he's not doing what they think he should be doing, and then the rest of his [spirit team] come through, they're giving their demonstrations and just because they don't demonstrate what people want him to demonstrate then they get angry with the poor chap. It's not his fault is it? And he's got the trust and faith to let the others come through and do what they want. He doesn't know what they are doing, or anything other than what people tell him afterwards. (Billy, through Jon, March 17, 2009)

To briefly summarise what I am trying to say here, when we see the medium's body during the incorporation of a particular spirit, we are no longer observing the medium's own conscious actions, but are instead observing the actions of the incorporating spirit. A *transformation* has taken place. From this perspective tricks, unconsciously performed by the medium, may be part of the conscious performance of the spirit—an element of their mode of expression.

To further explore how séance *performances* can have a dual nature, we now turn to psychical researcher Kenneth Batcheldor (1921–1988), whose research with "Spiritualist style" sitter groups working for the manifestation of psychokinesis (PK), explored the possibility that trickery might, in some way, assist in the development and manifestation of psi phenomena. He explains his rationale:

> ... it was inferred that artifacts [faked phenomena] ... acted as suggestions that paranormal events were already occurring. This would produce intense expectancy of further paranormal events, and this expectancy or belief might in turn release PK and cause genuine events to supervene. (1984)

Over the course of his experiments Batcheldor found that by introducing fake phenomena into the séance room he was able to influence the beliefs of his sitters (i.e., influencing them to believe that psi is real), so that they were eventually able to manifest genuine phenomena—to sort of kick-start the psychokinetic process. Trickery, then, can be understood as a modulator of both *experience* and *belief and so may actually perform an important function in séance performances.*

The detection of deliberate acts of trickery in the performances of mediums does not necessarily negate the entirety of their psychological, and parapsychological, repertoire. Nor should we assume that the detection of trickery necessarily detracts from the value and efficacy of the performance in the cultural/ontological matrix within which it occurs. Indeed, as we have seen in the case of the healer Quesalid, specific techniques of prestidigitation were effective in producing what could be considered genuine anomalous healing in sick individuals. Similarly, physical mediumship performances might also bring about genuine spiritual and psychophysiological benefits to sitters, whether or not the medium has introduced "artifacts" into the demonstration. As I have mentioned earlier, the sum of the séance seems much greater than its constituent parts.

If we are hoping to develop a non-reductive understanding of the practices of groups like the Bristol Spirit Lodge we will have to go beyond the confines of traditional Western rationalist interpretations of performance. Dominant academic culture makes it so easy to scoff at and dismiss such practices, but as researchers it is important that we try to overcome this limited view. Even if we are never *fully* able to enter into the ontological domain inhabited by those who regularly interact with spirits, by entertaining dual nature concepts, and incorporating perspectives from alternative ontological contexts, we can at perhaps move a little *closer* to that position.

The next section will examine the way that the body is used in the expression of personality, self, and discarnate spirits.

The medium's body

The body is the primary tool for the expression of our personalities and for the communication of our internal psychological states. This is achieved predominantly through the use of facial expressions, gestures, movements, and specific bodily postures (Argyle, 1987), but also through the transformational use of items of clothing, bodily decoration, and so on. The body is our interface with the physical world and our everyday means of communicating with each other, both verbally and non-verbally (Goffman, 1990; DePaulo, 1992, p. 203). Indeed, Eduardo Viveiros de Castro suggests that: "The body is the subject's fundamental expressive instrument and at the same time the object *par excellence*, that which is presented to the sight of others" (2002, p. 480). The way in which we use our bodies, therefore, is of key importance for the way that we are perceived as distinctive personalities.

In mediumship, the body is used to express more than one personality, and so it must be used in very specific ways in order for these different personalities to be perceived as distinct from the personality of the medium. During a séance the medium's body serves as the means for the "enactment" (Spanos, Menary, Gabora, DuBreuil, & Dewhirst, 1991, p. 308; Spanos, 1994, p. 147) or physical expression, of numerous, seemingly distinct personalities. I prefer to use the term personalities to refer to the spirits incorporated at the Bristol Spirit Lodge, rather than more neutral terms such as "agencies", primarily because this is how they are referred to and perceived by its members.

In many of the world's spirit possession traditions, including the Euro-American Spiritualist movement, a particular spirit or deity, when incorporated, is discerned through the performance of socially and culturally recognised behaviours that indicate the presence of a spirit, or personality, different from the medium's personality (Jules-Rosette, 1980, p. 2). Paul Stoller, for example, describes how the spirits incorporated by Songhay spirit mediums "assume ritualized postures and vocalize in ways characteristic of their families, which marks their powerful otherness" (1994, p. 65). Among the Kel Ewey Tuareg of Niger, women's trance performances involve a head dance known as *asul* which features "sideways movement of the head and neck, gradually becoming more vigorous and including the shoulders and torso" (Rasmussen, 1994, p. 74). Such behaviours might be thought of in terms of Marcel Mauss's notion of *habitus*, being culturally specific techniques of the body (Mauss, 1973, p. 75). For instance in the Afro-Brazilian religion of Batuque a medium *must* perform in a certain way if they are to be perceived as genuinely under the influence of an *encantado*, or supernatural being. Anthropologists Seth and Ruth Leacock describe this when they write:

> Although in the early moments of the trance there may be some uncontrolled movements, the medium must quickly gain control if his or her activity is to be interpreted as representing possession by a supernatural being. It is certainly not enough to fall on the floor and thrash around, or stagger about, or make incoherent sounds, or give other evidence of having some kind of unusual psychological experience. The meaning of this kind of behaviour is ambiguous in Batuque beliefs ... In order to prove that an *encantado* is really present, the medium must dance, sing the proper songs, and interact with the other participants in the ceremony in an acceptable

> manner. The behaviour that is most admired in the accomplished
> medium is very often the behaviour that appears the least frenzied
> and the most normal to the outside observer. (Leacock & Leacock,
> 1975, pp. 171–172)

To simply fall into trance, then, is not always enough to signify the presence of non-physical persons, though it is more often than not the first signifier. In order for spirits to be discerned, specific, culturally recognised behaviours are required (Csordas, 1990, p. 15), and these may take a long time to perfect. In this sense, therefore, the mediumship process may be understood as a complex form of *learned performance*. Levy, Mageo, and Howard, for example, write that "full possession behaviour is highly skilful", requiring "mastery of playing and of subtle, specialized kinds of communally significant communication" (1996, p. 18). Drawing on my own experience during a mediumship development session at the Bristol Spirit Lodge, in which my hand was apparently "possessed" (see next chapter), I would suggest that the process of learning to be a medium also involves knowing how to *relinquish* control of the body, without *losing* control—there is a delicate balance that has to be maintained during the trance demonstration. Bodily performance, therefore, plays a central role in the expression of the non-physical persons embodied by mediums in trance. In this context, as we have already seen, the word performance should not be read as an indicator that what the medium does is necessarily fake, fraudulent, or somehow "pretending" (Beattie, 1977, p. 2), rather it should be considered as a specific tool employed to allow ostensibly non-physical entities (whether ontologically distinct or aspects of the medium's subconscious) to express themselves in a socially and culturally recognised manner (Schechner, 1988, p. 175).

It should also be noted at this juncture that the use of the body as a focus point for the analysis of spirit possession does not necessarily help us to get any closer to understanding what spirit possession *really is*, or what it *means* to those who participate in it. Matthijs van de Port highlights this when he writes of his dissatisfaction:

> … this body that has now entered the anthropological text does not
> move us beyond the constructivist deadlock. To the contrary, all too
> often this body is merely a new object on which the constructivist
> project can feed itself and display its prowess. (2011, p. 28)

The recent emphasis on the body only takes us so far and is actually quite limiting. By focusing only on the body we are ignoring the much wider network of interrelated systems in operation during a spirit mediumship performance. As has been mentioned in previous chapters, no single explanatory or descriptive framework seems capable of doing justice to the complexity of the practice and experience of mediumship. A focus on the body and performance cannot, therefore, be taken as a *complete* solution to the problem, it simply highlights one interconnected part of the mediumship process as a whole. Is it possible, then, to move beyond the obvious observation that the body is used in spirit mediumship, to entertain new ideas about what is "possible" in the field, and to make headway into new ontological domains?

Blending with a spirt being

The term "blending" is frequently used by Western mediums and channellers, including members of the Bristol Spirit Lodge, to describe the *interconnectedness* of the medium's consciousness with that of the discarnate entity utilising their body as a vessel. Anthropologist Dureen Hughes has highlighted the positive connotations and sense of "harmony … between channel and entity" implied by the use of this term (1991, p. 166); though it is clear that this harmony develops over time—the initial experience can be quite terrifying (see next chapter).

As we have just discussed, when an entity is incorporated into the body of a medium it makes itself apparent to the outside world through manipulations of the medium's vocal tonality and physical demeanour. Afro-Brazilian Umbandaists, for example, believe that spirits and saints, known as *Orixas*, inhabit the bodies of spirit mediums during trance dance performances (St. Clair, 1971; V. Turner, 1985, pp. 129–130). Each Orixa has a favourite rhythm and a particular stylised dance, which are performed by musicians and mediums respectively, and which enable *differentiation* between the embodied *Orixas*. During the trance session, the medium's movements *are* the movements of the *Orixa* inhabiting the body; at that moment we could say that the *Orixa* and the medium are *blended*. Through performance the medium essentially *becomes* the *Orixa*. The medium *is* the spirit and the spirit *is* the medium. The dance performance becomes the the physical expression of the *Orixa*'s presence.

Similarly, according to the Yanomamo of the Orinoco Valley in Venezuela, the *shapori* (shaman) initiation process involves the *metamorphosis* (again the notion of *process* and *transformation*) of the initiate into a *hekura* spirit: "The shaman is correspondingly perceived by non-initiated Yanomami as something other than a human being; he is a living spirit in the flesh … [The] Yanomami term for shamanic initiation, *hekura prai*, can be translated as 'the metamorphosis of a human being into a hekura spirit, or human body into a cosmic body'" (Jokic, 2008a, pp. 38–39; see also Viveiros de Castro, 2002). While the *shapori* is inhabited by the spirits he carries out specific healing and divinatory tasks under their direct control and influence. To the outside observer this may appear to be an elaborate act, as if the *shapori* is "pretending" to be possessed by the *hekura*. To the Yanomami, however, the performance is a *blending together* of the human and spirit worlds: a performance that expresses and manifests the presence of non-physical entities in a culturally recognised manner.

What if, then, we were able to transpose something of this *transformational* perspective on shamanic and possession performance over into the domain of Western mediumship performances at the Bristol Spirit Lodge? Can we use lessons learned in alternative ontologies to interpret a different ethnographic context?

Recognising the bodily expression of spirit in Bristol

As with the *Orixas* of Umbanda and the *hekura* of the Yanomamo, the spirits at the Bristol Spirit Lodge also express themselves through the physical bodies of their hosts. In this section we will consider the processes involved in expression of discarnate entities, and how mediums and sitters *learn to recognise* the presence of distinctive spirit personalities.

When a spirit first makes itself known through an entranced medium at the Lodge the communication is often weak and it may take many developmental sittings for an individual spirit personality to fully express itself. Occasionally a personality will show the early signs of emerging (such as slight twitches of the medium's body following the onset of trance, or gurgling sounds indicative of an attempt to speak, for example), but might never reach its full expression as a regular communicator in the group. Such entities are sometimes referred to as "drop in communicators". Indeed, my own experience of falling into what the circle leader described as a "light trance state", during which my left arm moved of its own accord, was taken as a sign that a spirit entity was attempting to communicate through my own body (Hunter, 2009, 2012a), but never developed into a fully communicative personality.

It is the role of the circle leader to recognise these early signs and then to develop and encourage them through engaging them in *dialogue*. This is a process that involves drawing out and sustaining the subjective experiences of the trainee medium (usually dissociative experiences), of giving them a voice, and then of assisting in their development into fully formed spirit personalities. It could almost be thought of as a sort of *incubation* and *birthing process*—the social manifestation of spirits. The role of the circle leader at the Lodge is comparable, to a surprising degree, with that of the master of ceremonies in Kelantan Malay spirit mediumship practices, as described by Raymond Firth (1901–2002) in the 1960s. Firth writes that:

> The master of ceremonies plays a leading part in questioning the medium, interpreting what he says, and by his control of the musical accompaniment stimulates and guides the medium's actions. For the most part he adopts a quiet, rather neutral position in the verbal exchanges, agreeing with the putative spirit or commenting rather drily in a kind of "so, indeed" fashion ... Throughout he is recognised as the person having prime authority in the proceedings; at the symbolic level he is the "master of spirits", a shaman in the strict sense of the word. (1967, p. 199)

Firth's description of the role of the master of ceremonies matches almost exactly that assumed by Christine during séances. In drawing this comparison with Malay spirit possession rituals, I am not suggesting that what Christine and the Malay "master of ceremonies" are doing are *identical* practices. What I am suggesting, however, is that both culturally distinct modes of spirit communication make use of *underlying processes* that are necessary in order to bring spirit communicators into social reality. At the Bristol Spirit Lodge this process begins by first of all recognising the onset of trance, as Christine describes:

> Basically, sometimes within a séance situation they will crash out in spontaneous trance anyway, which is what happened with Sandy to start with. Then, often I'm unaware of it until time has passed,

and then I look over and I realise they're in that state. It's pretty obvious that they're in a trance state because they're unconscious. So it's very clear. If they are sitting for the purpose of development of trance then I would say the opening prayer, and encourage spirit to assist them in that way. Often as they're sitting they will feel the presence, and they will feel the presence of the spirit overtaking them really. I know that's happening, I can sense that's happening, but often their skin goes paler first, that's the first thing: skin goes paler, breathing changes. In some cases, when they're first aware of it, they will look somewhat alarmed or uncomfortable, and I become aware of that, and sometimes I find it amusing, but I can't help it. But, it's just interesting to see their reaction to this different feeling, a totally unfamiliar feeling. (Interview with Christine, 2013)

Christine's recognition of the trance state, therefore, depends on a combination of behavioural (the performative aspect discussed in the previous sections) and physiological observations (which could also be defined as broadly performative), and her own *sense* of an incorporating presence (the intuitive aspect, often facilitated by her guide FC). She further explains:

Some go with the flow easily, some resist it. In which case maybe it'll go away. Some just don't know what to do with it and are vaguely disconcerted by it. Some are just plain terrified, but that's unusual—it's just a case of "what the heck do I do with this, and what's it about?" But as they're usually sitting for trance, anyway, they would surely expect something to happen … there's lots of small things. (Interview with Christine, March 23, 2011)

Once the altered state of consciousness has been recognised, indicating that the medium is in the trance state (a *transitional* state), the circle leader will look out for further twitches, gestures, or patterns of movement, or particular sounds, in order to detect whether a spirit entity is attempting to communicate. Christine detects these changes, and hones in on them. She will continue to work on them until some form of interactive communication is achieved. For example, if a leg is seen to twitch, the circle leader may take note of this and might then ask, "Are you trying to move the medium's leg? If so, stamp twice to say yes."

Once a dialogue, however superficial, has been initiated, the personality of the spirit can begin to be expressed.

The strongest and most fully developed communicators generally form a group called a "spirit team". A medium will regularly channel the members of his or her spirit team, and these communicators come to be recognised by sitters as distinctive individual personalities. Because each personality must express itself through a single physical body, the spirits utilise exaggerated body movements and unusual vocal tones to differentiate themselves from one another. Occasionally the presence of a spirit is inferred simply by the physical posturing of the medium's body, and this posturing is recognised as signifying the presence of a distinct personality. Sandy explained how she first began manifesting spirits through her body:

> Sometimes, in the earliest days, they used to come through … presenting differently, and some of my movements would change. And depending on which spirit comes through depends on what I do with my hands, or, the one where I was dragging my leg, I just couldn't not drag my leg as I walked in. (Interview with Sandy, March 23, 2011)

Such exaggerated movements, postures, and vocalisations can often give the impression that the individual spirit personalities are caricatures, rather than complete personalities. It may, however, be a necessary part of the mediumship process (at least in the early stages of development), assisting in the development and expression in the social moment of strong, distinctive personalities: the exaggeration of postures, movements, and accents serves to signify the presence of a particular spirit-person. For example, a member of Sandy's spirit team called Elf (who we have already encountered in a previous section) is characterised by erratic movements of the arms and legs, as though swimming in the air, and he has a very high-pitched child-like voice. He is instantly recognisable by Christine and the group as soon as he begins to take control of Sandy's body. Graham the undertaker, another member of Sandy's spirit team, by contrast, presents as particularly large and heavy; he is broad-shouldered and has a deep, throaty voice that clearly distinguishes him from other members of the spirit team.

In some mediums (Sandy in particular) more than one spirit has, on occasion, presented *simultaneously* through the body of the medium (as Elf explained in Chapter 2). The psychical researcher Frederic Myers noted a similar capacity with the famous medium Eleonore Piper. He wrote: "In some cases ... two or more spirits may simultaneously control different portions of the same organism" (Myers, 1903, p. 248). In cases such as this, individual presences are inferred from the distinctive independent movements of certain body parts: for instance the legs may move in a manner distinctive to one particular personality, while the arms may behave in a completely different manner associated with the personality of another spirit. An illustrative example might be that Graham the undertaker would move his arms around heavily, moving slowly and lumberingly, whereas Elf might simultaneously be moving the legs around in an erratic and hyperactive manner—two spirit personalities manifesting simultaneously through a single physical body.

Anthropologist Nurit Bird-David describes a similar process of gestural expression of spirits in her analysis of the spirit possession performances of the south Indian Nayaka, in which nature spirits known as *devaru* are incorporated into the bodies of entranced mediums. She writes:

> The *devara* evoked often improvise on the same repetitive phrases. The saying, the voicing, the gesturing are important. These principal aspects of their behaviour are, in Bateson's terms ... meta-communication, namely, communicating that *devaru* are communicating, because the *devaru* are present as they move, talk, make gestures, etc. They are present as they communicate and socially interact with Nayaka. (1999, p. 76)

Exaggerated behaviours, then, can be thought of as a form of "meta-communication", signifying the fact that a distinct personality is present and communicating, and serving as a means to allow them to be communicated with as individuals in their own right, recognised as separate from the medium's personality by the sitters and the circle leader.

These are just some of the ways that the physical body is put to work in the séance to manifest the presence of distinctive spirit personalities. Once the presence has been recognised it must then be reinforced.

Dialogue and the reinforcement of spirit personalities

Over time the spirit teams of each medium will become regular fixtures at the Lodge's weekly séances and are treated in many ways as anyone else who attends regularly. Their personalities are continually checked against past recordings of communications as a means of ensuring the genuineness of the phenomenon. The Bristol Spirit Lodge website is full of recordings from séances, so it is easy enough to follow the development of individual spirit personalities. Christine has stated that she "will be looking to see if previous spirit communicators return and present themselves as previously. Any inconsistencies in voice tone or personality or information offered between the 'previous' and 'present' communications will be noticed (I compare audio recordings)" (personal communication with Christine, 2011). Through this regular interaction the spirit communicators become much more than abstractions; interaction enables them to manifest in a socially real and very tangible way. Social interaction essentially creates and sustains social entities.

Arguing along similar lines, Bird-David understands the *devaru* as relational persons, brought into social existence through interactions, specifically through conversation and dialogue. She writes that: "Keeping the conversation going is important because it keeps the Nayaka *devaru* interaction and in a sense the *devara* themselves 'alive'." Moreover, and remarkably similar to the practices of the Bristol Spirit Lodge, Bird-David describes the form this interaction takes as "highly personal, informal, and friendly", consisting of "joking, teasing, [and] bargaining". The conversations are said to include numerous repetitions or minor variations on a theme, in which the Nayaka and the *devaru* "nag and tease, praise and flatter, blame and cajole each other, expressing and demanding care and concern" (1999, p. 76). The interactions between spirits and sitters at the Bristol Spirit Lodge could equally be described in this way. Take the following séance transcript for example, which is a section of dialogue between Christine and the spirit Charlie:

Christine [circle leader]: Are you there yet Charlie?

Charlie [spirit]: Of course.

Christine: Is it OK to open the cabinet?

Charlie: If you wish.

Christine: I'll do it slowly [...] How are you?

Charlie: Very well, how are you?

Christine: Fine. We've been sitting in the dark. How was it for you?
Charlie: Wonderful, how was it for you?
Christine: Not too bad actually. I wouldn't say it was the best ever, but not too bad!
Charlie: Some people are never satisfied.

(Di Nucci & Hunter, 2009, pp. 158–159)

The tone of the interaction is very informal and is characteristic of the kinds of interactions that take place between the spirits, sitters, and circle leader. Charlie repeats Christine's questions immediately. This sort of quick back-and-forth exchange between the circle leader and the spirit will usually precede the more advanced, philosophical discussions which form the bulk of the communication (at least with those spirits who enjoy explaining their metaphysical systems). These quick dialogues might be understood, therefore, as a means to rapidly *build up* the personality of the communicator at the start of the séance through recognising and reinforcing the fact that another personality is present by engaging it in dialogue. It is almost as if the spirit needs rebooting, recharging, or revving up before any sustained dialogue can take place.

The idea that spirits require this sort of engagement in order to manifest is also common in other mediumship traditions, which suggests that it might be an important cross-cultural feature of the processes of mediumship development more generally. In her analysis of the Venezuelan mediumship tradition of Maria Lionza, for example, Placido describes how conversation provides the *means* for spirits to express themselves in the social moment:

> To exist … the spirits need to be able to speak. By allowing them to express themselves through the mediums and by listening to what they say, humans are somehow resuscitating them … It is through words and communication that the spirits are brought to life, in that it is during episodes of spirit possession that they are created, that they become social persons. (Placido, 2001, p. 214)

This emphasis on *interaction* with the spirits can be thought of as an analogue (if not pointing in quite the same ontological direction) of the socio-cognitive theory of dissociative identity disorder and past-life regression personalities, proposed by social psychologist Nicholas Spanos (1942–1994). According to this perspective the various personalities expressed during episodes of dissociative identity are conceived as "rule governed, contextually supported social constructions". Spanos argues that "secondary personality enactments" represent "joint constructions that are created, shaped, and maintained by the beliefs and expectations of significant others who constitute an interfacing audience, as well as by the actor who displays the secondary identity enactments" (Spanos, Menary, Gabora, DuBreuil, & Dewhirst, 1991, p. 308).

Despite the similarities in understanding the way in which these personalities are manifested in the Maria Lionza world view and the socio-cognitive model, there are clear differences in terms of the *ontological implications associated with these theories*. For the members of the Maria Lionza cult, amongst other mediumistic traditions (Stoller, 1994; Lambek, 1998; Bubandt, 2009), including the Bristol Spirit Lodge (Hunter, 2009, 2012d), the spirits are *very real* and play an important role in the group because "what they say matters" (Placido, 2001, p. 221), while for the socio-cognitivists the finding that alternative personality enactments are sustained through social interaction implies that they possess no form of independent ontological reality—confusing a *process* (social interaction) for a *complete explanation*.

I would not go so far as to conclude that the spirits communicated with at the Bristol Spirit Lodge are *simple* "social constructions", in fact they are perhaps better described as "complex social constructions". Rather I am suggesting an interpretation, based on the notion that ontologically distinct spirits *could* exist, and that these are precisely the kinds of social *processes through which they would make themselves known*. This leads to an understanding of the process of manifesting spirits as fundamentally interactive and social in nature, just as our own personalities are expressed and sustained in the world.

CHAPTER SEVEN

Mediumship and the experiential self

... our normal waking consciousness, rational consciousness as we call it, is but one special type of consciousness, whilst all about it, parted from it by the filmiest of screens, there lie potential forms of consciousness entirely different. We may go through life without suspecting their existence; but apply the requisite stimulus, and at a touch they are there in all their completeness, definite types of mentality which probably somewhere have their field of application and adaptation.

—William James, *The Varieties of Religious Experience* (2004, p. 335).

Certain domains of the mind, certain states of being, certain states of one's own consciousness, are so foreign-alien-weird-strange-unfamiliar to most other minds that they cannot listen to or read what one says or writes without becoming upset, or without using ready labels for the explorer, rendering one's efforts to communicate either negative or null and void.

—John C. Lilly, *The Deep Self* (1977, p. 72).

Mediumship development as consciousness exploration

Home-circles for the development of trance mediumship have seen a recent upsurge in popularity since the 1990s. The website *Spiritualist Resources*,[16] for example, features listings of numerous privately run home development circles, as well as psychic development circles within established Spiritualist churches in the United Kingdom and further afield. These home-circles represent an active—we might say *grass-roots*—effort to explore the extents and limitations of consciousness, the self, and the threshold between life and death. As has been alluded to before, the process of mediumship development could be understood as a sort of *folk-scientific experiment* investigating the nature of mind and reality. The development of mediumship itself might also be thought of as either a telescope looking outwards to spirits and non-local consciousness, or as a microscope looking inwards—as a tool for discovering the nature of mind and its relation to the physical body. To a certain extent, this understanding echoes that of nineteenth-century psychical researchers who saw mediums as scientific instruments, which has long been a feature of Spiritualism's "spiritual science" approach to the afterlife. The term "medium" itself also carries with it the notion of a technology. Emerging at roughly the same time as other technologies such as the telegraph, mediumship was frequently referred to as a "spiritual telegraph", providing a line of communication between the worlds and a scientific metaphor for understanding spiritual communication (Warner, 2006, p. 222). In this apparently "scientific" and "experimental" manner, mediumship development provides an opportunity for participants to *define for themselves* the nature of human personhood and consciousness—and of reality more generally—through their own *first-person experiential experimentation*.

Debates over the nature of consciousness and its relation to the physical body—including the question of whether or not consciousness can survive beyond the death of the body—have never been more culturally pervasive, and are intimately connected with the perceived opposition of science and religion that currently dominates mainstream Western culture (cf. Dawkins, 2006). The heated debates that rage between vocal sceptics and believers of the paranormal on the internet are just one example of this cultural phenomenon in action (McLuhan, 2010), as is the combative approach of the "new atheist" movement, epitomised by

---

[16] www.spiritualistresources.com/cgi-bin/circles/index.pl?page=1.

the writings of Richard Dawkins (2006), Christopher Hitchens (2007), and Sam Harris (2010). The furore that erupted in 2013 over the virtual denunciation by TED Foundation of lectures hosted on its platform on topics related to "non-local consciousness" by biologist Rupert Sheldrake (2013) and alternative historian Graham Hancock (2013), is also evidence of this cultural turbulence.[17] Their emphasis on "non-local consciousness" as a very real possibility was derided as "pseudoscientific" by the TED organisation's scientific advisory board.

Groups such as the Bristol Spirit Lodge operate in the borderlands between *both* science *and* religion, and are an example of how the contemporary debate over the nature of consciousness is played out, explored, and navigated in a very particular sociocultural context (in suburban Bristol)—equally as far removed from academic institutions and scientific laboratories as from the Church and other mainstream religious organisations.

With the proliferation of materialist neuroscientific approaches to the nature of consciousness, and the mainstream reduction of consciousness to an epiphenomenon of physiological brain function, or indeed the more extreme denial of consciousness altogether (see, for example, the work of philosophers such as Daniel Dennet), it would seem reasonable to also take into account the efforts of groups such as the Bristol Spirit Lodge to *experientially investigate* the qualitative nature of consciousness. See, for example, the publications of Kelly et al. (2007), Ward (2010), Nagel (2012), Sheldrake (2012), Tallis (2012), and Kastrup (2014), all of whom argue that the dominant quantitative materialist approach to consciousness is at best limited, and at worst deliberately ignorant of the implications of subjective experience—the so-called hard problem of consciousness (Nagel, 1974; Chalmers, 1995). If nothing else, an awareness of the experiences and folk-hypotheses of groups such as the Bristol Spirit Lodge (among others) can serve to supplement and balance the dominant materialist view of consciousness, and may be revealing of aspects of consciousness that would otherwise go unnoticed.

Spirit mediumship and the experiential self

This chapter explores the possibility that the self is an *experiential* phenomenon, as distinct from the classical anthropological understanding of the self as a prescribed cultural category. The notion of the self as

---

[17] See *Paranthropology* Vol. 4, No. 2 for an exploration of these events.

a *cultural* category has been prevalent in anthropology since (at least) the work of the French sociologist Marcel Mauss (1872–1950). This chapter will introduce key historical developments in the anthropology of selfhood from Mauss onwards, focusing on the different ways the self has been defined by ethnographers working in the field. We will also briefly survey the anthropological distinction between Western and non-Western models of the self to set the scene for the discussion that follows.

Against this background, I would like to suggest that the self is *something more* than a cultural category. This is not to say, of course, that culture plays no role in the development of self conceptions. Indeed I shall argue that, rather than being the source of self concepts, culture might best understood as a filtration system, or as a modulator, through which experiences are given meaning and interpreted. Often, however, cultural notions become fixed, and are passed on as given *fact*: they can be taken as normative, prescriptive descriptions of all that it is possible for the self to be. In such situations individuals who experience alternative modes of the self may find that their own experiential understanding of the nature of the self is at odds with the normative models of their host culture (unless, of course, their culture takes into account a wider perspective of the nature of self and consciousness; for instance see Laughlin's (2013) distinction between "monophasic" and "polyphasic" cultures).

This is nowhere more clearly demonstrated than in the context of post-industrial Euro-American society, where the dominant paradigms of materialist science define consciousness—and consequently the self—as little more than an epiphenomenon of physiological brain function—as a by-product and an illusion (cf. Crick, 1994). I argue that through adopting an understanding of the self as an experiential phenomenon (that is, as something that is *experientially constructed*, rather than culturally generated) it is possible to move away from overly reductive explanatory models towards something more complex. An approach that emphasises the self as something that is experientially defined also helps us to understand why and how different self-concepts develop cross-culturally. Embracing the experiential dimensions of consciousness and self requires that we consider the implications of the widest variety of self-experiences that are reported by human beings across the world—including those of mediums and other extraordinary individuals.

As has already been suggested, mediums at the Bristol Spirit Lodge *experimentally* and *experientially* explore the nature of consciousness and self through the practice and development of trance and physical mediumship, which involve the incubation of altered states of consciousness during which spirit personalities communicate with sitters in the context of séances (Hunter, 2012d). Ultimately, through the development of this practice, mediums (and sitters) adopt models of consciousness and the self that seem to exceed what anthropologists have historically referred to as the "Western" conception of the self, in spite of the fact that in their daily lives they are immersed in mainstream Western culture. There are, perhaps, interesting parallels here with the work of Tanya Luhrmann among American Evangelicals, whose experiences communing with God have similarly led to alternative conceptions of the self (Luhrmann, 2012). Furthermore, and intriguingly, these conceptions of the self appear to exceed the standard models of mainstream materialist science, which might suggest that this line of inquiry also has *ontological* implications—that we might be making inroads into other domains of *reality*.

What is the self? Definitions and dimensions

Marcel Mauss's famous paper "A Category of the Human Mind: the Notion of Person; the Notion of Self" (1938) is frequently used as a starting point in discussions of the anthropology of personhood and selfhood (cf. Carrithers, Collins, & Lukes, 1985), and this chapter will be no exception. In his writings, Mauss often employed the terms "self" and "person" interchangeably, which has become a common trait in the wider scholarly discourse. "What I wish to show you", Mauss writes, "is the succession of forms that this concept [the category of self] has taken on in the life of men in different societies, according to their systems of law, religion, customs, social structures and mentality" (Mauss, 1938, p. 3). The specific concern he addresses in his influential paper is the development of what he calls *conceptions* of self and person (i.e., cultural models), as opposed to the "conscious personality" itself (ibid.). This is where our approaches diverge. Mauss's main emphasis is on the evolution of different *cultural* notions of the "self", while the research presented here is focused on the *experiential core*—the self itself—that underlies such cultural notions: an ontological entity.

Mauss achieved *his* goal through a cross-cultural overview of different notions of the self, which he neatly divided into five distinct stages.

He begins with the self as "the subject" (being the state of human experience as an embodied entity, and the main focus of my inquiry), followed by "the role" (being the place and function of the person within a society), the "persona" (the character, or moral and legal entity), and onwards to the Christian "person" (an individual metaphysical entity), before finally arriving at the person defined as an individual, bounded "psychological being" in the modern, post-industrial, Euro-American sense (1938, pp. 1–23). For Mauss, then, the self was a constantly evolving *concept*—"imprecise, delicate and fragile"—and above all was *socially* and *culturally* constructed, eventually culminating with the model of the individual Western self we know today.

While I agree that self concepts do seem to become ingrained within a *particular* cultural context, I nevertheless feel that a focus on the self as purely culturally derived—that is, as a category of thought without any wider ontological implications—is to ignore a much deeper, and much more interesting, problem. Namely, what do alternative experiences of the self, even if they fly in the face of dominant cultural models, tell us about the ultimate nature of human consciousness itself? What is the experiential core that underlies the cultural conceptions of person and self that Mauss investigated? If the self is purely a cultural category, how is it that practitioners of mediumship, meditation, and shamanism (for example) come to develop conceptions of the self that seem to contradict mainstream cultural models? Of course it is entirely possible that subcultures with their own conceptions of the nature of the self can develop *within* society, but it is also true to say that many such subcultures (Spiritualism included) develop in response to direct personal experiences that challenge their accepted cultural models.

Writing some sixty years after Mauss's first tentative explorations of the self, anthropologist Melford Spiro took up the issue of defining the self in a paper titled "Is the Western Conception of the self 'Peculiar' Within the Context of the World's Cultures?" (1993). Spiro's article was written in response to influential papers by Clifford Geertz (1974), and Markus and Kitayama (1991), who had argued for a distinction between what they referred to as the bounded "Western" notion of the self and the "porous" non-Western self (more on this later). To begin his deconstruction of the debate, Spiro drew attention to the different ways in which the terms "person" and "self" have been used—and very often conflated—by theorists, psychologists, and anthropologists.

Spiro delineated seven possible things to which the label "self" is frequently applied:

- The *person*, or the *individual*, including the package of biological, psychological, social, and cultural characteristics by which he or she is constituted.
- The *cultural conception* of the person or individual.
- The cultural conception of some *psychic entity or structure* within the person, variously designated as "pure ego", "transcendental ego", "soul", and the like.
- The person's construal of such an entity as the centre or locus of his or her initiative, sensations, perceptions, emotions, and the like.
- The personality or the configuration of cognitive orientations, perceptual sets, and motivational dispositions that are uniquely characteristic of each person.
- The sense of self or the person's awareness that he or she is both separate and different from other persons. The former is often referred to as "self-other differentiation", the latter as "personal individuation".
- The self-representation or the mental representation of the attributes of one's own person as they are known, both consciously and unconsciously, to the person himself or herself. (1993, p. 114)

Although Spiro does not go on to propose any working definitions of his own—which might have helped to bring a little clarity to this area—he nevertheless highlights the fact that the focus of the majority of anthropological studies has been primarily on "cultural conceptions of the self" (1993, p. 143), in keeping with Mauss's tradition, rather than dealing with the self as a metaphysical or phenomenological entity. It is this phenomenological perspective that I am concerned with here, that is, *how the self is experienced from the subjective perspective.*

Spiro also criticised the often assumed binary distinction between the so-called "Western" and "non-Western" conceptions of the self, and my research would certainly seem to support this view. As we shall see in the next section, the ethnographic reality is far more complex than this simple either/or dichotomy gives it credit for. I also agree with Spiro's suggestion that the overemphasis on cultural conceptions, rather than on the phenomenological dimensions of the self (the many different ways in which the self is experienced, for example in different states of consciousness), is a cause for concern for anthropologists and anthropological theories of the self. It is my contention that an appreciation of the range of phenomenological dimensions of the self will ultimately help to shed light on the nature of self as a complex ontological entity.

As another example of an attempt to clear up some of the confusion around these terms, Grace Harris (1989) has proposed much more rigid definitions of the terms "individual", "self", and "person", arguing that the conflation of such labels in anthropological and ethnographic writing has been responsible for considerable problems in cross-cultural comparison and interpretation. How do we know that we are talking about the same thing in one context as our colleagues are talking about in another, for example? In order to counteract this confusing state of affairs, Harris offers the following definitions:

- *Individual*: "A concept of the individual is one focusing on a human being considered as a single member of the human kind" (1989, p. 600). This is a biologistic category.
- *Self*: "To work with a concept of self is to conceptualize the human being as a locus of experience, including experience of that human's own someoneness" (p. 601). This is a psychologistic category.
- *Person*: "Dealing with a concept of person entails conceptualizing the human or other being as an agent, the author of action purposively directed toward a goal" (p. 602). This is a sociologistic category.

Harris suggests that local variations of these three concepts are employed near-universally across human cultures, though whether this is actually the case is a point of contention. It could be argued, for example, that the models of personhood that emerge in Amerindian perspectivist cosmologies (as documented, for example, in A. Irving Hallowell (2002), Viveiros de Castro's (2002), and Eduardo Kohn's (2013) work) effectively blur any kind of neat distinction between these three components of the "self". With this in mind, then, in the context of this chapter at least, we are primarily concerned with what G. G. Harris calls the "self"—as distinct from the individual or person—in that our emphasis is on the phenomenology of the self, how the self is experienced, and how this experience subsequently influences the development of particular cultural models of self. We will return to this idea shortly.

Drawing on recent research in neurobiology, anthropologist Naomi Quinn (2006) critiques the "impoverishment of cultural anthropological theory with regard to the self" (p. 362), which she characterises as overly simplistic. Following neuroscientist Joseph LeDoux (2002) of the self as "the totality of what an organism is physically, biologically, psychologically, socially and culturally", Quinn proposes a definition of the self that emphasises "the intra-psychic—including psychological, biological, and cultural, and both explicit and implicit processes that comprise it". This view of the self "encompasses the physical organism, all aspects of psychological functioning, and social attributes" (Quinn, 2006, p. 363). Interestingly, however, Quinn is comfortable with the using the words "self" and "personality" interchangeably, though—to me at least—this seems to be a further unnecessary conflation of ideas. I would understand personality as the *outward expression of the self*— much as in Mauss's conception of the persona—and the self as the *inner phenomenological core of the person*. In spite of this difficulty, however, I agree with Quinn's general conclusion that the "self" consists of a variety of component parts, ranging from the intrapsychic and experiential (subjective) to the physical and biological (objective).

It is also clear that there are other facets of the self that are very often left out—or ignored—in these kinds of discussions, namely the so-called "transpersonal" dimensions of the self. Transpersonal anthropologist Charles Laughlin defines the transpersonal as "a movement in science toward seeing the significance of experiences had in life, that somehow go beyond the boundaries of ordinary ego-consciousness, as data" (2012, p. 70). The implication here, then, is that certain kinds of experiences that appear to contradict cultural expectations should not be simply brushed aside as essentially delusional, pathological, and irrational, but rather ought to be understood as data that might provide fruitful insights into the nature of consciousness, mind, and self. Daniels (2002), for example, argues that the different aspects of the soul/self encountered in different cultural traditions are "based on interpretations of a wide variety of human experiences, including life and death, dreams, out-of-body experiences, hauntings, possession, self-reflexive consciousness, inspiration and mystical experience". My own research also supports this view, and I will suggest that the experiences of trainee mediums in the development of their trances lead to expanded conceptions of self and consciousness.

By defining the self then as experiential (that is, defined by experience rather than by culture), we can overcome many of the problems associated with the cross-cultural study of selfhood. In addition to comparing cultural models (which is undoubtedly a useful approach in itself) we could also be comparing how the self is actually experienced by different groups and individuals, as well as the methods and techniques by which the experiential self is investigated and explored by our field-work informants. In this way we might also be able to learn something more about the nature of human consciousness, as distinct from specific cultural ideas (beliefs) about it, perhaps leading to the development of a "map", or topography, of consciousness.

Western/non-Western, bounded/porous

Now that we have surveyed some of the literature on the definition of self, we can turn to examine some of the classical distinctions between so-called "Western" and "non-Western" models of the self.

Willy de Craemer (1983), in a small-scale cross-cultural comparison of American, Bantu, and Japanese conceptions of the person, highlighted several key characteristics of what he considers the "Western" conception of the person, which includes characteristics of: (1) individuality, (2) rights, (3) autonomy, (4) self-determination, (5) privacy, and (6) specific roles and functions within society. In addition to these characteristic features of the Western person-concept, de Craemer also emphasises the relatively restricted extent to which the individual is located within a wider kinship group, which "does not usually include kin-like friends or patrons and clients as it does in many other societies". Furthermore, "Even within the confines of strict biological relatedness, what we count as kin, with whom we identify, has shrivelled over time and is now predominantly a matter of relationship to a spouse, parent, sibling, grandparent, and, to a lesser extent, aunt, uncle and cousin." de Craemer characterises this individualising of the person as running even deeper, arguing that "Relations with the deceased and the unborn, especially ancestors and descendants, so interpersonally and metaphysically important in African and Asian societies, all play a minimal role in the conscious conception and life of the American individual" (1983, p. 20). While this may be true generally, the reality on the ground is not quite so clear-cut, as we shall see. There are groups, even within the dominant Euro-American culture, who deliberately seek to foster relationships with the deceased, as well as other non-physical beings, and whose understanding of the self clearly exceeds the limitations of the "American individual".

Clifford Geertz also provides a very similar, and hugely influential, definition of the so-called "Western" person when he writes that the Western person is conceived as:

> ... a bounded, unique, more or less integrated motivational and cognitive universe, a dynamic center of awareness, emotion, judgement and action organized into a distinctive whole and set contrastively against other such wholes and against its social and natural background. (1974, p. 31)

For Geertz, then, the Western conception of the person is structured and defined by contrast with "other such wholes". It is bounded by the limitations of the physical body, which acts as a barrier between the inner "center of awareness" and the outer world of the natural and social spheres. The "Western" person is understood to be autonomous, bounded, and *in*-dividual (non-divisible). In Charles Taylor's terms, the Western self is "buffered" (2007, pp. 37–41), separated from the outside world. By contrast, Marilyn Strathern (1988) is famous for popularising the distinction between "individual" models of personhood (exemplified by the "Western" model), and "dividual" models (exemplified by "non-Western" models, and particularly Melanesian models). The key differences between these two modes of conceiving of the nature of the person have been briefly summarised by Karl Smith as follows:

> In the simplest terms, the individual is considered to be an indivisible self or person. That is, it refers to something like the essential core, or spirit of a singular human being, which, as a whole, defines that self in its particularity. To change, remove or otherwise alter any part of that whole would fundamentally alter the "self"; she/he would then be, effectively, a different person. By contrast, the dividual is considered to be divisible, comprising a complex of separable—interrelated but essentially independent—dimensions or aspects. The individual is thus monadic, while the dividual is fractal; the individual is atomistic, while the dividual is always socially embedded; the individual is an autonomous social actor, the author of his or her own actions, while the dividual is a heteronomous actor performing a culturally written script; the individual is a free-agent, while the dividual is determined by cultural structures; the individual is egocentric, while the dividual is sociocentric. (2012, p. 53)

Anthropologists have, therefore, attempted to highlight the variety of personhood concepts worldwide, but have not quite so often addressed the plurality of personhood concepts within a single society. In her discussion of cultural variations in theories of mind, psychologist Angeline Lillard, for example, explains how "variation in folk psychological thinking within the [Euro-American] community has not received adequate attention from researchers", and suggests that further research in this direction is required, a sentiment echoed more recently by Tanya Luhrmann (2011). Lillard proposes that differences in theories of mind within Euro-American society might arise as a consequence of individual, or subcultural, beliefs, for example "whether non-material sources like spirits or God can directly influence one's mind" (1998, p. 3). Taylor also agrees, arguing that what he calls the "buffered self" arises as a product of the disenchantment of the world (2007, p. 41). Cultural beliefs and expectations, then, seem to either *limit* or *expand* conceptions of the self. In spite of this, however, it is still possible to have experiences that seem to exceed the limitations expected by a particular cultural model, which would seem to imply that the self is not derived directly from culture—experience can also give rise to cultural models.

What we are dealing with, then, is a greater degree of intra-cultural variation in experiences and conceptualisations of self than the standard Western/non-Western dichotomy seems to allow for (cf. Spiro, 1993, pp. 144–145), and this appears, at least preliminarily, to be due not solely to the influence of culture (which does play a role in shaping our experience), but also due to the influence of *individual first-personal experiences*. Rane Willerslev (2004) explains:

> What I propose, in other words, is to reverse the order of analysis, so to speak, and begin from the assumption that people's everyday practical engagement with things is the crucial foundation upon which "intellectual culture," that is abstract cognition and conceptual representation, is necessarily premised. (p. 401)

Culture does not *create* our sense of self (though it certainly has an influence)—our sense of self is generated through our "practical engagement" with the world, and the *experiences* that gives rise to. Mediumship, as a distinctive mode of "practical engagement" with the world gives rise to certain kinds of experiences that cannot be accessed in any other way; such experiences may in turn lead to an expansion of notions of the self.

Mediumship experiences and the experiential self

We will now turn to examine some of the types of experience reported by developing mediums at the Bristol Spirit Lodge, before elaborating on how such experiences influence the development of models of self. In addition to accounts from mediums in training, I have also included a couple of references to my own subjective experiences as a participant-observer in mediumship development sittings. I felt that it was important that, as a researcher, I experienced, as far as possible, the kinds of experiences reported by my fieldwork informants.

Surrendering to trance

Some of the most unusual experiences reported by mediums themselves involve the hours and minutes leading up to the onset of their trance states and the formal beginning of the séance, when they are in a strange in-between state. Before entering the Lodge, for example, mediums often report strange bodily sensations and subtle alterations of their consciousness indicative of the presence of their spirit teams, who are understood to move closer to the medium in preparation before the séance begins. Emily begins to show visible signs of entering into an altered state of consciousness in the moments leading up to the beginning of the séance. She becomes slightly dazed and her legs and arms noticeably twitch and spasm; her movements are reminiscent of the tics exhibited by sufferers of Tourette's syndrome, though not quite as violent. Almost as soon as she is in the Lodge, and seated in the cabinet, she enters into her trance state—breathing deeply in and exhaling in short, stammering puffs. Christine reads the opening prayer, plays the music, and dims the red light so that it is dark, but still light enough to see Emily in the gloom of the cabinet. Before long she is on her feet—still in trance—with the spirits attempting to levitate her body. She bends far backwards without falling, an impressive feat, and quite eerie in the red glow of the séance room. She moves around the room—she is not confined to the cabinet like most of the other mediums at the Lodge—and then begins to speak in different voices.

Similarly, in the following extract, Sandy describes the qualitative sensations she feels when surrendering herself to the early stages of the trance state:

> I don't feel tired as such. But, you know if you're tired, you start kind of staring, and you're just not totally with it. If somebody's

chatting at you, you know they're chatting and you're kind of half with it and half not. That's how it starts. They've not taken over at that point. I'm just aware that they're going to be in the near future. And that happens before I get here ... There's this kind of, almost a daze, as if you're really tired and you're just going to go to sleep, and that's the first thing I notice. (Interview with Sandy, March 23, 2011)

Sandy describes a gradual process of her spirit team moving closer, beginning with an altered, drowsy state of consciousness, and progressing towards full trance and a dissociation from the external world. She describes a growing awareness of the presence of her spirit team leading up to the beginning of the séance, as they move into her field of awareness. Similarly, in the following extract, Rachael describes her own sensation of falling into trance over the course of an hour leading up to the start of the séance. She explains:

My head starts spinning. That's normally before I sit, it starts about an hour before, just a little bit, you kind of can't get your words in the right order sometimes, and your head doesn't really seem to connect with the rest of you for a little while ... by the time you're sat in the cabinet you're feeling quite calm ... and it's weird, it's almost like you're moving backwards inside your own head, and it's like your own head is bigger than it normally is and you're moving backwards into it. I don't seem to go anywhere else at the moment, I just seem to stay in myself, but it's kind of like my head's a lot like an alien [laughs], and I'm going backwards into my own head. (Interview with Rachael, June 16, 2012)

Rachael's description contains interesting references to anomalous bodily sensations. Her head feels larger than it normally is, and she senses herself falling backwards into it. The boundaries of the physical body are felt to expand outwards, or dissolve, or to lose their normal sense of proportion, and consciousness is *experienced* as more expansive than in her everyday waking state. She feels dizzy and hazy as the locus of her consciousness dissociates from her physical body—perhaps shifting to focus on inner processes, rather than the external world. This unusual bodily sensation—the evaporation of the boundaries of the physical body—is also echoed in Jon's description of the process of fall-ing into the trance state:

> Once we're out in the Lodge … I sit down [and] feel a calmness wash over and the music starts. I love the first couple of tracks but usually find they've gone very quickly … I'm still very much aware of the room but find that I've often missed bits of time … For the first half of the evening I have absolutely no awareness of what's going on externally … Often now, when they are talking I'll go back into myself and I get a strange sensation of vertigo and being detached from the conversation, not just intellectually but physi-cally as well. (Interview with Jon, in Hunter 2009, p. 74)

Again, Jon reports the dissolution of the usual boundaries of the physical body. Time is experienced differently, it seems to flow much quicker, or it stops and starts. His awareness shifts, like Rachael's, from the external world towards *internal* processes. Again, the boundaries are expanded so much that Jon has a "strange sense of vertigo" that "physically" detaches him from the conversations going on around him. My own experience of falling into trance during a development sitting at the Lodge also included many of the features of Sandy, Rachael, and Jon's experiences, which, to my mind at least, adds credence to the veracity of the experiences they reported to me—such experiences *are possible*.

My "possessed" hand

Approximately two months after my very first séance at the Bristol Spirit Lodge, in March 2009, I had my own "anomalous", or more precisely dissociative trance, experience in the Lodge, which added an extra per-sonal experiential dimension to my investigations. On this particular occasion the usual medium was unable to attend, so the circle leader decided that we should sit in a development circle instead, as a group, and invite spirits to make themselves known through any of the sitters present.[18] I decided that I would go along with this by sitting in quiet

---

[18] In retrospect, perhaps not the most "spiritually safe" of activities, but it was what the group was doing. The danger in opening yourself up in this way is that you can never be sure what "level" of entity might get involved.

meditation, relaxing, and enjoying the music and warm and supportive atmosphere of the séance room. I closed my eyes, focused my attention onto my breathing, and let down my barriers.

Eventually, after a short while of uneventful meditation, I felt my hands begin to tingle as they rested on the arms of the chair, and my heart rate began to quicken. It started to feel as though I was going to lose control of my body, as though I was on the verge of fainting or passing out, though still physically sitting comfortably in the chair. Gradually I felt as though I was becoming distanced from my physical body, as though I (the conscious "me") was somehow sitting just behind my own body. At the point when I felt most distanced from my physical form I heard Christine, the circle leader, say that she sensed a presence standing by me, a male presence that wanted to communicate. This unsettled me, because I too sensed an unusual, invisible though tangible presence to my left. I felt on the verge of losing control of my body. I panicked. I swore. I opened my eyes and snapped myself back into the room. I felt light-headed, and my heart was racing. I had to regain composure, calm down, and reassure myself that everything was OK. The group laughed.

When I finally managed to relax again I decided to begin my meditation one more time, just to see what would happen. This time around, the physical sensations I felt in the first meditation came on again much faster; my heart rate increased and the tingling in my hands returned. I began to feel the uneasy sensation of distancing from my body again, of smoothly and subtly sliding away from the physical, and at the point of greatest distance I felt as though there was an empty space within my body that seemed as though it could quite easily be filled by "something else". It was as though I had made room in my physical body by moving "myself" out of it, like a jug emptying itself of water ready to be refilled. I then felt what in my field notes I described as an "energy" moving into my left hand, and my index finger began to rise, seemingly of its own accord—a sensation of something other than myself. It felt as though my hand was being lifted by a cushion of air, pushed up from below. My second finger then began to move upwards as well, and soon my whole hand was quivering and twitching on the arm of the chair. I was aware of the movement, I could feel it, but I was also aware of the fact that I was in no way consciously willing it to happen. It was as though I was observing the movement, as if I were a spectator, but not with my eyes, which were shut throughout the experience: I was sensing it, feeling.

The motion in my hand became more vigorous, and soon my entire left arm was vibrating and shaking from side to side. All the while my head felt heavy and drooped down onto my chest. After some time, I cannot recall how long the experience lasted (it can't have been very long), my hand began to lower itself again; it felt as though whatever energy had caused it to move was becoming less intense, and as it did so my arm's movement became less vigorous. Soon it was only my two forefingers that remained up, and then these too returned to normal. When it all subsided I had "returned" and was fully in control of my body once again. I opened my eyes and looked around the red-lit séance room in stunned silence. I waited for Christine to read the closing prayer, which would ensure that any spiritual energies present in the room during the séance would be safely dissipated, so that I wouldn't leave with a spirit still attached. Once the prayer had been read we retired back into the house for tea and cake.

This was an unusual, quite shocking, experience for me. I was reluctant to surrender myself to the experience. I hadn't expected that something like this could possibly happen to me, and certainly not in a garden shed in the middle of suburban Bristol. But it did, and it was very *weird*. I now understand this experience, in the words of anthropologist Zeljko Jokic (2008a), as my "point of inter-subjective entry" into the experiential domain of trance mediumship. I had, so I was later told by Christine, experienced the early stages of trance mediumship development, what the ethnographic literature refers to as "spirit possession". For me, the experience I have just described demonstrates that, at the very least, there *are* genuine experiences that seem to suggest to the experiencer that the physical body can be temporarily controlled by something that (again, at the very least) *feels* as though it is an external controlling intelligence. My own experience of dissociative trance further reinforces my conviction that the altered states of consciousness experienced by the mediums I have encountered in the field are genuine, and that they *really do* experience a surrendering of their physical bodies to something that, at the very least, *feels like* an ontologically distinct discarnate spirit. All of this provided the driving force that motivated me to investigate further, and provided a valuable experiential insight into the *how processes* of trance and physical mediumship.

Experiences such as these seem to challenge the cultural notion of the physical body as an impermeable membrane between the inner and outer worlds, which is a hallmark of the so-called "Western" individual model of the self, and a Cartesian hangover. I *felt* a sense of presence move into my awareness, as if my consciousness was *a field extending out from my experiential centre*. Like Jon and Rachael, I felt an expanse open up within me, like a cavernous space, much larger than my physical body, and I can quite understand Jon's reported sense of vertigo.

Such experiences come as a shock to mediums in the early stages of development precisely because the dominant paradigms of Western materialist science, which are ubiquitous in mainstream post-industrial Euro-American culture and into which we have all been socialised through education and the media, do not prime us to expect them. If such sensations *are* mentioned at all, it is usually in the context of pathology, or horror movies. In the words of transpersonal anthropologist Charles D. Laughlin, Euro-American society participates in a predominantly *mono*-phasic culture, in which the ostensibly productive, everyday state of waking consciousness is promoted as the only acceptable, practical, economically viable, and "normal" state of consciousness (excepting, perhaps, the drunken state at certain socially and culturally prescribed times; only after work, for example). There is no framework within which to understand experiences of bodily dissolution and expanded awareness, except in the contexts of intoxication and pathology. *Poly*-phasic cultures, by contrast, can be said to embrace a variety of altered states of consciousness as normal, or at least not as abnormal, and have developed frameworks within which the kinds of sensations reported by developing mediums, for example, can be understood. What seems to be taking place at the Bristol Spirit Lodge, then, is the formation of a poly-phasic subculture, within which expanded experiences of self can be made sense of.

Porous bodies and field-like selves

We can say, then, that the kinds of experiences reported by those developing mediumship at the Lodge lead to a porous conception of the body. No longer is the body understood as an impermeable layer, as a solid boundary between the internal and external worlds. Instead, the body is experienced as permeable, so permeable in fact that under certain conditions non-physical entities can move into, occupy, and control it (see also Steffen, 2011). Christine describes the idea in the following terms:

> I think we just flow through each other. Or, we've got very blurred edges, we appear to be solid, but only our eyes are seeing this solid, this light reflection which causes us to appear solid. We're not. So, our boundaries aren't where we think they are. We are here to experience whatever this is, this life-form, this stage of life is. We are

> here … to experience, or to perceive things as solid and individual
> and it's a very little tiny part of a very big life. I think. Possibly.
> (Interview with Christine, June 16, 2012)

Christine conceives of the boundaries of the person as extending beyond the confines of the physical body, which self only appears to be solid. According to this perspective the "solid" and the "individual" are, to a certain extent, illusory. With a porous body, then, it is possible for things to flow into and out of the person. Anthropologist Fiona Bowie has characterised this, in the context of spiritualist trance séances, through describing the body as a "shared territory, holding the physical life-force of the medium and the conscious intelligence of visiting spirits" (Bowie, 2013b, p. 14).

In further discussions, Christine has described her model of consciousness as being somewhat "like an onion", that is, like "a whole split into millions and trillions of consciousnesses that can act together" (interview with Christine, February 25, 2013). This kind of pluralistic, dividual understanding of consciousness and the person recurs throughout the ethnographic literature (see, as one such example, Roseman (1990, p. 227) on the structure of the self among Senoi Temiar, which is described as consisting of "a number of potentially detachable selves").

In the following extract Emily further describes her own experience of the porosity of the body, and elaborates on how she subjectively experiences spirits moving into her "personal space":

> Then, usually around the table while we are waiting for the start,
> I will feel a presence around me kind of like an enveloping feel-
> ing, the first thing I feel is as if a friend is standing unseen nearby.
> I have an awareness of there being someone there, near me, that is
> a friend. I then feel them come closer into my personal "space" in
> some quiet gentle way. (Interview with Emily, February 13, 2013)

Emily's description of a sense of presence, unseen but *felt*, further suggests a model of the self as a non-physical field expanding outwards from the physical body, into which other entities can pass. Again, we see the idea that mediumship development is a gradual process, beginning with a sensed presence, and an interjection into "personal space", and finally resulting in the embodiment of distinctive spirit personalities, who communicate through the medium's body.

In the following extract, Rachael, who had been attending the Lodge for just over one year when I spoke to her in 2012, explained how before developing mediumship she would frequently experience the unusual, and often unpleasant, sensation of spirits moving through her body. She explains:

> When they actually make a personal entrance into your body, that's pretty bizarre. It would normally happen, um, in the middle of the night I'd wake up and there was something, it's a sort of odd feeling, it's like, um, if you can imagine taking off a polo necked jumper, but from inside yourself. It's like something's pulling, it's kind of gone in, and then it's kind of pulling out, and it's, oh, I can't explain it, but it's the weirdest, weirdest feeling. But it's quite horrible … It happened, um, on about three occasions through my thirties, and in the end I got talking to a medium and she said it sounds like a spirit entity in you, or something passing through you, and she said to contact the local Spiritualist church, but, I did that, but nobody there seemed to feel the same kind of thing: with mental mediumship it all seems to be outside of the person coming in through the mind and talking, it wasn't, with me it's a very physical thing … (Interview with Rachael, June 16, 2012)

For Rachael the process of developing mediumship allowed her to come to terms with experiences that had previously been disturbing to her. Where once the experience of spirits moving through her body had been unpleasant and spontaneous, primarily because she did not have a cultural framework through which to understand her experience, it is now both deliberately induced during formalised séances, and has become an enjoyable experience for her. She explains how mediumship development has made her "soft and squidgy" and "more open to other people" (interview with Rachael, February 25, 2013), again, a description of the self that accords particularly with the so-called "non-Western" model, but which has arisen through first-person experience rather than through cultural indoctrination.

Multiple intelligences and spiritual augmentation

Christine's notion that consciousness is "a whole split into millions and trillions of consciousnesses that can act together" is an example of what

I would call "spiritual augmentation", that is, the notion that spiritual beings can be thought of as augmentations of consciousness, coexisting and assisting with cognitive processes. In the following extract, for example, Sandy describes how the members of her spirit team assist her with memory and information recall:

> [The spirits] help me keep a clearer mind, and therefore I am able to make better decisions. I can utilise information that I've got … I did a degree in nutritional medicine, years ago I was a nurse and a midwife, and there's a lot of information in my head somewhere, but I can actually tap in on information that I've not used in years and years and years … the knowledge is mine but it can be used more efficiently. (Interview with Sandy, March 23, 2011)

Sandy told me this in the context of a wider discussion about an experience she had had several years before we met. Sandy explained that when her children were growing up they had been ill and were recommended a course of drugs by their doctor. Sandy eventually came to the conclusion that this course of action was only making the situation worse, and so decided to personally oversee a reduction in the amount of drugs she was giving to her children, noting along the way that they seemed to be getting better the fewer drugs they were taking. Eventually, however, Sandy reached the point where she was beginning to doubt the action she was taking, that was until she was affirmed in her actions by a mysterious, seemingly disembodied, voice. She explains:

> One day I was, um, laid on the bed upstairs and um, I was really, I was mulling over it, and I was thinking right I really don't know if I should be doing this, I don't know if I, you know, where this can take me, you know, this is my kids, so this is important stuff you know. And so, um, and suddenly I heard the voice and it said, "You've gotta keep going." And it was out loud, you see, and I kinda looked round and my son was asleep on the bed [laughs]. Come on, I don't know, who said this, you know? And I just didn't know, and I didn't know whether to tell anybody that I'd heard this voice, but it was an out-loud voice. In fact it was the only time I've heard that out-loud voice, I haven't heard that out-loud voice since. In fact I don't really hear a voice since. But this was an out-loud voice, it was a definite voice, and, um, and I thought wow, OK then … The whole

thing was managed, and when Joseph started to come through he said that he'd been with me for a long time, and, you know, previously he was a medicine man in a previous life, and he was a healer, and he was here to heal and that was what he was doing ... and so he said he did it. (Interview with Sandy, March 23, 2011)

The reassuring and practical, supportive tone of Sandy's experience accords well with a general pattern in auditory "hallucinations" of this nature—namely that they are *helpful hallucinations*. Tanya Luhrmann, for instance, drawing on her own research with members of a Charismatic Christian church and the work of others in similarly structured fieldwork situations, explains how "whether internal or external, the voices focused on immediate issues. They offered practical direction, not grand metaphysical theology. Many, though not all, had the experiences during emotional turmoil" (2011, p. 74).

Here Christine, the circle leader, describes how her spirit guide, known as Fuzzy Critter, influences her decision making:

> As time went on in trusting Fuzzy Critter, and these telepathic voices, I did get to a point where I knew it was separate from me ... It was a separate personality. The words he uses are better than mine ... his language is different to mine ... His general way of working, it's not me, in fact sometimes I'll argue with him ... I have a sense, he seems to approach me from this side of my shoulder, this side of my head [left]. I, in my own mind, feel that he's a bit like a fluffy owl sitting on my shoulder ... Sometimes it's annoying if I'm doing housework and he wants to communicate with me, and I get this feeling. It's a bit like having something playing with your hair, or whispering in your ear when you're trying to do something. (Interview with Christine, November 18, 2009)

Again, we see here examples of what anthropologists have labelled a "dividual"—or "porous"—self, emerging from a Western post-industrial context. The locus of the self can be entered by discarnate spirits, who may offer their assistance in a range of different everyday situations and decision-making processes.

CHAPTER EIGHT

Conclusions

> We shall pick up an existence by its frogs ... if there is an underlying oneness of all things, it does not matter where we begin, whether with stars, or laws of supply and demand, or frogs, or Napoleon Bonaparte. One measures a circle, beginning anywhere.
>
> —Charles Fort, *The Book of the Damned* (2008, p. 554)

> Strangeness which is the essence of beauty is the essence of truth, and the essence of the world.
>
> —Arthur Machen, *The London Adventure*

The following sections will give summaries of the book's primary conclusions about the Bristol Spirit Lodge, séances, the manifestation of spirits, and the experiential self. We will also briefly summarise some of the key methodological and theoretical conclusions that have arisen over the course of the preceding, before offering suggestions for further work in the direction of a non-reductive anthropological approach to the paranormal.

The Bristol Spirit Lodge

The Bristol Spirit Lodge is an active part in the "New Age of Physical Mediumship". Its roots can be traced back to the Scole Experiment of the 1990s, which essentially reinvigorated interest in the development of physical mediumship after a lull following the Second World War. It is also a continuation of a long tradition of Spiritualist activity in Bristol that goes back to the earliest days of the Victorian Spiritualist craze. In a sense, then, what is happening at the Bristol Spirit Lodge is both new and old.

Christine established the Lodge out of her own scientific curiosity following anomalous experiences (witnessing apparent materialisations of spirit forms and hearing disembodied voices that she clearly recognised) during a physical mediumship séance at Jenny's Sanctuary in Banbury. Christine's scientific curiosity lays the groundwork for an understanding of the practices of the Bristol Spirit Lodge as *experimental* in nature. Christine's approach as the founder of the Lodge, as well as the circle leader during séances, is a scientific one—she is an experimenter investigating the nature of consciousness and the afterlife through mediumship development sessions in her back garden.

Members of the Lodge can broadly be characterised as "seekers". They do not think of séances as specifically religious events (though they may have religious sentiments themselves), rather they see themselves as searchers after the truth. Mediumship is understood as a natural capacity of human beings, and is there to be explored and put to use. In this respect, sitters at the Lodge consider themselves to be doing good work in helping to bridge the divide between the living and the dead. They are doing a positive act for humanity, furthering our understanding of ourselves and the hereafter, and reconnecting our world with the spiritual realm that envelopes and penetrates it.

The mediums at the Bristol Spirit Lodge show considerable dedication to the development of their mediumistic abilities. They do not get paid for working in séances, which are private, and attend (often more than once a week) at their own expense and purely out of a desire to develop themselves. All mediums at the Lodge—including my primary informants Sandy, Jon, Rachael, and Emily—have come to the development of trance and physical mediumship following a lifetime of anomalous experiences, which subsequent mediumship development has helped them to make sense of and incorporate into their lives.

My fieldwork and interviews with mediums at the Bristol Spirit Lodge have convinced me of their sincerity, and that when they enter into their trance states they are experiencing a genuine altered state of consciousness. I did not get the impression that they were "faking it" or deliberately trying to mislead anyone, and therefore took their experiences (and the implications of those experiences) seriously.

Séances and spirits

I have characterised séances at the Bristol Spirit Lodge as a form of experimental consciousness exploration, but in addition to this they are *also* performances. Through the discussion presented in Chapter 6, I have come to understand performance and dialogue as fundamental processes in the manifestation of spirits in social reality.

First, a physical body is necessary to express the presence of spirits. Christine uses bodily clues (changes in skin tone, twitches, convulsions, and gestures), coupled with her own intuitive sense, to recognise the onset of trance states and the emergence of particular spirit personalities in the mediums she works with. The trance state allows for a dissociation (to varying degrees) of the medium's everyday sense of self, which must be relinquished during the séance (something I personally resisted when my hand was possessed). The emerging personalities are expressed through more overt performative elements, such as altered postures and vocal tonality, to indicate their independence from the medium's personality. The medium must surrender control of their body to the incoming spirits, who are then engaged in dialogue—first by Christine as the circle leader, and then by the rest of the attendant sitters. Through dialogue the spirits become stronger, and over time their personalities are more completely expressed during séances. In this respect, the practices of the Bristol Spirit Lodge share similarities with what Nurit Bird-David (1999) has called "relational" ontologies. Mediumship brings the spirits into a social relationship with the living, and it is the resultant dialogue that supports the spirits' existence in social reality. When the dialogue ends, at the close of the séance, the spirits return from where they came until their next opportunity to manifest. The processes by which spirits become manifest in social reality are, in themselves, certainly social, but I am not trying to suggest that the spirits are "just social constructions".

Anthropologist Sidney Greenfield, in an effort to understand the role of spirit beings in the process of Spiritist psychic surgery in Brazil, drew upon the writings of psychologist and parapsychologist Lawrence LeShan who put forward a third way to begin conceptualising the nature of spirit controls in trance mediumship (2008, pp. 160–161). LeShan identified two explanations that dominate the debate over the nature of spirit controls—either they are the product of multiple personality disorder (now known as dissociative identity disorder), or they are "real" spirits. LeShan suggests, however, a third way of thinking about these entities. He proposes that they might best be understood as "functional entities", which he explains:

> ... do not have any length, breadth, or thickness. They cannot be detected by any form of instrumentation, although their effects often can be ... They do not have continuous existence whether or not they are being mentally conceptualized ... they exist only when they are held in the mind, only when being conceptualized, only when being considered to exist. (1995, p. 167)

Other examples of functional entities include mathematical postulates, such as, for example, square roots, which do not exist but which are nevertheless *real* in that they help us to solve real-life problems. Greenfield summarises this idea when he writes that a "functional entity, therefore, is what we agree it is and/or does and when it does it" (2008, p. 161). Combined with some of the ideas we have been exploring about the role of performance, dialogue, and social interaction, this perspective suggests that spirit controls are manifested to perform specific functions for the duration that the dialogue is sustained.

Towards a psychoid model of mind-matter interaction

The relational model of mediumship summarised above also resonates with Frederic Myers's model of consciousness, in which consciousness consists of *at least* two streams—the *subliminal* and the *supraliminal*. Myers argued in favour of interpreting spirit possession as a "shifting of the psychical centre of the personality of the [medium] himself" to allow emergences from the subliminal into the supraliminal, much like bubbles breaching the surface of the ocean. This is not, however, to suggest a *purely psychological* explanation for mediumship and the spirits it expresses:

> I propose to extend the meaning of the term [subliminal] ... to make it cover *all* that takes place beneath the ordinary threshold, or say, if preferred, outside the ordinary margin of consciousness; not only those faint stimulations whose very faintness keeps them submerged, but much else which psychology as yet scarcely recognises; sensations, thoughts, emotions, which may be strong, definite, and independent, but which, by the original constitution of their being, seldom emerge into that *supraliminal* current of consciousness which we habitually identify with *ourselves*. (Myers, 1903, pp. 13–14)

Myers did not deny the possibility that *external, non-physical* influences might be at play in mediumistic states. Indeed, his theory of the subliminal mind differs considerably from the Freudian notion of the *unconscious* in its inclusion of aspects *external to the individual*. Myers's model provides a framework for understanding such phenomena "without reducing them to epiphenomena of psychopathology ... or ruling out influences beyond the self" (Taves, 1999, p. 258; see also Alvarado, 2002, p. 23). From this perspective the spirit personalities expressed through spirit mediumship performances might be interpreted in Carl Jung's terms as *psychoid manifestations*. Jung identified the *psychoid* as a transcendent entity that manifests at the junction of unconscious (non-physical) and external (physical) influences—a bridge between mind and matter (Addison, 2009). Psychologist Jon Mills refers to the psychoid as a "liaison between mind and body" (Mills, 2014, p. 237). Like Myers's notion of the subliminal mind, Jung's conception of the unconscious also includes aspects external to the *individual* psyche. He wrote that "A psychological truth is ... just as good and respectable a thing as a physical truth [because] no one knows what 'psyche' is, and one knows just as little how far into nature 'psyche' extends" (Jung, 1977, p. 157). Recent developments in the theory of *panpsychism*, which posits consciousness as a fundamental property of matter (Velmans, 2007), may support Jung's suggestion that mind extends *beyond* the body, as do theories of non-local consciousness and the extended mind. Perhaps Myers, Jung, the Spiritualists and members of the Bristol Spirit Lodge (not to mention the numerous other varieties of shaman and magico-religious practitioners) were onto something in their collective experiential exploration of the extents and limitations of consciousness. From this perspective, then, spiritual beings might be understood as a co-creation of internal biological, psychological (subliminal and supra-liminal), and cultural influences interacting with ontologically distinct external stimuli, with spirits emerging at the intersection. Such an inter-pretation would account for both pan-cultural similarities (the role of common biological structures and ontologically distinct entities), as well as cross-cultural differences (the influence of psychological and cultural filters).

The experiential self

The examples cited in Chapter 7 offer just snapshots of the wide range of experiences reported by developing mediums at the Bristol Spirit Lodge. They serve as a useful illustration of some of the ways in which anomalous experiences (trance experiences in this instance) can lead to the development of expanded conceptions of consciousness and the self.

Lillard's (1998) suggestion that variations in theories of mind might arise from specific cultural beliefs about the influence of spirits, dei-ties, and so on, naturally begs the question of where such beliefs come from in the first place. Of course, the cultural diffusion of ideas clearly does take place, and specific ideas and beliefs are undoubtedly trans-mitted through social groups, families, and communities, but many such beliefs also have an experiential source. Folklorist David J. Huf-ford (1982), for example, has written extensively on the experiential source for a wide variety of supernatural assault traditions, arguing that such traditions emerge in direct response to first-hand experiences, specifically of sleep paralysis. Beliefs about the nature of the self, then, might also arise from first-hand personal experience, built up over time and incorporating or rejecting new experiential insights. Just as culture shapes the experience of sleep paralysis (while retaining the essence of the experience), so too does culture shape our ideas of the self—but it is not the source. Psychedelic experiences, for example, may lead to expanded notions of the nature of the self, just as experi-ences with mediumship might also lead to different models. An under-standing of the self as arising through direct first-hand experiences, as opposed to the notion that conceptions of the self are purely culturally constructed, goes some way towards explaining the much greater vari-ety of intra-cultural conceptions of the self commented on by Lillard

(1998), and further noted by Luhrmann (2011). It also raises important questions about what, if anything, should be considered a "normal" self-conception, and clearly has implications for both psychology and psychiatry, especially with regard to diagnosis and treatment (Hunter, 2016a). Through engaging with the way that self and consciousness are experienced phenomenologically, rather than through cultural categories, we can further advance the anthropology of consciousness, and begin to move away from dealing with problematic notions of "belief" (see Hunter, 2015a, 2015b), towards a greater appreciation of distinctive phenomenological experiences. In other words, what I am suggesting is that people do not simply believe that the self can survive death, or that it consists of multiple parts, or that it is porous and permeable, rather they experience it to be so, and through this experiencing *know* that consciousness is far more expansive than the dominant cultural models of Western materialism allows itself to admit.

Key methodological conclusions

There are several key points that have emerged over the course of the preceding chapters, which must now be synthesised into a model and conclusion. The key features of this emergent perspective include:

- An emphasis on *complexity* and a rejection of *reductionism*
- An emphasis on *ontology* (reality/realities) over *culture* and *belief*
- An emphasis on *subjective experience* as epistemologically valid
- An emphasis on *processes*
- An emphasis on *participation*
- An openness to the possibility of *psi* and *non-local consciousness*
- An emphasis on *interdisciplinary perspectives* on complex phenomena.

Through the preceding analysis of spirit mediumship practices and experiences at the Bristol Spirit Lodge, coupled with my own auto-ethnographic observations, and by reviewing the theoretical and explanatory literature on spirit possession and mediumship, it has become clear that mediumship is a particularly *complex* phenomenon that cannot be reduced to a single causal explanation. To name just a few explanations that have been applied to mediumship: fraud, DID, social protest, spirit communication, psi, bereavement counselling, cognitive category error, epilepsy, psychological defence mechanism, and so on. It seems more likely that the truth lies somewhere in between—in Charles Fort's "intermediate" space—an ontologically flooded state, with multiple influencing factors, processes, and worlds. Focusing on the *processes* involved in mediumistic practices (such as performance, dialogue, psycho-biological processes, as well as possible spirit and psi processes) provides an opportunity to develop a comparative approach to mediumship that cuts through apparent (surface) differences between traditions to access core features and underlying structures.

As a consequence of this emphasis on the processes involved in bringing spirits into social reality, questions of *belief* become problematic. We are dealing with something more than abstract belief. Shifting our emphasis to *ontology*—to an appreciation that we are not simply dealing with beliefs, but *whole ways of being*—allows for a much more nuanced understanding of practices such as spirit mediumship, and encourages us to engage with them on their own terms as researchers. It allows us to see connections between *multiple* processes operating simultaneously, while not giving any one of them pre-eminence. Ritual, performance, psi, altered states of consciousness, psychoneuroimmunological processes, cognitive processes, trickery, alterations of brain function, spirits—all (and more) are *simultaneously* at play.

Treating subjective experience as a valid means of accessing information about ourselves and the world(s) we inhabit means that we must take seriously the possibility that the experiences reported by trance mediums in altered states of consciousness (as well as the experiences of countless other magico-religious practitioners and explorers of consciousness) might tell us something useful about the world, and in particular about the nature of consciousness itself. This approach is challenging to the dominant materialist epistemology/ontology, which assumes that we can only gain valid knowledge (i.e., empirically verifiable and falsifiable knowledge), about the world/consciousness through *objective, quantitative* methods. This results in mind being *reduced* to physiological functioning, and the rejection of a wide range of "damned facts" about the nature of consciousness (to use Charles Fort's term).

Shifting emphasis away from notions of the self as "culturally" determined—for example the preoccupation with Western and non-Western models of the self—towards an *experiential* understanding helps to explain both what Lillard (1998) has called the many "intra-cultural variations" in self concepts, as well as the huge variety of self concepts that can exist within a single culture. Our sense of self is not something that is simply given to us by the cultures we inhabit (though perhaps elements of it are through socialisation processes), but rather is something we *learn about* and *develop* through *experience*. This helps to explain how understandings of the nature of self that seem to go against the established cultural models can and do emerge in groups such as the Bristol Spirit Lodge.

Furthermore, and in addition to the above, the evidence from experimental parapsychology seems to suggest that psi effects *are* real (if not always on a *macro* scale),[19] and hints that rather than being firmly located in and produced by the brain, consciousness *may* actually be non-local in nature, or more widely dispersed throughout matter than our usual models tend to want to allow (Radin, 2006). Given that most anthropological theorising has operated on the materialist assumption that psi effects do not exist—hence magic, witchcraft, shamanism, spirit possession, and so on are delusional—and that consciousness is a by-product of physiological functioning and nothing more (i.e., limited to the brain), then surely anthropology's dominant theories may need to be modified to take into account the wider context. As Winkelman (1982) has suggested, the evidence from parapsychology calls for a reassessment of traditional anthropological theories of magic and spirit possession (as well as, necessarily, many other areas of anthropological inquiry).

Finally, in light of the fact that we are dealing with a particularly complex phenomenon in the study of spirit mediumship, it is clear that *multiple perspectives* are required in order to understand it. I would, therefore, call for much greater interdisciplinary collaboration in future studies of mediumship and spirit possession. Perspectives from psychology, neuroscience, performance studies, social-functionalism, biology, and parapsychology *all* offer *pieces* of the puzzle, and *taken together* move us *closer* (if not all the way) to a more complete understanding. To isolate particular processes from wider networks of influence is to revert back to a form of reductionism.[20]

Closing remarks: towards a non-reductive anthropology of the paranormal

Some of these conclusions may seem tangential from the perspective of mainstream social anthropology; they may even be challenging. Nevertheless, it is my contention that they get right to the heart of what

---

[19] Just as we once thought quantum effects, like entanglement, were.
[20] Further explorations in this direction are presented in the book *Greening the Paranormal: Exploring the Ecology of Extraordinary Experience* (Hunter, 2019).

we are dealing with in the phenomenon of spirit mediumship. Through attempting to understand the *mechanisms* and *processes* through which spirit possession operates we can move towards a much more nuanced understanding of the practices of groups such as the Bristol Spirit Lodge (as well as countless others), instead of reducing them down to a system of ultimately erroneous beliefs. By attempting to understand how spirit mediumship *could be possible*—as I have tried to do in this book—the anthropologist approaches an ontological perspective. Such an interpretation is a useful starting point for any analysis of spirit mediumship, and is particularly well suited to ethnographic approaches in that it does not rule out native understanding—rather it draws from it, borrows concepts, and expands on ideas in order to understand the phenomenon and expand the limits of anthropological theory. It provides an inclusive framework that is amenable to scientific theorising and investigation while also being cross-culturally applicable, and most importantly resists the temptation to reduce phenomena down to simple explanations. It helps us to understand core-features of mediumship practices without *reducing* the complexity of the phenomena as they exist within their natural ontological network, and it helps us to understand the diversity of spirit mediumship practices present throughout the world as complex (though interrelated) wholes in themselves.

To conclude, the ideas presented in this book are intended as a springboard for further ethnographic engagement with those things we consider "paranormal", in whatever context. It is an encouragement to think differently about a subject that, from the mainstream materialist perspective, is nonsense. It is an effort to overcome what Edith Turner (1993) called "positivist denial". It is not, however, a definitive statement on the reality of the paranormal. The overarching purpose of this book is to encourage researchers to explore a wide range of possibilities in their investigations, and to nudge anthropology forward into new areas of ontological inquiry, perhaps even towards a *metaphysical anthropology*. It is my hope that this thesis will encourage future researchers not to feel limited in their conclusions by the theoretical models that currently dominate scholarly discourse. There *may well* be a lot more going on beyond the veil. Reality doesn't always play by our rules.

REFERENCES

Addison, A. (2009). Jung, vitalism and "the psychoid": An historical reconstruction. *Journal of Analytic Psychology, 54*: 123–142.

Alvarado, C. S. (1993). Gifted subjects' contribution to psychical research: The case of Eusapia Palladino. *Journal of the Society for Psychical Research, 59*: 269–292.

Alvarado, C. S. (2002). Dissociation in Britain during the late nineteenth century: The Society for Psychical Research, 1882–1900. *Journal of Trauma and Dissociation, 3*(2): 9–33.

Alvarado, C. S. (2011). Eusapia Palladino: An autobiographical essay. *Journal of Scientific Exploration, 25*(1): 77–101.

Angoff, A., & Barth, D. (1974). *Parapsychology and Anthropology: Proceedings of an International Conference.* New York: Parapsychology Foundation.

Argyle, M. (1987). Innate cultural aspects of human non-verbal communication. In: C. Blakemore & S. Greenfield (Eds.), *Mindwaves: Thoughts on Intelligence, Identity and Consciousness* (pp. 55–74). Oxford: Basil Blackwell.

Azaunce, M. (1995). Is it schizophrenia or spirit possession? *Journal of Social Distress and the Homeless, 4*(3): 255–263.

Barrett, J. L. (2000). Exploring the natural foundations of religion. *Trends in Cognitive Sciences, 4*(1): 29–34.

Bartlett, R. (2008). *The Natural and the Supernatural in the Middle Ages.* Cambridge: Cambridge University Press.

Bartolini, N., Chris, R., Mackian, S., & Pile, S. (2013). Mediums, crystals, candles and cauldrons: alternative spiritualities and the question of their esoteric economies. *Social and Cultural Geographies, 14*(4): 1–22.

Batcheldor, K. J. (1984). Contributions to the theory of PK induction from sitter-group work. *Journal of the American Society for Psychical Research, 78:* 105–122.

Bateson, G., & Bateson, M. C. (2005). *Angels Fear: Towards an Epistemology of the Sacred.* Cresskill, NJ: Hampton.

Beattie, J. (1977). Spirit mediumship as theatre. *RAIN: Royal Anthropological Institute News, 20:* 1–6.

Becker, J. (1994). Music and trance. *Leonardo Music Journal, 4:* 41–51.

Bednarowski, M. F. (1980). Outside the mainstream: Women's religion and women religious leaders in nineteenth century America. *Journal of the American Academy of Religion, 48*(2): 207–232.

Beischel, J. (2010). The reincarnation of survival research. *Edgesience, 3:* 10–12.

Beischel, J., Mosher, C., & Boccuzzi, M. (2014). The possible effects on bereavement of assisted after-death communication during readings with psychic mediums: a continuing bonds perspective. *OMEGA: Journal of Death and Dying, 70*(2): 169–194.

Beischel, J., & Rock, A. J. (2009). Addressing the survival vs. psi debate through process-focused mediumship research. *Journal of Parapsychology, 73:* 71–90.

Beischel, J., & Schwartz, G. (2007). Anomalous information reception by research mediums demonstrated using a novel triple-blind protocol. *Explore: The Journal of Science and Healing, 3*(1): 23–37.

Bem, D. (2011). Feeling the future: Experimental evidence for anomalous retroactive influences on cognition and affect. *Journal of Personality and Social Psychology, 100:* 407–425.

Bennett, G. (1987). *Traditions of Belief: Women, Folklore and the Supernatural Today.* London: Penguin.

Berger, P. L. (1971). *A Rumour of Angels: Modern Society and the Rediscovery of the Supernatural.* London: Penguin.

Berlotti, T., & Magnani, L. (2010). The role of agency detection in the invention of supernatural beings: An abductive approach. In: L. Magnani, W. Carnielli, & C. Pizzi (Eds.), *Model-Based Reasoning in Science and Technology* (pp. 239–262). Berlin: Springer.

Bird-David, N. (1999). Animism revisited: Personhood, environment, and relational epistemology. *Current Anthropology, 40S:* 67–79.

Biscop, P. (1985). *There Is No Death: Belief and the Social-Construction of Reality in a Canadian Spiritualist Church—A Study in the Anthropology of*

Knowledge. Unpublished PhD thesis, Simon Fraser University, Burnaby, BC, Canada.

Blackmore, S. (1992). *Beyond the Body: An Investigation into Out-of-the-Body Experiences.* Chicago, IL: Academy of Chicago Publishers.

Blackmore, S. (2011). *A 21ˢᵗ Century Séance.* presentation, 22 November, Goldsmith's University, London.

Blanes, R., & Espírito Santo, D. (2013). *The Social Life of Spirits.* Chicago, IL: Chicago University Press.

Blum, D. (2007). *Ghost Hunters: The Victorians and the Hunt for Proof of Life After Death.* London: Arrow.

Boddy, J. (1988). Spirits and selves in northern Sudan: The cultural therapeutics of possession and trance. *American Ethnologist, 15*(1): 4–27.

Bourguignon, E. (1973). A framework for the comparative study of altered states of consciousness. In: E. Bourguignon (Ed.), *Religion, Altered States of Consciousness and Social Change* (pp. 3–37). Columbus, OH: Ohio State University Press.

Bourguignon, E. (2007). Spirit possession. In: C. Casey & R. B. Edgerton (Eds.), *A Companion to Psychological Anthropology* (pp. 374–388). Oxford: Blackwell.

Bourguignon, E., Bellisari, A., & McCabe, S. (1983). Women, possession trance cults, and the extended nutrient-deficiency hypothesis. *American Anthropologist, 85*(2): 413–416.

Bowker, J. (1973). *The Sense of God: Sociological, Anthropological and Psychological Approaches to the Origin of the Sense of God.* Oxford: Clarendon.

Bowie, F. (2003). An anthropology of religious experience: Spirituality, gender and cultural transmission in the Focolare Movement. *Ethnos, 68*(1): 49–72.

Bowie, F. (2010). Methods for studying the paranormal (and who says what is normal anyway?). *Paranthropology: Journal of Anthropological Approaches to the Paranormal, 1*(1): 4–6.

Bowie, F. (2012). Devising methods for the ethnographic study of the afterlife: Cognition, empathy and engagement. In: J. Hunter (Ed.), *Paranthropology: Anthropological Approaches to the Paranormal* (pp. 99–106). Bristol, UK: Paranthropology.

Bowie, F. (2013a). Building bridges, dissolving boundaries: Towards a methodology for the ethnographic study of the afterlife, mediumship and spiritual beings. *Journal of the American Academy of Religion, 81*(3): 698–733.

Bowie, F. (2013b). *Material and Immaterial Bodies: Ethnographic Reflections on a Trance Séance.* Available online: https://academia.edu/2186310/Material_and_Immaterial_Bodies_Ethnographic_Reflections_on_a_Trance_Seance (accessed April 16, 2020).

Bowie, F. (2015). Miracles. In: M. Cardin (Ed.), *Ghosts, Spirits and Psychics: The Paranormal from Alchemy to Zombies* (pp. 161–166). Santa Barbara, CA: ABC-CLIO.

Bowker, J. (1973). *The Sense of God: Sociological, Anthropological and Psychological Approaches to the Origin of the Sense of God.* Oxford: Clarendon.

Boyer, P. (2001). *Religion Explained.* London: Heinemann.

Braude, S. (1988). Mediumship and multiple personality disorder. *Journal of the Society for Psychical Research, 55*(813): 177–195.

Braude, S. (1997). *The Limits of Influence: Psychokinesis and the Philosophy of Science.* New York: University Press of America.

Braude, S. (2003). *Immortal Remains: The Evidence for Life After Death.* Oxford: Rowman & Littlefield.

Braude, S. (2014). Investigations of the Felix Experimental Group: 2010–2013. *Journal of Scientific Exploration, 28*(2): 285–343.

Bristol Evening Post. (1979, 1 March). Medium sized target.

Bristol Evening Post. (1980, 28 February). Church in search for home.

Broughton, R. (1991). *Parapsychology: The Controversial Science.* London: Rider.

Brower, M. B. (2010). *Unruly Spirits: The Science of Psychic Phenomena in Modern France.* Urbana, IL: University of Illinois Press.

Brown, M. F. (1997). *The Channeling Zone: American Spirituality in an Anxious Age.* Cambridge, MA: Harvard University Press.

Bubandt, N. (2009). Interview with an ancestor: Spirits as informants and the politics of possession in North Maluku. *Ethnography, 10*(3): 291–316.

Budden, A. (2003). Pathologizing possession: An essay on mind, self and experience in dissociation. *Anthropology of Consciousness, 14*(2): 27–59.

Burger, E. (2012). Magic, science and religion: A conversation with Eugene Burger. *Paranthropology: Journal of Anthropological Approaches to the Paranormal, 3*(4): 29–31.

Byrne, G. (2010). *Modern Spiritualism and the Church of England, 1850–1939.* Woodbridge, UK: Boydell.

Cardeña, E., Lynn, S. J., & Krippner, S. C. (Eds.) (2000). *The Varieties of Anomalous Experience: Examining the Scientific Evidence.* Washington, DC: American Psychological Association.

Cardeña, E., van Duijl, M., Weiner, L. A., & Terhune, D. B. (2009). Possession/trance phenomena. In: P. F. Dell & J. A. O'Neil (Eds.), *Dissociation and the Dissociative Disorders* (pp. 171–181). New York: Routledge.

Cardeña, E. (2014). Call for an open, informed study of all aspects of consciousness. *Frontiers in Human Neuroscience, 8*(17).

Cardin, M. (Ed.) (2015). *Ghosts, Spirits and Psychics: The Paranormal from Alchemy to Zombies.* Santa Barbara, CA: ABC-CLIO.

Carrazana, E., DeToledo, J., Tatum, W., Rivas-Vasquez, R., Rey, G., & Wheeler, S. (1999). Epilepsy and religious experience: Voodoo possession. *Epilepsia*, 40(2): 239–241.

Carrithers, M., Candea, M., Sykes, K., Holbraad, M., & Venkatesan, S. (2010). Ontology is just another word for culture: Motion tabled at the 2008 Meeting of the Group for Debates in Anthropological Theory. *Critique of Anthropology*, 30(2): 152–200.

Carrithers, M., Collins, S., & Lukes, S. (1985). *The Category of the Person: Anthropology, Philosophy, History*. Cambridge: Cambridge University Press.

Castaneda, C. (1968). *The Teachings of Don Juan: A Yaqui Way of Knowledge*. London: Penguin, 1976.

Castillo, R. J. (1994). Spirit possession in South Asia, dissociation or hysteria? Part 1: Theoretical background. *Culture, Medicine and Psychiatry*, 18: 1–21.

Castillo, R. J. (1995). Culture, trance and the mind-brain. *Anthropology of Consciousness*, 6(1): 17–32.

Castro, M., Burrows, R., & Wooffitt, R. (2014). The paranormal is (still) normal: The sociological implications of a survey of paranormal experiences in Great Britain. *Sociological Research Online*, 19(3): 16.

Caswell, J. M. (2014). Consciousness, cross-cultural anomalies and a call for experimental research in paranthropology. *Journal of Consciousness Exploration and Research*, 5(1): 331–340.

Caswell, J. M., Hunter, J., & Tessaro, L. W. E. (2014). Phenomenological convergence between major paradigms of classic parapsychology and cross-cultural practices: An exploration of paranthropology. *Journal of Consciousness Exploration and Research*, 5(5): 467–482.

Census. (2001). Census Standard Tables: Table T53—Theme Table on Religion—BRISTOL. Available from: https://bristol.gov.uk/documents/20182/35004/Religion%202001.pdf/345a99fb-083b-4425-96be-22215f2e6f41 (accessed 30 August 2017).

Chalmers, D. (1995). Facing up to the problem of consciousness. *Journal of Consciousness Studies*, 2(3): 200–219.

Churchland, P. S. (1982). Mind-brain reduction: New light from the philosophy of science. *Neuroscience*, 7(5): 1041–1047.

Clarke, D. (1995). Experience and other reasons given for belief and disbelief in paranormal and religious phenomena. *Journal of the Society for Psychical Research*, 60(841): 371–384.

Cohen, E. (2008). What is spirit possession? defining, comparing and explaining two possession forms. *Ethos*, 73(1): 101–126.

Cohen, E., & Barrett, J. L. (2011). In search of "folk anthropology": The cognitive anthropology of the person. In: J. Wentzel van Huyssteen & E. P. Wiebe (Eds.), *In Search of Self: Interdisciplinary Perspectives on Personhood* (pp. 104–124). Cambridge, MA: Wm. B. Eerdmans.

Comte, A. (1976). The positive philosophy. In: K. Thompson & J. Tunstall (Eds.), *Sociological Perspectives* (pp. 18–32). London: Penguin.

Conan, M. (2007). Introduction: the cultural agency of gardens and landscapes. In: M. Conan (Ed.), *Sacred Gardens and Landscapes: Ritual and Agency*. Washington, DC: Dumbarton Oaks Research Library.

Conan Doyle, A. (1926). *A History of Spiritualism*. Fairford, UK: The Echo Library, 2006.

Cooper, I. S. (1989). *Theosophy Simplified*. Wheaton, IL: Quest.

Corbin, H. (1964). Mundus imaginalis or the imaginary and the imaginal. *Cahiers internationaux de symbolisme, 6*: 3–26.

Cox, J. L. (2008). Community mastery of the spirits as an African form of shamanism. Available from: http://basr.ac.uk/diskus/diskus9/cox.htm (accessed July 02, 2020).

Crabtree, A. (1988). *Multiple Man: Explorations in Possession and Multiple Personality*. London: Grafton.

Crapanzano, V. (2005). Spirit possession: An overview. In: L. Jones (Ed.), *Encyclopedia of Religion* (pp. 8687–8694). London: Macmillan.

Crick, F. (1994). *The Astonishing Hypothesis: The Scientific Search for the Soul*. New York: Touchstone.

Crookes, W. (1874). *Researches in the Phenomena of Spiritualism*. London: J. Burns.

Csordas, T. J. (1987). Health and the holy in African and Afro-American spirit possession. *Social Science and Medicine, 24*(1): 1–11.

Csordas, T. J. (1990). Embodiment as a paradigm for anthropology. *Ethos, 18*(1): 5–47.

Daniels, M. (2002). The transpersonal self: 1. A psychohistory and phenomenology of the soul. *Transpersonal Psychology Review, 6*(1): 17–28.

Davison, G. C., Neale, J. M., & Kring, A. M. (2004). *Abnormal Psychology*. Hoboken, NJ: John Wiley & Sons.

Dawkins, R. (2006). *The God Delusion*. London: Transworld.

Dawson, A. (Ed.) (2010). *Summoning the Spirits: Possession and Invocation in Contemporary Religion*. London: I. B. Tauris.

Dawson, L. L. (1998). *Comprehending Cults: The Sociology of New Religious Movements*. Oxford: Oxford University Press.

de Craemer, W. (1983). A cross-cultural perspective on personhood. *The Milbank Memorial Fund Quarterly: Health and Society, 61*(1): 19–34.

de Heusch, L. (1971). *Pourquoi l'épouser? et autres essais*. Paris: Gallimard.

Delorme, A., Beischel, J., Michel, L., Boccuzzi, M., Radin, D., & Mills, P. J. (2013). Electrocortical activity associated with subjective communication with the deceased. *Frontiers in Psychology, 4*(834).

de Martino, E. (1975). *Magic: Primitive and Modern*. London: Tom Stacey.

De Mille, R. (1979). Explicating anomalistic anthropology with help from Castaneda. *Zetetic Scholar*, 3–4: 69–70.

De Mille, R. (2000). *Casteneda's Journey: The Power and the Allegory*. Bloomington, IN: iUniverse.

DePaulo, B. M. (1992). Nonverbal behavior and self-presentation. *Psychological Bulletin*, 111(3): 203–243.

Deren, M. (2004). *Divine Horsemen: The Living Gods of Haiti*. New York: McPherson.

Descartes, R. (1968). *Discourse on Method and The Meditations*. London: Penguin.

Di Nucci, C. (2009). *Spirits in a Teacup: Questioning the Reality of Life After Death Has Led One Housewife Along an Adventurous Path Towards Discovery*. Bristol, UK: The Bristol Spirit Lodge.

Di Nucci, C., & Hunter, J. (2009). *Charlie: Trance Communications and Spirit Teachings*. Bristol, UK: The Bristol Spirit Lodge.

Donovan, J. M. (2000). A Brazilian challenge to Lewis' explanation of cult mediumship. *Journal of Contemporary Religion*, 15(3): 361–377.

Durkheim, E. (2008). *The Elementary Forms of the Religious Life*. Oxford: Oxford University Press.

Edwards, H. (1940). *The Mediumship of Arnold Clare*. London: The Psychic Book Club.

Edwards, H. (1978). *The Mediumship of Jack Webber*. Guildford, UK: The Harry Edwards Spiritual Healing Sanctuary.

Eliade, M. (1989). *Shamanism: Archaic Techniques of Ecstasy*. London: Arkana.

Emmons, C. F. (2008). On becoming a spirit medium in a "rational" society. *Anthropology of Consciousness*, 12(1): 71–82.

Emmons, C. F., & Emmons, P. (2012). *Science and Spirit: Exploring the Limits of Consciousness*. Bloomington, IN: iUniverse.

Escolar, D. (2012). Boundaries of anthropology: Empirics and ontological relativism in a field experience with anomalous luminous entities in Argentina. *Anthropology and Humanism*, 37(1): 27–44.

Espírito Santo, D. (2011). Process, personhood and possession in Cuban spiritism. In: A. Dawson (Ed.), *Summoning the Spirits: Possession and Invocation in Contemporary Religion* (pp. 93–108). London: I. B. Tauris.

Evans, H. (1987). *Gods, Spirits, Cosmic Guardians: A Comparative Study of the Encounter Experience*. Wellingborough, UK: Aquarian.

Evans-Pritchard, E. E. (1937). *Witchcraft, Oracles and Magic Among the Azande*. Oxford: Oxford University Press, 1976.

Evans-Pritchard, E. E. (1965). *Theories of Primitive Religion*. Oxford: Oxford University Press, 1972.

Favret-Saada, J. (1977). *Deadly Words: Witchcraft in the Bocage*. Cambridge: Cambridge University Press.

Ferrari, F. M. (2014). *Ernesto de Martino on Religion: The Crisis and the Presence.* Abingdon, UK: Routledge.

Firth, R. (1967). Ritual and drama in Malay spirit mediumship. *Comparative Studies in Society and History, 9*(2): 190–207.

Foley, K. (1985). The dancer and the danced: Trance dance and theatrical performance in West Java. *Asian Theatre Journal, 2*(1): 28–49.

Fort, C. (2008). *The Book of the Damned: The Complete Works of Charles Fort.* London: Tarcher.

Foy, R. (2007). *In Pursuit of Physical Mediumship.* London: Janus.

Foy, R. (2008). *Witnessing the Impossible: The Only Complete and Accurate Eyewitness Account of the Amazing Physical Psychic Phenomena Experienced at Scole, Norfolk, UK and Overseas During the Scole Experiment: 1992–1998.* Diss, UK: Torcal.

Frazer, J. G. (1944). *Magic and Religion.* London: Watts.

Frazer, J. G. (1993). *The Golden Bough: A Study in Magic and Religion.* Ware, UK: Wordsworth.

Freed, S. A., & Freed, R. S. (1964). Spirit possession as illness in a North Indian village. *Ethnology, 3*(2): 152–171.

Freeman, J. R. (1998). Formalised possession among the Tantris and Teyyams of Malabar. *South Asia Research, 18*(1): 73–98.

Freud, S., & Breuer, J. (1895d). *Studies on Hysteria.* London: Penguin, 1974.

Fry, P. (1986). Male homosexuality and spirit possession in Brazil. *Journal of Homosexuality, 11*(3–4): 137–153.

Gaskill, M. (2001). *Hellish Nell: Last of Britain's Witches.* London: Harper Collins.

Gauld, A. (1982). *Mediumship and Survival: A Century of Investigations.* London: Granada.

Geertz, C. (1974). From the native's point of view: On the nature of anthropological understanding. *Bulletin of the American Academy of Arts and Sciences, 28*(1): 26–45.

Geley, G. (2006). *Clairvoyance and Materialisation: A Record of Experiments.* Whitefish, MT: Kessinger.

Giesler, P. V. (1984). Parapsychological anthropology: I. Multi-method approaches to the study of psi in the field setting. *Journal of the American Society for Psychical Research, 78*(4): 289–330.

Gilbert, H. (2010). A sociological perspective on "becoming" a spirit medium in Britain. *Rhine-Online: Psi News Magazine, 2*(1): 10–12.

Giles, L. L. (1987). Possession cults on the Swahili coast: A re-examination of theories of marginality. *Africa: Journal of the International African Institute, 57*(2): 234–258.

Glass-Coffin, B. (2012). The future of a discipline: considering the ontological/methodological future of the anthropology of consciousness,

Part IV: Ontological relativism or ontological relevance: An essay in honor of Michael Harner. *Anthropology of Consciousness*, *23*(2): 113–126.

Goff, D. C., Brotman, A. W., Kindlon, D., Waites, M., & Amico, E. (1991). The delusion of possession in chronically psychotic patients. *Journal of Nervous and Mental Disease*, *179*(9): 567–571.

Goffman, E. (1990). *The Presentation of Self in Everyday Life*. London: Penguin.

Gomm, R. (1975). Bargaining from weakness: Spirit possession on the South Kenya coast. *Man*, *10*(4): 530–543.

Goodman, F. D. (1999). Ritual body postures, channeling and ecstatic body trance. *Anthropology of Consciousness*, *10*(1): 54–59.

Gould, S. J. (2007). Two separate domains. In: M. Peterson, W. Hasker, B. Reichenbach, & D. Basinger (Eds.), *Philosophy of Religion: Selected Readings* (pp. 549–558). Oxford: Oxford University Press.

Goulet, J.-G., & Miller, B. G. (Eds.) (2007). *Extraordinary Anthropology: Transformations in the Field*. Lincoln, NE: University of Nebraska Press.

Graham, F. (2011). Commentary on "Reflecting on Paranthropology." *Paranthropology: Journal of Anthropological Approaches to the Paranormal*, *2*(3): 20–21.

Graham, F. (2014). Vessels for the gods: Tang-ki spirit mediumship in Singapore and Taiwan. In: J. Hunter & D. Luke (Eds.), *Talking With the Spirits: Ethnographies from Between the Worlds* (pp. 325–346). Brisbane, Australia: Daily Grail.

Graham, R. (2017). *UFOs: Reframing the Debate*. Guildford, UK: White Crow.

Greeley, A. (1975). *The Sociology of the Paranormal*. London: Sage.

Greenfield, S. (2008). *Spirits with Scalpels*. Walnut Creek, CA: Left Coast.

Greenwood, S. (2013). On becoming an owl: Magical consciousness. In: G. Samuel & J. Johnston (Eds.), *Religion and the Subtle Body in Asia and the West: Between Mind and Body* (pp. 211–223). Abingdon, UK: Routledge.

Greenwood, S. (2015). The dragon and me: Anthropology and the paranormal. *Paranthropology: Journal of Anthropological Approaches to the Paranormal*, *6*(1): 4–25.

Grindal, B. T. (1983). Into the heart of Sisala experience: Witnessing death divination. *Journal of Anthropological Research*, *39*(1): 60–80.

Grosso, M. (2016). *The Man Who Could Fly: St. Joseph of Copertino and the Mystery of Levitation*. Lanham, MD: Rowman & Littlefield.

Guthrie, S. (1980). A cognitive theory of religion. *Current Anthropology*, *21*(2): 181–203.

Guthrie, S. (1993). *Faces in the Clouds: A New Theory of Religion*. Oxford: Oxford University Press.

Hageman, J. H., Peres, J. F. P., Moreira-Almeida, A., Caixeta, L., Wickramasekera II, I., & Krippner, S. (2010). The neurobiology of trance and mediumship in Brazil. In: S. Krippner & H. L. Friedman (Eds.),

Mysterious Minds: The Neurobiology of Psychics, Mediums and Other Extraordinary People (pp. 85–112). Oxford: Praeger.

Hallowell, A. I. (2002). Ojibwa ontology, behaviour, and world view. In: G. Harvey (Ed.), *Readings in Indigenous Religions* (pp. 18–48). London: Continuum.

Halloy, A. (2010). Comments on "The Mind Possessed: The Cognition of Spirit Possession in an Afro-Brazilian Religious Tradition" by Emma Cohen. *Religion and Society: Advances in Research, 1*: 164–176.

Hancock, G. (2013). The war on consciousness. Available online at http://m.youtube.com/watch?v=Y0c5nlvJH7w (accessed May 21, 2017).

Hanegraaff, W. J. (1998). *New Age Religion and Western Culture: Esotericism in the Mirror of Secular Thought*. New York: State University of New York Press.

Hansen, G. P. (1990). Deception by test subjects in psi research. *Journal of the American Society for Psychical Research, 84*(1): 25–80.

Hansen, G. P. (2001). *The Trickster and the Paranormal*. Bloomington, IN: Xlibris.

Hansen, G. P. (2010). Rationalization, secularization and the paranormal: On the "elimination" of magic from the world. *Proceedings of the 2010 Annual Conference of the Academy for Spirituality and Paranormal Studies*: 117–128.

Harner, M. (1990). *The Way of the Shaman*. San Francisco, CA: Harper.

Harner, M. (2013). *Cave and Cosmos: Shamanic Encounters with Another Reality*. Berkeley, CA: North Atlantic.

Harpur, P. (2002). *The Philosophers' Secret Fire: A History of the Imagination*. London: Penguin.

Harris, G. G. (1989). Concepts of individual, self, and person in description and analysis. *American Anthropologist, 91*(3): 599–612.

Harris, R. (1968). *The Rise of Anthropological Theory*. London: Routledge & Kegan Paul.

Harris, S. (2010). *The Moral Landscape*. London: Black Swan.

Hartley, R. (2007). *Helen Duncan: The Mystery Show Trial*. London: HPR.

Harvey, G. (2005). *Animism: Respecting the Living World*. London: Hurst.

Haule, J. R. (2011). *Jung in the 21st Century, Vol. II: Synchronicity and Science*. London: Routledge.

Hawking, S. (1988). *A Brief History of Time: From the Big Bang to Black Holes*. London: Bantam.

Haynes, R. (1982). *The Society for Psychical Research: 1882–1982, A History*. London: MacDonald.

Heath, P. R. (2000). The PK zone: A phenomenological study. *Journal of Parapsychology, 64*: 53–72.

Heathcote-James, E. (2001). *Seeing Angels*. London: John Blake.

Henare, A., Holbraad, M., & Wastell, S. (Eds.) (2006). *Thinking Through Things: Theorising Artefacts Ethnographically*. London: Routledge.

Hitchens, C. (2007). *God Is Not Great: How Religion Poisons Everything.* London: Atlantic.

Holbraad, M., & Pedersen, M. A. (2017). *The Ontological Turn: An Anthropological Exposition.* Cambridge: Cambridge University Press.

Holbraad, M., Pedersen, M. A., & Viveiros de Castro, E. (2014). The politics of ontology: Anthropological positions. Available from: https://culanth.org/fieldsights/462-the-politics-of-ontology-anthropological-positions (accessed January 13, 2014).

Holt, N. J., Simmonds-Moore, C., Luke, D., & French, C. C. (2012). *Anomalistic Psychology.* Basingstoke, UK: Palgrave Macmillan.

Howard, A. J. (2013). Beyond belief: Ethnography, the supernatural and hegemonic discourse. *Practical Matters, 6*: 1–17.

Hufford, D. J. (1982). *The Terror That Comes in the Night: An Experience-Centred Study of Supernatural Assault Traditions.* Philadelphia, PA: University of Pennsylvania Press.

Hufford, D. J. (1995). Beings without bodies: An experience-centred theory of the belief in spirits. In: B. Walker (Ed.), *Out of the Ordinary: Folklore and the Supernatural* (pp. 1–45). Logan, UT: Utah State University Press.

Hufford, D. J. (2013). Modernity's defences. Paper presented at the Esalen Institute, Big Sur, California, October.

Hughes, D. J. (1991). Blending with an other: An analysis of trance channeling in the United States. *Ethos, 19*(2): 161–184.

Hughes, D. J., & Melville, N. T. (1990). Changes in brainwave activity during trance channeling: A pilot study. *Journal of Transpersonal Psychology, 22*(2): 175–189.

Hume, D. (2000). *An Enquiry Concerning Human Understanding: A Critical Edition.* Oxford: Clarendon.

Hume, L. (1998). Creating sacred space: Outer expressions of inner worlds in modern Wicca. *Journal of Contemporary Religion, 13*(3): 309–319.

Hunter, J. (2009). *Talking With Spirits: An Experiential Exploration of Contemporary Trance and Physical Mediumship.* Unpublished undergraduate dissertation, University of Bristol.

Hunter, J. (2010). Contemporary mediumship and séance groups in the UK: Speculations on the Bristol Spirit Lodge. *Psychical Studies: Journal of the Unitarian Society for Psychical Studies, 76*: 7–13.

Hunter, J. (2011a). Talking with the spirits: Anthropology and interpreting spirit communicators. *Journal of the Society for Psychical Research, 75*.3(904): 129–142.

Hunter, J. (2011b). The anthropology of the weird: Ethnographic fieldwork and anomalous experience. In: G. Taylor (Ed.), *Darklore Vol. VI* (pp. 243–254). Brisbane, Australia: Daily Grail.

Hunter, J. (2012a). *Talking With Spirits: Personhood, Performance and Altered Consciousness in a Contemporary Spiritualist Home-Circle.* Unpublished M.Litt. dissertation, University of Bristol.

Hunter, J. (Ed.) (2012b). *Paranthropology: Anthropological Approaches to the Paranormal.* Bristol, UK: Paranthropology.

Hunter, J. (2012c). Contemporary physical mediumship: Is it part of a continuous tradition? *Paranthropology: Journal of Anthropological Approaches to the Paranormal,* 3(1): 35–43.

Hunter, J. (2012d). Expressions of spirithood: Performance and the manifestation of spirits. *Anomaly: Journal of Research into the Paranormal,* 46: 144–156.

Hunter, J. (2013). Numinous conversations: Performance and manifestation of spirits in spirit possession practices. In: A. Voss & W. Rowlandson (Eds.), *Daimonic Imagination: Uncanny Intelligence* (pp. 391–403). Newcastle-upon–Tyne, UK: Cambridge Scholars.

Hunter, J. (2014a). Mediumship and folk models of mind and matter. In: J. Hunter & D. Luke (Eds.), *Talking With the Spirits: Ethnographies From Between the Worlds* (pp. 99–131). Brisbane, Australia: Daily Grail.

Hunter, J. (2014b). Can science see spirits? Neuroimaging studies of mediumship and spirit possession. Available from: https://dailygrail.com/2014/05/can-science-see-spirits/ (accessed 9 January 2018).

Hunter, J. (2015a). "Spirits are the problem": Anthropology and conceptualising spiritual beings. *Journal for the Study of Religious Experience,* 1(1): 76–86.

Hunter, J. (2015b). "Between realness and unrealness": Anthropology, parapsychology and the ontology of non-ordinary realities. *Diskus: Journal of the British Association for the Study of Religion,* 17(2): 4–20.

Hunter, J. (2016a). Engaging the anomalous: Reflections from the anthropology of the paranormal. *European Journal of Psychotherapy and Counselling,* 18(2): 170–178.

Hunter, J. (Ed.) (2016b). *Damned Facts: Fortean Essays on Religion, Folklore and the Paranormal.* Paphos, Cyprus: Aporetic.

Hunter, J. (2019). *Greening the Paranormal: Exploring the Ecology of Extraordinary Experience.* Milton Keynes, UK: August Night.

Hunter, J., & Luke, D. (Eds.) (2014). *Talking With the Spirits: Ethnographies from Between the Worlds.* Brisbane, Australia: Daily Grail.

Hustvedt, A. (2011). *Medical Muses: Hysteria in Nineteenth Century Paris.* New York: Bloomsbury.

Hutton, R. (2007). *Shamans: Siberian Spirituality and the Western Imagination.* London: Continuum.

Huxley, F. (1967). Anthropology and ESP. In: J. R. Smythies (Ed.), *Science and ESP* (pp. 281–302). London: Routledge & Kegan Paul.

Inglis, B. (1989). *Trance: A Natural History of Altered States of Mind*. London: Grafton.

Jackson, M. (Ed.) (1996). *Things As They Are: New Directions in Phenomenological Anthropology*. Bloomington, IN: Indiana University Press.

Jahn, R. G., & Dunne, B. J. (1997). Science of the subjective. *Journal of Scientific Exploration*, 11(2): 201–224.

James, W. (2004). *The Varieties of Religious Experience*. New York: Barnes & Noble.

Jansen, R. (2010). The soul seeker: A neuroscientist's search for the human essence. *Texas Observer*, 28 May, pp. 17–20.

Jaynes, J. (1976). *The Origin of Consciousness in the Breakdown of the Bicameral Mind*. Boston, MA: Houghton Mifflin.

Jilek-Aall, L. (1999). Morbus sacer in Africa: Some religious aspects of epilepsy in traditional cultures. *Epilepsia*, 40(3): 382–386.

Johnson, R. C. (1955). *Psychical Research*. London: English Universities Press.

Jokic, Z. (2008a). Yanomami shamanic initiation: The meaning of death and postmortem consciousness in transformation. *Anthropology of Consciousness*, 19(1): 33–59.

Jokic, Z. (2008b). The wrath of the forgotten Ongons: Shamanic sickness, spirit embodiment, and fragmentary trancescape in contemporary Buriat shamanism. *Sibirica*, 7(1): 23–50.

Jones, S. H., Adams, T. E., & Ellis, C. (2016). *Handbook of Autoethnography*. London: Routledge.

Jules-Rosette, B. (1980). Ceremonial trance behaviour in an African church: Private experience and public expression. *Journal of the Scientific Study of Religion*, 19(1): 1–16.

Jung, C. G. (1977). *Psychology and the Occult*. London: Routledge, 2007.

Kant, I. (1766). *Dreams of a Spirit-Seer*. London: Macmillan, 1963.

Kardec, A. (2006). *The Spirits' Book*. New York: Cosimo.

Kastrup, B. (2011). *Meaning in Absurdity: What Bizarre Phenomena Can Tell Us About the Nature of Reality*. Alresford, UK: Iff.

Kastrup, B. (2014). *Why Materialism Is Baloney: How True Skeptics Know There Is No Death and Fathom Answers to Life, the Universe and Everything*. Alresford, UK: Iff.

Keel, J. A. (2013). *The Eight Tower: On Ultraterrestrials and the Superspectrum*. San Antonio, TX: Anomalist.

Keen, M. (2001). The Scole investigation: A study in critical analysis of paranormal physical phenomena. *Journal of Scientific Exploration*, 15(2): 167–182.

Keen, M., Ellison, A., & Fontana, D. (1999). *The Scole Report*. London: Saturday Night, 2011.

Keener, C. S. (2010). Spirit possession as a cross-cultural experience. *Bulletin for Biblical Research, 20*(2): 215–236.

Kehoe, A. B., & Giletti, D. H. (1981). Women's preponderance in possession cults: The calcium-deficiency hypothesis extended. *American Anthropologist, 83*(3): 549–561.

Kelly, E. F., Kelly, E. W., Crabtree, A., Gauld, A., Grosso, M., & Greyson, B. (2007). *Irreducible Mind: Toward a Psychology for the 21st Century.* Lanham, MD: Rowman & Littlefield.

Kelly, E. F., & Locke, R. G. (2009). *Altered States of Consciousness and Psi: An Historical Survey and Research Prospectus.* New York: Parapsychology Foundation.

Keyes, D. (1995). *The Minds of Billy Milligan.* London: Bantam.

Kilson, M. (1971). Ambivalence and power: Mediums in Ga traditional religion. *Journal of Religion in Africa, 4*: 171–177.

Klass, M. (2003). *Mind Over Mind: The Anthropology and Psychology of Spirit Possession.* Oxford: Rowman & Littlefield.

Klimo, J. (1987). *Channeling: Investigations on Receiving Information from Paranormal Sources.* Los Angeles, CA: Jeremy P. Tarcher.

Kohn, E. (2013). *How Forests Think: Toward an Anthropology Beyond the Human.* Berkeley, CA: University of California Press.

Koss-Chioino, J. (2010). Introduction: Do spirits exist?. *Anthropology and Humanism, 35*(2): 131–141.

Kripal, J. J. (2010). *Authors of the Impossible: The Paranormal and the Sacred.* Chicago, IL: University of Chicago Press.

Kripal, J. J. (2011). *Mutants and Mystics: Science Fiction, Superhero Comics and the Paranormal.* Chicago, IL: University of Chicago Press.

Kripal, J. J. (2014). *Comparing Religions: Coming to Terms.* Chichester, UK: John Wiley & Sons.

Krippner, S. (2002). Stigmatic phenomena: An alleged case in Brazil. *Journal of Scientific Exploration, 16*(2): 207–224.

Krippner, S. (2008). Learning from the spirits: Candomblé, Umbanda and Kardecismo in Recife, Brazil. *Anthropology of Consciousness, 19*(1): 1–32.

Krippner, S., & Kirkwood, J. (2008). Sacred bleeding: The language of stigmata. In: J. Harold Ellens (Ed.), *Miracles: God, Science and Psychology in the Paranormal (Vol. 1)* (pp. 154–175). Westport, CT: Praeger.

Kuhn, T. (1973). *The Structure of Scientific Revolutions.* Chicago, IL: University of Chicago Press.

Lachman, G. (2014). *Revolutionaries of the Soul: Reflections on Magicians, Philosophers and Occultists.* Wheaton, IL: Quest.

Lachman, G. (2017). Faculty X and other times and places. In: C. Stanley (Ed.), *Proceedings of the First International Colin Wilson Conference* (pp. 115–125). Newcastle-upon-Tyne, UK: Cambridge Scholars.

Laidlaw, J. (2007). A well-disposed social anthropologist's problems with the cognitive science of religion. In: H. Whitehouse & J. Laidlaw (Eds.), *Religion, Anthropology & Cognitive Science* (pp. 211–245). Durham, NC: Carolina Academic.

Lajoie, D. H., & Shapiro, S. I. (1992). Definitions of transpersonal psychology: The first twenty-three years. *Journal of Transpersonal Psychology, 24*(1): 79–98.

Lambek, M. (1998). The Sakalava Poiesis of history: Realizing the past through spirit possession in Madagascar. *American Ethnologist, 25*(2): 106–127.

Lamont, P. (2005). *The First Psychic: The Peculiar Mystery of a Notorious Victorian Wizard*. London: Abacus.

Lamont, P., & Wiseman, R. (1999). *Magic in Theory: An Introduction to the Theoretical and Psychological Elements of Conjuring*. Hatfield, UK: University of Hertfordshire Press.

Lang, A. (1900). *The Making of Religion*. Available from: https://ebooks. adelaide.edu.au/l/lang/andrew/making_of_religion/index.html (accessed September 1, 2017).

Lang, A. (1894). *Cock Lane and Common Sense*. Charleston, SC: Bibliobazaar, 2010.

Laszlo, I. (2007). *Science and the Akashic Field: An Integral Theory of Everything*. Rochester, VT: Inner Traditions.

Latour, B. (2013). *An Inquiry Into Modes of Existence*. Cambridge, MA: Harvard University Press.

Laughlin, C. D. (1997). The cycle of meaning: Some methodological implications of biogenetic structural theory. In: S. Glazier (Ed.), *Anthropology of Religion: Handbook of Theory and Method* (pp. 471–488). Westport, CT: Greenwood.

Laughlin, C. D. (2012). Transpersonal anthropology: What is it, and what are the problems we face in doing it? In: J. Hunter (Ed.), *Paranthropology: Anthropological Approaches to the Paranormal* (pp. 69–98). Bristol, UK: Paranthropology.

Laughlin, C. D. (2013). Dreaming and reality: A neuroanthropological account. *International Journal of Transpersonal Studies, 32*: 64–78.

Leacock, S., & Leacock, R. (1975). *Spirits of the Deep: A Study of an Afro-Brazilian Cult*. New York: Anchor.

LeDoux, J. (2002). *Synaptic Self: How Our Brains Become Who We Are*. New York: Penguin Viking.

Lehman, A. (2009). *Victorian Women and the Theatre of Trance: Mediums, Spiritualists and Mesmerists in Performance*. London: McFarland.

LeShan, L. (1995). When is Uvani? *Journal of the American Society for Psychical Research, 89*: 165–175.

Lévi-Strauss, C. (1986). *Structural Anthropology, Volume I*. London: Penguin.

Levy, R. I., Mageo, J. M., & Howard, A. (1996). Gods, spirits, and history. In: J. M. Mageo & A. Howard (Eds.), *Spirits in Culture, History, and Mind* (pp. 11–28). London: Routledge.

Lewis, I. M. (1971). *Ecstatic Religion: An Anthropological Study of Spirit Possession and Shamanism*. London: Penguin.

Lewis, I. M. (1983). Spirit possession and biological reductionism: A rejoinder to Kehoe and Gilleti. *American Anthropologist, 85*: 412–413.

Lillard, A. (1998). Ethnopsychologies: Cultural variations in theories of mind. *Psychological Bulletin, 123*(1): 3–32.

Lilly, J. C. (1977). *The Deep Self: Profound Relaxation and the Tank Isolation Technique*. New York: Warner.

Lindberg, D. C. (1996). *The Beginnings of Western Science*. Chicago, IL: University of Chicago Press.

Littlewood, R. (1995). The return of multiple consciousnesses. In: A. P. Cohen & N. Rapport (Eds.), *Questions of Consciousness* (pp. 153–177). London: Routledge.

Littlewood, R., & Bartocci, G. (2005). Religious stigmata, magnetic fluids and conversion hysteria: On survival of "vital force" theories in scientific medicine. *Transcultural Psychiatry, 42*: 596–609.

Long, J. K. (Ed.) (1974). *Extrasensory Ecology: Anthropology and Parapsychology*. London: Scarecrow.

Luhrmann, T. M. (2011). Toward an anthropological theory of mind. *Suomen Antropologi: Journal of the Finnish Anthropological Society, 36*(4): 5–69.

Luhrmann, T. M. (2012). *When God Talks Back: Understanding the American Evangelical Relationship with God*. New York: Alfred A. Knopf.

Luke, D. (2010). Anthropology and parapsychology: Still hostile sisters in science? *Time and Mind: The Journal of Archaeology, Consciousness and Culture, 3*(3): 245–266.

Luke, D. (2012). Experiential reclamation and first-person parapsychology. *Paranthropology: Journal of Anthropological Approaches to the Paranormal, 3*(2): 4–14.

Machen, A. (1924). *The London Adventure*. London: Martin Secker.

Mackian, S. (2011). Crossing spiritual boundaries: encountering, articulating and representing otherworlds. *Methodological Innovations Online, 6*(3): 61–74.

Mackian, S. (2012). *Everyday Spirituality: Social and Spatial Worlds of Enchantment*. Basingstoke, UK: Palgrave Macmillan.

Malik, A. (2009). Dancing the body of God: Rituals of embodiment from the central Himalayas. *SITES: A Journal of Social Anthropology and Cultural Studies, 6*(1): 80–96.

Malinowski, B. (1974). *Magic, Science and Religion*. London: Condor.

Maraldi, E., Machado, F. R., & Zangari, W. (2010). Importance of a psycho-social approach for a comprehensive understanding of mediumship. *Journal of Scientific Exploration, 24*(2): 181–196.

Maraldi, E., Zangari, W., Machado, F. R., & Krippner, S. (2014). Anomalous mental and physical phenomena of Brazilian mediums: A review of the scientific literature. In: J. Hunter & D. Luke (Eds.), *Talking With the Spirits: Ethnographies from Between the Worlds* (pp. 257–300). Brisbane, Australia: Daily Grail.

Markus, H. R., & Kitayama, S. (1991). Culture and the self: Implications for cognition, emotion and motivation. *Psychological Bulletin, 98*(2): 224–253.

Marton, Y. (2010). A rose by any name is still a rose: The nomenclature of the paranormal. *Paranthropology: Journal of Anthropological Approaches to the Paranormal, 1*(1): 11–13.

Matthews, E. (2005). *Mind: Key Concepts in Philosophy*. London: Continuum.

Mauss, M. (1938). Une catégorie de l'esprit humain: La notion de personne celle de "moi". *Journal of the Royal Anthropological Institute of Great Britain and Ireland, 68*: 263–281.

Mauss, M. (1973). Techniques of the body. *Economy and Society, 2*(1): 70–88.

McClenon, J. (1993). The experiential foundations of shamanic healing. *Journal of Medicine and Philosophy, 18*: 107–127.

McClenon, J., & Nooney, J. (2002). Anomalous experiences reported by field anthropologists: Evaluating theories regarding religion. *Anthropology of Consciousness, 13*(12): 46–60.

McLuhan, R. (2010). *Randi's Prize: What Sceptics Say About the Paranormal, Why They Are Wrong and Why It Matters*. Leicester, UK: Matador.

McTaggart, L. (2001). *The Field: The Quest for the Secret Force of Life*. London: Harper Collins.

Mead, M. (1974). An anthropological approach to different types of commu-nication and the importance of differences in human temperaments. In: J. K. Long (Ed.), *Extrasensory Ecology: Parapsychology and Anthropology* (pp. 45–52). London: Scarecrow.

Meintel, D. (2007). When the extraordinary hits home: Experiencing spiri-tualism. In: J.-G. Goulet & B. G. Miller (Eds.), *Extraordinary Anthropol-ogy: Transformations in the Field* (pp. 124–157). Lincoln, NE: University of Nebraska Press.

Meintel, D. (2014). Spirits in the city: Examples from Montreal. In: J. Hunter & D. Luke (Eds.), *Talking With the Spirits: Ethnographies from Between the Worlds* (pp. 73–98). Brisbane, Australia: Daily Grail.

Melechi, A. (2008). *Servants of the Supernatural: The Night Side of the Victorian Mind*. London: William Heinemann.

Mesulam, M. M. (1981). Dissociative states with abnormal temporal lobe EEG: Multiple personality and the illusion of possession. *Archives of Neurology, 38*: 176–181.

Mills, J. (2014). Jung as philosopher: Archetypes, the psychoid factor and the question of the supernatural. *International Journal of Jungian Studies*, 6(3): 227–242.

Monroe, R. A. (1972). *Journeys Out of the Body*. London: Souvenir.

Moore, R. L. (1972). Spiritualism and science: Reflections on the first decade of the spirit rappings. *American Quarterly*, 24(4): 474–500.

Moreira-Almeida, A., Neto, F. L., & Cardeña, E. (2008). Comparison of Brazilian spiritist mediumship and dissociative identity disorder. *Journal of Nervous and Mental Disease, 196*(5): 420–424.

Moreman, C. M. (2010). *Beyond the Threshold: Afterlife Beliefs and Experiences in World Religions*. London: Rowman & Littlefield.

Muldoon, S., & Carrington, H. (1973). *The Phenomena of Astral Projection*. London: Rider.

Myers, F. W. H. (1903). *Human Personality and Its Survival of Bodily Death*. Norwich, UK: Pelegrin Trust, 1992.

Nagel, T. (1974). What is it like to be a bat? *Philosophical Review, 84*(4): 435–450.

Nagel, T. (2012). *Mind and Cosmos: Why the Materialist Neo-Darwinian Conception of Nature Is Almost Certainly Wrong*. Oxford: Oxford University Press.

Nahm, M. (2014). The development and phenomena of a circle for physical mediumship. *Journal of Scientific Exploration, 28*(1): 229–283.

Natale, S. (2011). The medium on the stage: Trance and performance in nineteenth century spiritualism. *Early Popular Visual Culture, 9*(3): 239–255.

Neher, A. (1990). *The Psychology of Transcendence*. New York: Dover.

Nelson, G. K. (1969). *Spiritualism and Society*. London: Routledge & Kegan Paul.

Nelson, G. K. (1972). The membership of a cult: The Spiritualist National Union. *Review of Religious Research, 13*(3): 170–177.

Nelson, G. K. (1975). Towards a sociology of the psychic. *Review of Religious Research, 16*(3): 166–173.

Newport, F., & Strausberg, M. (2001). Americans' belief in psychic and paranormal phenomena up over last decade. Available from: http://gallup.org/poll/4483/americans-belief-psychic-paranormal-phenomena-over-last-decade.aspx (accessed October 14, 2015).

Noll, R. (1985). Mental imagery cultivation as a cultural phenomenon: the role of visions in shamanism. *Current Anthropology, 26*(4): 443–461.

Northcote, J. (2004). Objectivity and the supernormal: The limitations of bracketing approaches in providing neutral accounts of supernormal claims. *Journal of Contemporary Religion, 19*(1): 85–98.

Obeyesekere, G. (1984). *Medusa's Hair: An Essay of Personal Symbols and Religious Experience*. Chicago, IL: University of Chicago Press.

Olson, C. (2011). *Religious Studies: The Key Concepts*. Abingdon, UK: Routledge.

Ong, A. (1988). The production of possession: Spirits and the multinational corporation in Malaysia. *American Ethnologist, 15*(1): 28–42.

Oohashi, T., Kawai, N., Honda, M., Nakamura, S., Morimoto, M., Nishina, E., & Maekawa, T. (2002). Electroencephalographic measurement of possession trance in the field. *Clinical Neurophysiology, 11*(3): 435–445.

Oppenheim, J. (1985). *The Otherworld: Spiritualism & Psychical Research in England, 1850–1914*. Cambridge: Cambridge University Press.

Osborne, G., & Bacon, A. M. (2015). The working life of a medium: A qualitative examination of mediumship as a support service for the bereaved. *Mental Health, Religion & Culture, 18*(4): 286–298.

Otto, R. (1958). *The Idea of the Holy*. Oxford: Oxford University Press.

Palecek, M., & Risjord, M. (2013). Relativism and the ontological turn within anthropology. *Philosophy of the Social Sciences, 43*(1): 3–23.

Palmer, T. (2014). *The Science of Spirit Possession*. Newcastle-upon-Tyne, UK: Cambridge Scholars.

Pearsall, R. (2004). *The Table-Rappers: The Victorians and the Occult*. Stroud, UK: Sutton.

Peres, J. F., Moreira-Almeida, A., Ciaxeta, L., Leao, F., & Newberg, A. (2012). Neuroimaging during trance state: A contribution to the study of dissociation. *PLoS ONE, 7*(11): 1–9.

Piaget, J. (1964). Part 1: Cognitive development in children: Piaget, development and learning. *Journal of Research in Science Teaching, 2*(3): 176–186.

Pierini, E. (2016). Becoming a spirit medium: Initiatory learning and the self in the Vale do Amanhecer. *Ethnos, 82*(2): 1–25.

Placido, B. (2001). "It's all to do with words": An analysis of spirit possession in the Venezuelan cult of Maria Lionza. *Journal of the Royal Anthropological Institute, 7*(2): 207–224.

Polidoro, M. (2001). *Final Séance: The Strange Friendship Between Houdini and Conan Doyle*. New York: Prometheus.

Prince, W. F. (1926). A review of the Margery mediumship. *American Journal of Psychology, 37*(3): 431–441.

Pyysiäinen, I., & Anttonen, V. (2002). *Current Approaches in the Cognitive Science of Religion*. London: Continuum.

Quinn, N. (2006). The self. *Anthropological Theory, 6*(3): 362–384.

Radin, D. (2006). *Entangled Minds*. New York: Paraview Pocketbooks.

Randall, J. L. (1975). *Parapsychology and the Nature of Life: A Scientific Appraisal*. London: Souvenir.

Rasmussen, S. J. (1994). The "head dance," contested self, and art as balancing act in Tuareg spirit possession. *Africa: Journal of the International African Institute, 64*(1): 74–98.

Ray, O. (2004). How the mind hurts and heals the body. *American Psychologist, 59*(1): 29–40.

Rhine, J. B., & Rhine, L. E. (1927). One evening's observation on the Margery mediumship. *Journal of Abnormal and Social Psychology, 21*(4): 401–421.

Richard, M. P., & Adato, A. (1980). The medium and her message: A study of spiritualism in Lily Dale, New York. *Review of Religious Research, 22*(2): 186–197.

Richet, C. (1923). *Thirty Years of Psychical Research: A Treatise on Metapsychics.* London: Macmillan.

Rock, A. J. (Ed.) (2013). *The Survival Hypothesis: Essays on Mediumship.* Jefferson, NC: McFarland.

Rock, A. J., & Beischel, J. (2008). Quantitative analysis of mediums' conscious experiences during a discarnate reading versus a control task: a pilot study. *Australian Journal of Parapsychology, 8*: 157–179.

Rogo, D. S. (1988). *The Infinite Boundary: Spirit Possession, Madness, and Multiple Personality.* Wellingborough, UK: Aquarian.

Rose, R. (1956). *Living Magic: The Realities Underlying the Psychical Practices and Beliefs of Australian Aborigines.* Chicago, IL: Rand McNally.

Roseman, M. (1990). Head, heart, odor, and shadow: The structure of the self, the emotional world, and ritual performance among Senoi Temiar. *Ethos, 18*(3): 227–250.

Rosenthal, N., Fingrutd, M., Ethier, M., Karant, R., & McDonald, D. (1985). Social movements and network analysis: A case study of nineteenth-century women's reform in New York State. *American Journal of Sociology, 90*(5): 1022–1054.

Roxburgh, E., & Roe, C. (2011). A survey of dissociation: Boundary-thinness, and psychological wellbeing in spiritualist mental mediums. *Journal of Parapsychology, 75*(2): 279–300.

Roxburgh, E., & Roe, C. (2013). A mixed methods approach to mediumship research. In: A. J. Rock (Ed.), *The Survival Hypothesis: Essays on Mediumship* (pp. 220–234). Jefferson, NC: McFarland.

Ryle, G. (2009). *The Concept of Mind.* Abingdon, UK: Routledge.

Salamone, F. (2002). The tangibility of the intangible. *Anthropology and Humanism, 26*(2): 150–157.

Sartori, P., Badham, P., & Fenwick, P. (2006). A prospectively studied near-death experience with corroborated out-of-body perceptions and unexplained healing. *Journal of Near-Death Studies, 25*(2): 69–84.

Schechner, R. (1988). *Performance Theory.* London: Routledge.

Schmeidler, G. (1943). Predicting good and bad scores in a clairvoyance experiment: A preliminary report. *Journal of the American Society for Psychical Research, 37*: 103–110.

Schmidt, B., & Huskinson, L. (Eds.) (2010). *Spirit Possession and Trance: New Interdisciplinary Perspectives*. London: Continuum.

Schrenck-Notzing, A. (1920). *Phenomena of Materialisation: A Contribution to the Investigation of Mediumistic Teleplastics*. London: Kegan Paul, Trench, Trubner.

Schroll, M. A. (Ed.) (2016). *Transpersonal Ecosophy, Vol. 1: Theory Methods and Clinical Assessments*. Llanrhaeadr-ym-Mochnant, UK: Psychoid.

Schroll, M. A., & Krippner, S. (2016). Differentiating experiences from events, and validity from authenticity in the anthropology of consciousness. In: M. A. Schroll (Ed.), *Transpersonal Ecosophy, Vol. 1: Theory Methods and Clinical Assessments* (pp. 217–230). Llanrhaeadr-ym-Mochnant, UK: Psychoid.

Schroll, M. A., & Schwartz, S. A. (2005). Whither psi and anthropology? An incomplete history of SAC's origins, its relationship with transpersonal psychology and the untold stories of Castaneda's controversy. *Anthropology of Consciousness*, 16(1): 6–24.

Schwartz, S. A. (2000). Boulders in the stream: The lineage and founding of the Society for the Anthropology of Consciousness. Available from: http://stephanaschwartz.com/wp-content/uploads/2010/02/Boulders-in-the-stream-SA.pdf (accessed April 26, 2020).

Scole Group (1996). *A Basic Guide to the Development and Practice of the New Physical Psychic Phenomena Using Energy*. Scole, UK: New Spiritual Science Foundation.

Seligman, R. (2005). Distress, dissociation, and embodied experience: Reconsidering the pathways to mediumship and mental health. *Ethos*, 33(1): 71–99.

Seligman, R. (2010). The unmaking and making of self: Embodied suffering and mind-body healing in Brazilian Candomblé. *Ethos*, 38(3): 297–320.

Shanafelt, R. (2004). Magic, miracle, and marvels in anthropology. *Ethnos*, 69(3): 317–340.

Sheldrake, R. (2005). The sense of being stared at: Is it real or illusory? *Journal of Consciousness Studies*, 12(6): 10–31.

Sheldrake, R. (2012). *The Science Delusion: Freeing the Spirit of Inquiry*. London: Coronet.

Sheldrake, R. (2013). The science delusion. Available from: https://youtube.com/watch?v=JKHUaNAxsTg (accessed September 14, 2017).

Shorter, E. (1994). *From the Mind into the Body: The Cultural Origins of Psychosomatic Symptoms*. New York: Free Press.

Shushan, G. (2009). *Conceptions of the Afterlife in Early Civilizations: Universalism, Constructivism and Near-Death Experience*. London: Continuum.

Sinclair, U. (2001). *Mental Radio*. Charlottesville, VA: Hampton Roads.

Skultans, V. (1974). *Intimacy and Ritual: A Study of Spiritualism, Mediums and Groups.* London: Routledge & Kegan Paul.

Smith, K. (2012). From dividual and individual selves to porous subjects. *Australian Journal of Anthropology, 23*: 50–64.

Solomon, G., & Solomon, J. (1999). *The Scole Experiment: Scientific Evidence for Life After Death.* London: Judy Piatkus.

Somer, E. (2006). Culture bound dissociation: A comparative analysis. *Psychiatric Clinics of North America, 29*: 213–226.

Sommer, A. (2009). Tackling taboos—from Psychopathia sexualis to the materialisation of dreams: Albert von Schrenck-Notzing (1862–1920). *Journal of Scientific Exploration, 23*(3): 299–322.

Spanos, N. P. (1994). Multiple identity enactment and multiple personality disorder: A sociocognitve perspective. *Psychological Bulletin, 116*(1): 143–165.

Spanos, N. P., Menary, E., Gabora, M. J., DuBreuil, S. C., & Dewhirst, B. (1991). Secondary identity enactments during hypnotic past-life regression: A sociocognitive perspective. *Journal of Personality and Social Psychology, 61*(2): 308–320.

Spencer, H., 1897. *Principles of Sociology.* New York: D. Appleton.

Spiro, M. (1986). Cultural relativism and the future of anthropology. *Cultural Anthropology, 1*(3): 259–286.

Spiro, M. (1993). Is the Western conception of the self "peculiar" within the context of the world cultures? *Ethos, 21*(2): 107–153.

Stark, R. (1984). The rise of a new world faith. *Review of Religious Research, 26*(1): 18–27.

St. Clair, D. (1971). *Drum and Candle: Accounts of Brazilian Voodoo and Spiritism.* New York: Bell.

Steffen, V. (2011). Intrusive agents and permeable selves: Spirit consultation in Denmark. In: S. Fainzang & C. Haxaire (Eds.), *Of Bodies and Symptoms: Anthropological Perspectives on Their Social and Medical Treatment* (pp. 79–96). Tarragona, Spain: URV.

Steinmeyer, J. (2004). *Hiding the Elephant: How Magicians Invented the Impossible.* London: Heinemann.

Steinmeyer, J. (2008). *Charles Fort: The Man Who Invented the Supernatural.* London: Heinemann.

Stemman, R. (2005). *Spirit Communication: A Comprehensive Guide to the Extraordinary World of Mediums, Psychics and the Afterlife.* London: Piatkus.

Stocking, G. W. (1971). Animism in theory and practice: E. B. Tylor's unpublished notes on "spiritualism." *Man, 6*(1): 88–104.

Stoller, P. (1994). Embodying colonial memories. *American Anthropologist, 96*(3): 634–648.

Stoller, P., & Olkes, C. (1989). In *Sorcery's Shadow: A Memoir of Apprenticeship Among the Songhay of Niger*. Chicago, IL: University of Chicago Press.

Storm, L., & Rock, A. J. (2009). Shamanic-like journeying and psi: I. Imagery cultivation, paranormal belief, and the picture-identification task. *Australian Journal of Parapsychology, 9*(2): 165–192.

Straight, B. (2007). *Miracles and Extraordinary Experience in Northern Kenya*. Philadelphia, PA: University of Pennsylvania Press.

Strathern, M. (1988). *The Gender of the Gift: Problems with Women and Problems with Society in Melanesia*. Los Angeles, CA: University of California Press.

Strieber, W., & Kripal, J. J. (2016). *The Super Natural: A New Vision of the Unexplained*. New York: Jeremy P. Tarcher/Penguin.

Sudduth, M. (2013). Is postmortem survival the best explanation of the data of mediumship? In: A. J. Rock (Ed.), *The Survival Hypothesis: Essays on Mediumship* (pp. 40–64). Jefferson, NC: McFarland.

Swanton, J. R. (1953). A letter to anthropologists. *Journal of Parapsychology, 17*: 144–152.

Swatos, W. H. (1990). Spiritualism as a religion of science. *Social Compass, 37*(4): 471–482.

Tabori, P. (1968). *Companions of the Unseen*. New York: New York University Press.

Taggart, S. (2019). *SEANCE*. Lopen, UK: Fulgur.

Tallis, R. (2012). *Aping Mankind: Neuromania, Darwinitis and the Misrepresentation of Humanity*. Durham, UK: Acumen.

Tart, C. (2000). Investigating altered states on their own terms: State-specific science. In: M. Velmans (Ed.), *Investigating Phenomenal Consciousness: New Methodologies and Maps* (pp. 255–278). Amsterdam, the Netherlands: John Benjamins.

Taves, A. (1999). *Fits, Trances and Visions: Experiencing Religion and Explaining Experience from Wesley to James*. Princeton, NJ: Princeton University Press.

Taves, A. (2006). Where (fragmented) selves meet cultures: Theorising spirit possession. *Culture and Religion, 7*(2): 123–138.

Taylor, C. (2007). *A Secular Age*. Cambridge, MA: Harvard University Press.

Thomas Jefferson University (2012). Brazilian mediums shed light on brain activity during a trance state. Available from: http://sciencedaily.com/releases2012/11/121117184543.htm (accessed 11 January 2013).

Time Magazine (1972, 19 June). The occult revival: A substitute faith.

Tobert, N. (2016). *Cultural Perspectives on Mental Wellbeing: Spiritual Interpretations of Symptoms in Medical Practice*. London: Jessica Kingsley.

Turner, E. (1992). *Experiencing Ritual: A New Interpretation of African Healing*. Philadelphia, PA: University of Pennsylvania Press.

Turner, E. (1993). The reality of spirits: A tabooed or permitted field of study? *Anthropology of Consciousness*, 4(1): 9–12.

Turner, E. (2002). A visible spirit form in Zambia. In: G. Harvey (Ed.), *Readings in Indigenous Religions*. London: Continuum.

Turner, E. (2010). Discussion: ethnography as a transformative experience. *Anthropology and Humanism*, 35(2): 218–226.

Turner, E. (2012). *Communitas: The Anthropology of Collective Joy*. New York: Palgrave Macmillan.

Turner, V. (1985). *On the Edge of the Bush: Anthropology as Experience*. Tucson, AZ: University of Arizona Press.

Turner, V. (2002). Liminality and communitas. In: M. Lambek (Ed.), *A Reader in the Anthropology of Religion* (pp. 358–373). Oxford: Blackwell.

Tylor, E. B. (1930). *Anthropology: An Introduction to the Study of Man and Civilization*. London: C. A. Watts.

Vallee, J. (1969). *Passport to Magonia: From Folklore to Flying Saucers*. Brisbane, Australia: Daily Grail, 2014.

van de Castle, R. L. (1976). Some possible anthropological contributions to the study of parapsychology. In: G. Schmeidler (Ed.), *Parapsychology: Its Relation to Physics, Biology, Psychology and Psychiatry* (pp. 151–161). Metuchen, NJ: Scarecrow.

van de Castle, R. L. (1977). Anthropology and psychic research. *Phoenix: New Directions in the Study of Man*, 1(1): 27–35.

van de Port, M. (2011). *Ecstatic Encounters: Bahian Candomblé and the Quest for the Really Real*. Amsterdam, the Netherlands: Amsterdam University Press.

van Dusen, W. (1994). *The Presence of Other Worlds: The Psychological/Spiritual Findings of Emanuel Swedenborg*. West Chester, PA: Chrysalis.

Velmans, M. (2007). The co-evolution of matter and consciousness. *Synthesis Philosophica*, 22(44): 273–282.

Viveiros de Castro, E. (2002). Cosmological deixis and Amerindian perspectivism. In: M. Lambek (Ed.), *A Reader in the Anthropology of Religion*. Oxford: Blackwell.

Viveiros de Castro, E. (2014). Who's afraid of the ontological wolf?: Some comments on an ongoing anthropological debate. Available from: https://sisu.ut.ee/sites/default/files/biosemio/files/cusas_strathern_lecture_2014.pdf (accessed September 14, 2017).

Voas, D., & Crocket, A. (2005). Religion in Britain: Neither believing nor belonging. *Sociology*, 39(1): 11–28.

Voss, A. (2015). A matter of spirit: An imaginal perspective on the paranormal. In: J. Hunter (Ed.), *Strange Dimensions: A Paranthropology Anthology* (pp. 151–168). Llanrhaeadr-ym-Mochnant, UK: Psychoid.

Voss, A. (2017). *Delectare, Docere, Movere*: soul-learning, reflexivity and the third classroom. In: A. Voss & S. Wilson (Eds.), *Re-enchanting the Academy* (pp. 113–138). Seattle, WA: Rubedo.

Voss, A., & Rowlandson, W. (2013). Introduction. In: A. Voss & W. Rowlandson (Eds.), *Daimonic Imagination: Uncanny Intelligence* (pp. 1–5). Newcastle-upon-Tyne, UK: Cambridge Scholars.

Walliss, J. (2001). Continuing bonds: Relationships between the living and the dead within contemporary spiritualism. *Morality*, 6(2): 127–145.

Ward, K. (2010). *More Than Matter: What Humans Really Are*. Oxford: Lion Hudson.

Warner, M. (2006). *Phantasmagoria: Spirit Visions, Metaphors, and Media into the Twenty-first Century*. Oxford: Oxford University Press.

Watters, E. (2011). *Crazy Like Us: The Globalization of the Western Mind*. London: Constable & Robinson.

Went, C. W. (1960). Parapsychology and anthropology. *Manas*, 13(15): 1–6.

Wescott, R. W. (1977). Paranthropology: A nativity celebration and a communion commentary. In: J. K. Long (Ed.), *Extrasensory Ecology: Parapsychology and Anthropology* (pp. 331–347). London: Scarecrow.

Whorf, B. L. (1956). *Language, Thought and Reality*. Cambridge, MA: MIT Press.

Whitehead, A. N. (1978). *Process and Reality*. London: Free Press.

Willerslev, R. (2004). Spirits as "ready to hand": A phenomenological analysis of Yukaghir spiritual knowledge and dreaming. *Anthropological Theory*, 4(4): 395–413.

Willerslev, R. (2012). Laughing at the spirits in North Siberia: Is animism being taken too seriously? Available from: http://e-flux.com/journal/36/61261/laughing-at-the-spirits-in-north-siberia-is-animism-being-taken-too-seriously (accessed 4 June 2017).

Williams, B., & Roll, W. (2007). Spirit controls and the brain. *Proceedings of Presented Papers: The Parapsychological Association Convention 2007*, pp. 170–186.

Wilson, C. (1981). *Poltergeist!: A Study in Destructive Haunting*. London: New English Library.

Wilson, D. G. M. (2011). *Spiritualist Mediums and Other Traditional Shamans: Towards an Apprenticeship Model of Shamanic Practice*. Unpublished PhD Thesis, University of Edinburgh.

Wilson, D. G. M. (2013). *Redefining Shamanisms: Spiritualist Mediums and Other Traditional Shamans as Apprenticeship Outcomes*. London: Continuum.

Wilson, I. (1988). *The Bleeding Mind: An Investigation into the Mysterious Phenomenon of Stigmata*. London: Weidenfeld & Nicolson.

Wilson, L. (2011). The anthropology of the possible: The ethnographer as sceptical enquirer. *Paranthropology: Journal of Anthropological Approaches to the Paranormal, 2*(4): 4–9.

Wilson, P. J. (1967). Status ambiguity and spirit possession. *Man, 2*(3): 366–378.

Wilson, R. A. (n. d.). Toward understanding E-prime. Available from: http://nobeliefs.com/eprime.htm (accessed April 26, 2020).

Wilson, R. A. (1987). *The New Inquisition: Irrational Rationalism and the Citadel of Science*. Phoenix, AZ: Falcon.

Winkelman, M. (1982). Magic: A theoretical reassessment. *Current Anthropology, 23*(1): 37–66.

Winkelman, M. (1986). Trance states: A theoretical model and cross-cultural analysis. *Ethnos, 14*(2): 174–203.

Winkelman, M. (1999). Joseph K. Long: obituary. *Anthropology News, 40*(9): 33.

Winkelman, M. (2000). *Shamanism: The Neural Ecology of Consciousness and Healing*. Westport, CT: Bergin & Garvey.

Winkelman, M. (2004). Spirits as human nature and the fundamental structures of consciousness. In: J. Houran (Ed.), *From Shaman to Scientist: Essays on Humanity's Search for Spirits* (pp. 59–96). Oxford: Scarecrow.

Wittkower, E. D., Douyon, L. & Bijou, L. (1964). Spirit possession in Haitian Vodun ceremonies. *Acta Psychotherapeutica et Psychosomatica, 12*(1): 72–80.

Young, D. E. (2012). Dreams and telepathic communication. In: J. Hunter (Ed.), *Paranthropology: Anthropological Approaches to the Paranormal* (pp. 15–180). Bristol, UK: Paranthropology.

Young, D. E., & Goulet, J.-G. (Eds.) (1994). *Being Changed by Cross-Cultural Encounters: The Anthropology of Extraordinary Experience*. Peterborough, ON, Canada: Broadview.

Zingrone, N. (1994). Images of woman as medium: power, pathology and passivity in the writings of Frederic Marvin and Cesare Lombrosso. In: L. Coly & R. A. White (Eds.), *Women and Parapsychology: Proceedings of an International Conference* (pp. 90–121). New York: Parapsychology Foundation.

INDEX

255